RESEARCH AND PRACTICE
IN THE PRIMARY CLASSROOM

RESEARCH AND PRACTICE IN THE PRIMARY CLASSROOM

Edited by
**Brian Simon and
John Willcocks**

ROUTLEDGE & KEGAN PAUL
London, Boston and Henley

First published in 1981
by Routledge & Kegan Paul Ltd
39 Store Street,
London WC1E 7DD
9 Park Street,
Boston, Mass. 02108, USA and
Broadway House,
Newtown Road,
Henley-on-Thames,
Oxon RG9 1EN
Printed in Great Britain by
Biddles Ltd, Guildford
© Introduction, Editorial Matter and
Authors' Contributions:
Brian Simon, John Willcocks, Maurice Galton,
Paul Croll and Anne Jasman 1981
Other contributions
© Routledge & Kegan Paul Ltd 1981

British Library Cataloguing in Publication Data

Simon, Brian
Research and practice in the primary classroom.
1. Education, Elementary - England
I. Title   II. Willcocks, John
372.9'42   LB1555

ISBN 0-7100-0850-3

CONTENTS

v

Part III RESEARCH AND THE TEACHER   131

10 Curriculum change and research in a middle   133
    school
    David Johnston

11 Teachers' assessments in classroom research   144
    Anne Jasman

12 Empirical research and educational theory   161
    Ruth Jonathan

13 ORACLE: its implications for teacher training   176
    Maurice Galton and Brian Simon

Bibliography   190

Index   195

CONTRIBUTORS

Patricia Ashton taught in primary schools, a college of education, and at Leicester University School of Education before becoming a Senior Research Fellow at the Open University where she is currently engaged in a DES-funded project on school-focused initial and in-service education, and helping to prepare a new INSET course on practical curriculum evaluation.

Deanne Boydell was a research consultant to the ORACLE programme. She was associated with the the SSRC - funded research into primary classrooms at Leicester University School of Education from its inception in 1970, and worked full time on the exploratory studies until 1975.

Paul Croll worked as a Research Fellow on the ORACLE project at the University of Leicester, specializing in computing and statistical analysis. He is now directing a research project on the Assessment and Incidence of Special Educational Needs also at the University of Leicester.

Angela Delafield was an observer on the ORACLE programme. Both before and since then she has had a wide range of teaching experience, in England and abroad, with children and adults in several areas of special educational need. She is currently training as an educational psychologist.

Maurice Galton is a Senior Lecturer in Education at the School of Education, University of Leicester. He is now directing phase II of the ORACLE project, is a co-author of 'Inside the Primary Classroom' and joint editor with Brian Simon of its sequel 'Progress and Performance in The Primary Classroom'.

Anne Jasman lectures in Teaching Studies at Worcester College of Higher Education. She taught at Bosworth Community College in Leicestershire before joining the ORACLE research team in 1976. She is particularly concerned with the application in schools and teacher training of systematic observation and methods of assessment and evaluation.

David Johnston is a General Adviser for Primary Education in Derbyshire. He has been a headteacher at two primary schools, most recently at a combined Nursery first and middle school (3-12 years). His particular interests include the development of primary science, activities for the more able child and the management of schools.

Ruth Jonathan is a Lecturer in the Philosophy of Education at Edinburgh University. She has previously taught languages abroad and in England, as well as philosophy and psychology. Her particular interest is the potential contribution of speculative thought to educational theorizing, and she has been concerned in both empirical and speculative research in education.

Sylvia Leith is Associate Professor in the Department of Curriculum at the University of Manitoba. She spent a year (1978-9) as visiting fellow at the University of Leicester School of Education, where she worked on a topic related to the ORACLE programme, concerning the assessment of project work.

Brian Simon has recently retired from his Chair in Education at the University of Leicester. He has written widely on the history of education, on psychological questions and on contemporary educational issues. He acted as joint director (with Maurice Galton) of the ORACLE programme.

Sarah Tann has been working as a Research Associate on an SSRC project, 'The Community College in its Setting' based at Leicester University School of Education. Before joining the ORACLE programme in 1976 she taught for five years, in a multi-racial junior school in Malaysia and in the Chichester College of Further Education.

John Willcocks was an educational psychologist before becoming Senior Research Fellow on the ORACLE research programme. Since then he has worked at the Institut National de Recherche Pédagogique in Paris on an SSRC research exchange scheme.

INTRODUCTION

Brian Simon and John Willcocks

The ORACLE research programme was the first large-scale observational study of primary school classrooms to be undertaken in
this country. Funded by the Social Science Research Council over
the period 1975-80, it was concerned primarily to study the relative effectiveness of different teaching approaches across the
main subject areas of the primary school. The findings of the
main study are presented in three other volumes: 'Inside the
Primary Classroom' (1980), which deals specifically with patterns ·
of activity and instruction; 'Progress and Performance in the
Primary Classroom' (1980), which concentrates on the relative
effectiveness of different teaching styles in relation to the pupil
types which were also identified; and 'Transfer from the Primary
Classroom' (1981), which presents the findings from longitudinal
studies of pupil and teacher consistency and of transfer to
secondary school.

The research programme brought together a large number of
people - researchers, observers, teachers and other university
and local authority staff - from a wide range of disciplines and
theoretical orientations; and their exchange of ideas and insights
over the five-year period gave rise to a variety of studies, both
speculative and empirical, some of which have been assembled in
the present volume. We have selected themes which we believe to
be of interest and importance to teachers, teacher educators and
their students; but we have also been aware of the requirements
of readers from the research community. Consequently, some of
the chapters contain sections of a technical nature; but these are
always accompanied by an account in straightforward language of
the purpose of the techniques used, and the conclusions to be
drawn from them. By these means our contributors have tried to
present their arguments and findings in a way which will interest
both the general and the specialist reader. All the chapters are
related directly to major contemporary problems or issues in the
general area of the primary classroom, its teachers and its children.

Part I, The Primary Classroom, Yesterday and Today, begins
with a discussion by Brian Simon of what has been called 'the
primary school revolution'. His systematic review of the historical
evidence leads to a conclusion which many readers may find surprising. The section continues with two chapters which, through
the use of survey techniques, seek to estimate the degree and
direction of change during the 1970s in two specific areas: Patricia
Ashton traces shifts in teachers' perceptions of the relative importance of different aims in primary education, and Deanne Boydell

gives an account of changes that have taken place during these
years in the way teachers organize their classrooms for teaching/
learning purposes. Both chapters bring out what appear to be
significant shifts in opinions and practice over this period, and
document these changes in a rigorous manner.

While these chapters form a distinct unity within Part I, those
by Sarah Tann and Sylvia Leith, both reporting studies related
to the ORACLE programme, focus on important issues for the
primary classroom. A main finding of the ORACLE research related to group work: it appeared that, although children are
normally seated in groups round tables in primary classrooms today, very little collaborative group work takes place. Sarah
Tann's chapter summarizes her own research into collaborative
group work in both primary and lower secondary classrooms.
Sylvia Leith takes up another issue related to the ORACLE research, that of project or topic work which, as indicated in an
earlier volume ('Inside the Primary Classroom', pp. 76-80) takes
up a relatively large amount of pupils' time in primary classrooms.

Part II, The Teacher and the Child, is chiefly concerned with
teachers' strategies and perceptions. Patricia Ashton reports
the results of her research into the way teachers attempt to form
or influence desired types of personal and social behaviour in the
classroom. John Willcocks contributes a chapter based on his
study of the ways in which teachers conceptualize and perceive
anxiety in their pupils, while Maurice Galton and Angela Delafield
report an original study, again arising from the ORACLE programme, concerned with the extent to which teachers' perceptions
of their pupils' abilities appear to affect pupil achievement in the
classroom - a study arising from Rosenthal and Jacobson's 'Pygmalion in the Classroom', and the controversy which followed its
publication in 1968.

The ORACLE data also permitted an analysis of the vexed question of the relation between social class and achievement in the
school system. The chapter by Paul Croll summarizes present
knowledge in this field and proceeds to a detailed analysis of
the light which the ORACLE findings throw on this question.

The four chapters in Part III relate in various ways to the
question of research and the teacher. David Johnston reflects on
the impact on his school of certain curriculum development projects,
and of participation in the ORACLE research programme. Anne
Jasman contributes a detailed article on the teacher-based assessment techniques developed for the ORACLE programme, and outlines the problems and issues involved in the development of procedures to assess pupils on a wider range of criteria than have
normally been used in process-product studies. Chapter 13 by
Maurice Galton and Brian Simon attempts to draw out some of
the main implications of the ORACLE studies for teacher education,
while Ruth Jonathan contributes a chapter raising important theoretical issues concerning observational research of the ORACLE
type.

This volume is once again a combined effort by the research

team as a whole, assisted by others who worked closely with the project in one way or another. Particular mention must be made of the groups of teachers who devoted considerable time and energy to helping in the planning and execution of some of the projects described in the book. It is certainly no exaggeration to say that without their co-operation and hard work those projects could not have been completed or even, in some cases, begun. We are also happy to acknowledge the efficient and consistently cheerful assistance of the project secretaries, Diana Stroud and Jaya Katariya, who have prepared the volume for publication. For the compilation of the bibliography and the index our thanks are due to Jaya Katariya and Elizabeth Willcocks respectively. We acknowledge also the support of the Social Science Research Council which funded the programme to which the researches reported in the volume are closely related.

Part I
THE PRIMARY
CLASSROOM, YESTERDAY
AND TODAY

1 THE PRIMARY SCHOOL REVOLUTION: myth or reality?[*]

Brian Simon

I want to attempt a cool, historical appraisal of primary school developments in the 1960s. In particular to answer the question: was there a primary school revolution, and, if so, how do we assess it?

There is no doubt that some thought there was, that anarchy and disorder were becoming the rule, leading to chaos and dark night. Nor is there any doubt that, as what many call the 'educational backlash' got under way in the 1970s, the brunt of the attack fell for a time at least on the primary schools. This campaign, taken up and propagated by the mass media (including both the popular press and the minority press) reached a climax in October 1976 with 'The Times's' notorious leader on the 'wild men of the classroom' (equating these with trade union disrupters) who must be brought to heel, implicitly labelling all primary school teachers in this way. The leader was sparked by the Tyndale affair, and was one of the features paving the way for Callaghan's Ruskin speech, which warned against 'modern methods' in the primary school.

We may first remind ourselves of the main stages in the build-up of this image of the primary school - as undergoing a 'revolution' where anything goes, all forms of activity are legitimate.

I

Black Paper I 'Fight for Education' was published in 1969. Generally it received a bad press and in particular was slammed by Ted Short, Secretary of State for Education, who referred to the authors as 'thugs'. Nevertheless it is now clear that this publication marked an important new phase in terms of a new type of populist educational ideology - having as its purpose halting, and if possible turning back, those developments in the 1960s which tended to open up the system, rendering it more egalitarian and

*Text of a lecture given in December 1979 to the History of Education Society's annual conference on 'Education in the Sixties'. The proceedings of the conference have been published under this title by the society and are available, at £6.50 (including postage) from Mrs B.J. Starkey, HES, 4, Marydene Drive, Evington, Leicester, LE5 6HD.

We are grateful to the Committee of the Society for permission to reprint the lecture in this volume (Eds).

7

less hierarchic. Here the word 'revolution' makes its appearance.
I quote from the Letter to M.P.s:

> Since the war revolutionary changes have taken place in English
> education – the introduction of free play methods in primary
> schools [this comes first – BS], comprehensive schemes, the
> expansion of higher education, the experimental courses at new
> universities . . . .

> At primary school some teachers are taking to an extreme the
> belief that children must not be told anything, but must find
> out for themselves . . . at the post-eleven stage there is a
> strong impetus to abolish streaming, and the grammar school
> concepts of discipline and hard work are treated with contempt
> . . . the new fashionable anarchy flies in the face of human
> nature [sic – BS], for it holds that children and students will
> work from natural inclination rather than the desire for reward.

1969, of course, saw the climax of the movement of student unrest in universities and colleges, including the Hornsey College
of Art affair where the students successfully took control of their
own education for several months in the summer and autumn of
1968, radically changing its character (The Hornsey Affair, 1969).
Black Paper I linked student unrest to the primary school, referring to an article by Timothy Raison, now Minister of State at the
Home Office, but then editor of 'New Society', published in the
'Evening Standard' earlier. The roots of student unrest, Raison
is quoted as saying, are to be found as early as the primary
school. Referring to the 'anarchistic beliefs' of the Hornsey students, Raison wrote: 'I sometimes wonder whether this philosophy
. . . does not owe at least something to *the revolution in our primary schools*' (my italics – BS). So there the seed of the idea was
planted. And of course Raison should know. He was, after all, a
member of the Plowden Committee and a signatory to its report.
On Timothy Raison's hypothesis a few points may be made which
may· help to clear the air. If the student unrest or revolt of 1968-9
was partly due to the primary school 'revolution', that revolution
must be dated back at least ten to fifteen years, that is, to 1958
and earlier, when the students at Hornsey and elsewhere would
have been in primary schools being inducted into their anarchistic
attitudes. The Black Paper I Letter to M.P.s in fact claims the
'introduction of free play methods' was one of the revolutionary
changes that had taken place 'since the war' – that is, from 1945.
But this seems historically inaccurate. Of course it is the case
that the Hadow reports of 1931 and 1933 (on the primary school
and infant and nursery schools respectively) had both stressed
a 'child-centred' approach with the famous phrase on 'activity
and experience' central to each of them. Indeed Professor R.J.W.
Selleck, has argued that a kind of watered-down progressivism
had become the 'intellectual orthodoxy' among training college
lecturers, HMIs, etc. by 1939 (Selleck 1972), but the reality, as
opposed to the rhetoric, appears to have been rather different.
It is quite true that there was a move towards 'free activity',

or modern methods, in the late 1940s, epitomised by M.V. Daniel's
'Activity in the Primary School' (1947), and this may have had a
permanent impact on practice as Alec Ross argued in 1960 even
if, as he says, 'the time was not a propitious one for experiment'
(Ross 1960 p.33). But at that time the 11-plus examination was
still the rule throughout the country, Leicestershire's reorganization was only just beginning, only 150 comprehensive schools
were in existence; the move to abolish streaming in the primary
schools was in its first stages. The students of 1968 were, in
fact, the products of the streamed, divided, hierarchical system
from which we only began to emerge in a significant way in the
mid 1960s – products of the system which the Black Paper writers
look back to with such cloying nostalgia. In 'Inside the Primary
School' (1967) Blackie, a senior HMI, confirms this. Asked by
foreign visitors to arrange visits to 'activity' schools, HMIs, to
whom the request was referred, 'found great difficulty in discovering any'. Change was taking place in the period 1947 to
1953, but 'slowly, cautiously', and, as he puts it, 'sensibly'
(p.11).

To interpret Raison's argument and that of the Black Paperites
charitably, we should remind ourselves that the Plowden Report,
basing itself on theories relating to the inherent curiosity of
children and their innate desire to learn, on the need for individualization of the teaching/learning process, on the pedagogical
value of discovery methods, with the teacher leading from behind, had been published only two years earlier in 1967. At that
time, this report appeared to represent a wide consensus as to
the ideal nature of primary education, and, indeed, to reflect
what was going on in the schools – or, at least, the main trends
or tendencies. The fact that the publication of the report coin-
cided fairly closely with the student unrest (an international
phenomenon, incidentally) may have led Raison to speculate on
the relationship between the two, a speculation taken up for their
own purposes by the Black Paper editors. In this way the myth
was perpetrated that the one was responsible for the other when,
of course, that could not be the case.

Nevertheless, the idea that primary school methods, or teachers,
were getting out of hand, a point of view that was presented in a
sustained critique in the whole series of Black Papers (five or
six in all), caught on, and, of course, exploded in the mass
media with the Tyndale affair covering the years 1974 to 1976.
Though this is outside our period, it bears closely on developments in the 1960s, so it is as well to remind ourselves of the
way these rather dramatic events unfolded, especially around
1975-6.

The Tyndale affair broke in the press first in 1974. Though the
key issue at stake was who, in the last resort, controls the
schools, the extreme version of 'progressive' teaching methods
espoused by the leading teachers underlay the conflicts. Given
that, following the Jencks and Coleman Reports which, briefly,
reached the conclusion that schools made no difference, as well

as the massive cut-backs in educational plans and spending in
the late 1960s, the early 1970s marked a period of disenchant-
ment with education as a panacea for social ills. In this situation
the Tyndale affair provided a focus for public discontent and
frustration on much wider issues than education alone. This was
the context of the rise of the populist agitator, Rhodes Boyson,
now a Minister of State, and of the politicization of the whole
critique of the educational advances of the 1960s, including in
particular comprehensive schooling. Just after the Tyndale affair
had drawn to its close, and in the atmosphere thus created, in
May 1976, Neville Bennett's small-scale research project (Bennett
1976), which appeared to show that formal teaching was more
effective than informal, received a highly unusual degree of mass
media coverage. In October that year, as mentioned at the start,
the high point of near hysteria was reached with 'The Times'
leader. There followed the HMI's so-called 'Yellow Paper' which
also (characteristically, and in contrast to earlier strong HMI
support for such methods) now appeared to challenge the spread
of new methods in the primary school, drawn up to brief the
Prime Minister, and Callaghan's Ruskin College speech, in which
he specifically warned against the way some teachers used these
methods in the classroom ('Education', 22 October 1976). From
this developed the Green Paper (July 1977), the Great Debate,
the Assessment of Performance Unit (although this had been set
up earlier), the imposition of mass testing by several local authorities, and new HMI/DES initiatives relating to the curriculum and
school organization. Primary education, to say the least, had come
under a cloud – or rather had now been forced into the limelight,
as a national political issue.

II

The question we have to resolve is what the basis was of all this?
What had, in fact, been going on? Had there been a fundamental
change in practice and procedures in primary schools? Was the
child-centred, 'discovery' approach widely implemented? Were
children being left on their own to determine their own curricula
and activities? Was there a neglect of 'the basics' – of the skills
of numeracy and literacy – and a more central focus on other
areas embodying different objectives – creativity, self-expression?
    First, there is no doubt that some people perceived this to be
the case. I refer here in particular to a whole series of more or
less distinguished American educationists who visited this country,
toured the key areas of the break-out, if one may use the term
(Oxfordshire, Leicestershire, the West Riding, Bristol and London
in particular), and then wrote about their experiences, generally
focusing on the concepts and practices of advanced British schools
as a model from which Americans could learn with advantage. This
phenomenon is, in my view, more part of the American history of
education than the British, for, in the late 1960s and early 1970s,

the crisis of schooling in the United States was at its height. The British primary school, it was thought by many, while not necessarily copyable, was linked with the move towards what the Americans call 'open' education, and could provide insights of value.

So we have Joseph Featherstone's famous series of 'New Republic' articles printed under the heading: The Primary School Revolution in Britain, in 1967 - and there we have that word again. These were reprinted with other articles in a book entitled 'Schools Where Children Learn', (1971a). Featherstone also wrote the introductory volume to the series entitled 'British Primary Schools Today' (1971b), a co-operative endeavour by American and British educators aiming to publicize modern procedures across both sides of the Atlantic. 1970 saw the publication of Charles Silberman's 'Crisis in the Classroom: the Remaking of American Education', a project massively funded by the Carnegie Corporation. Over 100,000 copies of the hardback edition were sold together with 240,000 copies of the paper-back edition; the book was also awarded seven prizes. This drew greatly on the author's British experience, even if of a subjective, episodic character. He followed this up by publishing, in 1973, the 'Open Classroom Reader', another massive compilation drawing heavily on British writers. The same year (1970) saw the publication of Vincent Rogers's 'Teaching in the British Primary School', again produced for American readers but contributed, in a series of articles, by the leading British educators with experience of the primary school, with a strongly adulatory introduction by Rogers, Professor of Education at the University of Connecticut and a convinced proponent of new forms of education. 1971 saw the publication of Lisa and Casey Murrow's 'Children Come First', subtitled 'The Inspired Work of English Primary Schools', also based on descriptions of activities in selected British primary schools, while in the same year Lilien Weber's useful and comprehensive 'The English Infant School and Informal Education' was also published in England. This, actually worked on in 1965-6, differs from the others in that it focused very specifically on the infant school which Lilien Weber saw as the centre of the thrust towards what she describes as 'informal' education.

It is certainly the case that some of these writings were propagandist in character and tended, therefore, to convey what was, perhaps, a rosy-hued version of developments in British primary schools in general; the common tendency of these authors, who visited many schools predominantly in the areas already mentioned, was to identify with these developments and processes and to persuade fellow Americans of their viability. 'I visited these two schools in Oxfordshire', writes Vincent Rogers, 'and I have not been quite the same since' (Rogers 1970). Silberman's influential book is built up largely of vignettes of teacher and pupil interaction, or activities, derived from visits again to selected, or recommended schools. He claimed that: 'In every formal classroom that I went to visit in England, children were restless, were whispering to one another when the teacher was not looking, were ignoring the lesson or baiting the teacher or annoying other children', while in the schools organised on the basis of informal schooling 'the joyfulness is pervasive; in almost every classroom visited, virtually every child appears happy and engaged. One simply does not see bored or restless or unhappy youngsters, or youngsters with the glazed look' (Silberman 1970, pp. 228-9). Featherstone, although he used the term 'revolution' in the primary schools, is careful to underline that it is Plowden's 10 per cent 'best' ('outstanding') schools that he is talking about, and, as far as junior schools are concerned, makes clear that many of these are as arid, poverty-stricken, and dull as he perceives most American education to be. For him, however, as with Vincent Rogers and, of course, Plowden, it is the 'best' schools that represent the trend, to which other schools are likely to approximate. Thus, although the American literature does provide welcome evidence, largely in the form of descriptive material of an unsystematic character, as to processes and procedures in what may be called the most advanced primary schools, we need to be aware of its provenance before accepting it at face value.

Suppose we turn now (before attempting an examination of such 'hard' evidence as we can find) to British educationists and writers - what can we learn from them of relevance to our theme? How did they perceive, describe and define changes in primary education in these years? In 1971 Sir Alec Clegg wrote a booklet for the National Association of Elementary School Principals (NEA) in the United States. It was entitled 'Revolution in the British Primary School', which seems to settle the matter at least as far as Sir Alec was concerned. The paper is reproduced in Silberman's Reader, which states that Sir Alec 'is widely acknowledged as one of the giants of British education', and 'one of the leaders of the quiet revolution that has transformed British primary education since World War II'. Many would agree with this evaluation, and, in this paper, Clegg outlines what he sees as the central changes in attitudes and approach that have taken place. Children no longer sit in rows facing the blackboard; the teacher gives formal lessons less frequently; learning is based on experiences rather than subjects; children work at their own pace on topics they choose from 'a range carefully prepared by the teacher' so that the 'integrated day has superseded the day cut up into subject times'; spelling lists and mechanical sums are now rarely used; the teacher encourages pupils to seek knowledge themselves rather than telling everything; there are few set books and more individual books and resources. In spite of indications to the contrary, Clegg continues, 'there is no doubt that the change in English primary schools is a momentous one'. 'Our primary schools, at their best, are models of the kind of social communities in which we would all wish to live.' (It is interesting to note that, in a section entitled 'What have we gained from the revolution in our primary schools', Clegg states badly that these developments have nothing to do with 'educational philosophers' -

Caldwell Cook and Dewey are cited - and owe nothing to the progressive school movement of the 1920s and 1930s (Silberman 1973,
pp. 71, 82).)

Evidently, then, Clegg perceived that an educational revolution
had already taken place in our primary schools, and of course the
West Riding achieved a national reputation as one of the main
centres of this break-out.[1] We now turn briefly to another such
centre, Leicestershire. According, once again, to its then
Director of Education, Stewart Mason, the abolition of the 11-plus
in the experimental areas where the Leicestershire Plan was first
tried out had its immediate and most direct effect on the primary
schools. Mason linked new developments in the primary schools
directly with the abolition of streaming consequent on the elimination of the 11 plus. The increased flexibility which resulted, he
says, has led to the inclusion of a second language, greater concern with creative writing, the arts, music and drama, while 'the
most striking change of all is taking place in the teaching of
mathematics'. 'The ozone of enthusiasm and tang of enquiry are
in the air,' he concluded, 'and one cannot help breathing them
in' (Mason 1960, p. 29). This, it is worth noting, was written
as early as 1960; but Leicestershire was ahead of most other
areas in the country in its comprehensive plan implemented systematically in succeeding areas in the county from the late 1950s on-
wards.

These, then, are the impressions, or perceptions, of two directors of education in areas where the revolution in the primary
school has generally been considered to have been taken furthest.
It may be relevant here to quote from Maurice Kogan, commenting
on the way educational policy is sometimes formed through the
interaction between teachers, local authority administrators, inspectors and advisers and even councillors. 'No-one who has wit-
nessed the powerful cultural and social networks established within some local education authorities where, for example, primary
education was changing its ways in the 1940s and 1950s can fail
to have seen how policy was being made by the sanctioning and
encouragement of progressive educational practices' (Kogan 1978,
pp. 128-9).

One of the most authoritative, and probably influential, writers
assessing British primary schools in the 1960s was the then Chief
Inspector for Primary Education, John Blackie, who also acted as
an assessor to the Plowden Committee. His book, 'Inside the
Primary School', written officially and published by HMSO in 1967
(the Plowden Report was published in January that year) popular-
ized the Plowden message (and was shot through with its ideology,
of which more later). In a later book, entitled 'Changing the
Primary School: an Integrated Approach' (1974), the author states
that 'this little book' ('Inside the Primary School'), reprinted in
1968, 1969, 1972, 'has sold 70,000 copies in the U.K. and U.S.A.'
(and that an American edition was also published in 1971). The
book was intended, he said, for parents and the general public,
'but has proved popular among teachers'. In 'Inside the Primary

School', Blackie paints a picture of the ideal type primary school, and discusses present trends. There is a chapter on 'Exploring the World' focusing on discovery methods and first-hand experience; another on creating ('the creative instinct, the desire to make something new for oneself, is unique in man'); another on a foreign language. In his later book, 'Changing the Primary School', Blackie makes clear his own position at the start. The first chapter opens with the remark that 'the assumption on which this book is written is that primary schools ought to be changed', while the second chapter follows this up by saying that 'anyone who recommends a revolutionary change in an educational system might be expected to do two things', and proceeds to do them.

The whole question of the role of HMIs in supporting and propagating the 'primary school revolution' is an interesting one that deserves serious consideration. Important here, for instance, must be the role of Christian Schiller, who appears (to the outside observer) as a kind of prophet. Many of his carefully worked out but apparently spontaneous talks are given in the privately printed book, 'Christian Schiller in his Own Words' (edited by Christopher Griffin-Beale, 1979). Here is an example:

The most important thing that has happened as far as the children are concerned is that we treat them differently. We have come to think of them differently - we no longer think of them as objects into which you push something called knowledge, and if it doesn't go easily, give it a knock. We think of them as individuals growing, learning, and learning as part of growing. We have come to think of them differently and so we have come to act towards them differently. And in turn they have come to act differently towards us. For centuries, boys and girls crept like snails unwillingly to school. In many, many primary schools now the children not only come willingly, they want to come and when they are there they enjoy what they do - and they do so much. For one thing, they learn and even like learning.

And here are the last words of his closing lecture at the annual Plowden Conference of 1975:

We have pioneers now. It is very difficult to see ahead. It will be difficult without any doubt. We've got a long long way to go - a very long way to go. All sorts of new problems will come. I have been voyaging a long time, but I never thought that I could live to see the voyage get so far forward as it has. So may it be with you. 'Not farewell, fareforward, voyagers!

And if Christian Schiller, with his stress on human potential, appears evangelical, there is also the influence of such HMIs as Edith Biggs who certainly had her feet firmly planted on the ground. Her 'Mathematics in Primary Schools' (Schools Council Curriculum Bulletin no. 1), published in 1965, sold 165,000 copies in four years. Her activities are generally regarded as highly influential in bringing about methodological and organizational change in the primary schools - specifically in the area of mathematics or number on which, as we shall see, primary school pupils

spend a lot of their time.
Material has now been presented on how some directors of
education and HMIs, both influential groups, assessed the situation. And here is a benevolently inclined summary of these
developments made in 1978 by Maurice Kogan, one-time secretary
to the Plowden Committee (Kogan 1978, pp. 55-6):
There had been perhaps twenty or thirty years of triumphant
progress by the primary schools in which it seemed that all
that was good was happening through them. A powerful human-
itarianism seemed to suffuse the best of the primary schools.
To the visitor they seemed unbelievably good in their relationships between adults and children, able to elicit powerful interest on the part of the pupils, and yet still be highly productive
in work that was both creative and skilful. Successive reading
surveys since 1948 had shown that 11 year olds in 1964 were
reaching the standards that children 17 months older in 1948
had attained. Against evidence such as this it was difficult for
attacks on the primary schools to be sustained. The new mathematics in the primary schools seemed exciting and impressively
difficult to those brought up in traditional maths.
The Plowden Committee's Report, Kogan goes on, celebrated
the achievement of the primary schools in several hundred pages.
So let us now turn to that Committee and its Report, a very characteristic product of the 1960s.
The Plowden Committee, of course, was sitting at a particular
moment in time. Appointed in August 1963 by Lord Boyle, then,
as Sir Edward, Minister of Education, it got to work just a month
or two before the Robbins Committee reported with its great expansionist programme, immediately and enthusiastically accepted
in full by Sir Alec Douglas-Home, then Conservative Prime
Minister. The Plowden Committee reported in January 1967, that
is, just before the Labour government ran into really severe
economic difficulties, and began to cut education as well as other
public expenditure, postponing the raising of the school leaving
age. It is clearly evident from their Report that the Committee's
general perspective was one of continuous economic growth, full
employment, enhanced affluence and the more or less inevitable
emergence of a more egalitarian society, where human potential,
which they saw as unlimited, would find realization. 'Unemploy-
ment has been almost non-existent since the war, except in some
areas and for a small minority of workers,' they write. 'Incomes
have risen, nutrition has improved, housing is better, the health
service and the rest of the social services have brought help
where it is needed' (Plowden Report, 1, p. 29). Most of the children,
they add, 'are now physically healthy, vigorous, curious and
alert'. This was, perhaps, the last point in time (1965-6) when
such a general optimism expressed something of a consensus. This
is the context of the committee's deliberations, and it is, perhaps,
reflected in what might be called the educational optimism of the
committee's theoretical outlook, and of the practical proposals concerning the role of both teachers and pupils, and of classroom

procedures generally. It is on this aspect that I want to concentrate, as most relevant to the present topic.

The committee specifically identify with what they called, and
so, presumably, perceived, as a number of trends already extant
in the schools, and to some degree claim to base their proposals
on these; however, their theoretical standpoint is also, and perhaps more particularly, grounded on the concept of the unique
make-up of each individual child, as set out in detail in the first
chapter of their report. Not only is each child unique in his rate
of development across three dimensions, physical, intellectual,
emotional, but also children generally have an innate, enquiring,
discovery-oriented, searching character or 'nature'. This is central to their reasoning, as Richard Peters has pointed out (Peters
1969). From this is derived the immense stress on the need to
individualize the work and activities of the children, and so of the
teachers' involvement with the children. Class teaching should
be reduced, work should be individualized, grouping should be
used if only as an economy of teacher time. Education is a process
of discovery or enquiry, and this is what is central to learning.
The teacher must lead from behind, stimulating, encouraging, unobtrusively guiding. Each child's activities must be appropriate
for that particular child, having these particular rates of development, at this particular moment in time. Such was the blueprint
of the role of the ideal-type teacher, and of the pupil, as set
out by Plowden.

It can hardly be denied that this was a highly 'progressive'
picture or syndrome, one that was built on, developed, and took
further the 'child-centred' ideology of the past, and, it was
claimed, one which reflected what was actually happening in the
schools themselves - or at least the main trends there. I suggest,
given the context of the time, it was this picture of the schools
that made a major impact. No one was in a position to know what
actually went on in the schools, or ever will be presumably.
Plowden stated what should happen; how many mistook the rhetoric for the reality?

III

We come now to the most difficult part of this chapter. What was
really happening in the primary schools in the 1960s? I have just
said that no one can really know. And that is clearly true. But
can we attempt a reconstruction?

First, what can be culled from the Plowden Report itself? There
is first the survey the HMIs undertook on behalf of the committee.
This categorizes the 20,000 plus primary schools in the country
under nine mutually exclusive categories. Characteristically, no
explanation is given as to how the HMIs set about this job, and
little information on what they were actually asked to do. Table
1.1 is derived from the section of the Report which describes the
results of the survey.

Table 1.1 Plowden Report: HMI categorization of primary schools
Total schools = 20,664

Category	Description	No. of schools	% of primary school population	No. of pupils
1	'In most respects a school of outstanding quality' 'Pacemakers and leaders of educational advance'	109	1	29,000
2	'A good school with some outstanding features' 'High quality, far above average, but . . .'	1,538	9	–
1 + 2	10 per cent in 2 categories of excellence			
3	'A good school in most respects without any special distinction'	4,155	23	–
1+2+3	'One third of the children in primary schools go to schools which are quite clearly good'			
4	'A school without many good features, but showing signs of life with seeds of growth in it' 'Promising'	3,385	16	–
5	'A school with too many weaknesses to go in category 2 or 3, but distinguished by specially good personal relationships' ('Often with large numbers of immigrant children')	1,384	6	–
6	'A decent school without enough merit to go in category 3 and yet too solid for category 8' 'run of the mill' schools	6,058	28	–
7	'Curate's egg school, with good and bad features'	2,022	9	–
8	'A school markedly out of touch with current practice and knowledge, and with few compensating features'	1,309	5	–
9	'A bad school where children suffer from laziness, indifference, gross incompetence or unkindness on the part of the staff'	28	0.1	4,333

Note: Plowden lumps together:
  (i) Categories 1 + 2 = 'excellent' (10 per cent)
  (ii) Categories 1 + 2 + 3 = 'clearly good' (one-third)
  (iii) Categories 6 + 8 + 9 = 'run of the mill' and 'bad' (one-third)

  This leaves another third (categories 4, 5, 7).

Source: Constructed from Plowden Report, 1, pp. 101-2.

What transpires is that the HMIs held that 10 per cent of
schools were good and even outstanding. And that in all about
one-third of the schools were good in terms of the general, but
rather vague, criteria used. The bulk of these, 23 per cent, are
defined as schools that are 'good ., . . in most respects without
any special distinction'. Of the remaining two-thirds (that is, the
large majority) 16 per cent were in Category 4, that is, there was
hope they might improve, 28 per cent were in Category 6, defined
as 'decent . . . run of the mill' schools (a description that sounds
intentionally derogatory), 6 per cent (Category 5) were good on
personal relations but were poverty stricken or swamped by
'immigrants', while 9 per cent were defined as 'curate's egg
schools' (Category 7), a definition that is difficult to make much
sense of, containing both 'good and bad features'. These latter
categories cover about 60 per cent of all primary schools of all
types.

Presumably, or perhaps, the 10 per cent best schools can be
equated with schools in which the primary school 'revolution' had
taken place - or should the 23 per cent in Category 3 also be included? It may be best to confine this assessment to Categories 1
and 2, to regard schools in Category 3 as half-way there, and
those in Category 4 as hopefully (according to Plowden) also
going the same way.

However this may be, it would seem that, in 1964 or 1965, when
the survey was made, only a minority of primary schools had been
transformed along 'modern lines', though an uncertain proportion
of others was perceived as following in that way. The report gives
a description of three schools at this stage 'run successfully on
modern lines', which, it is said, might fall into any of Categories
1, 2 and 3. These are an infant, a junior mixed, and a junior
mixed and infants' (JMI) school. These descriptions might prove
useful, but they give little indication, for instance, relating to
teaching styles or what goes on inside the classroom. It is the
feel or tone of the school or classroom as a whole that they describe, and seem most interested in, rather than the teaching/
learning process going on within them (Plowden Report 1, pp.
103-6).

Further information, though also of a rather imprecise character, can be gleaned from some of the surveys carried through for
the Plowden Committee in 1964, reported in volume 2. In a sample
survey, for instance, HMIs were asked to rate schools on a five-
point scale on the extent to which they were 'in line with modern
educational trends'. 3 per cent of the sample were rated as 'very
good' as far as acceptance of these trends was concerned, 18 per
cent as 'good', 47 per cent as 'average', 29 per cent as 'below
average', and 3 per cent as 'poor'.[2] Summing the first two categories together gives 21 per cent in either the 'very good' or
'good' categories. The 'modern educational trends' which the
HMIs were specifically asked to take into consideration were four:
(i) 'Permissive discipline?' (ii) 'Provision for individual rates of
progress?' (iii) 'Readiness to reconsider the content of education?'

(iv) 'Awareness of the unity of knowledge?' While this gives an interesting indication of the Plowden Committee's perceptions as to what in fact were the most significant modern educational trends, it is difficult to know what to make of the quantitative evidence provided. HMIs were instructed, in answering this and similar questions involving five-point scales, to 'allow for a national distribution of (i) 5 per cent (ii) 20 per cent (iii) 50 per cent (iv) 20 per cent (v) 5 per cent.' This seems fairly effectively to prejudge the situation. Perhaps the most significant figure, taking this instruction into account, is the 29 per cent 'below average' schools, since this is significantly greater than the recommended statistical pattern of 20 per cent only.

The same survey also reported that 55 per cent of this sample of schools classified children by 'age and achievement', that is, used streaming, while 43 per cent classified children by age only, which implies non-streaming; the remaining 2 per cent classifying children by 'other means'.[3] Further information gained shows that, in the words of the report, 'junior schools were much more likely than the others to be streamed', that 'three-fifths of J.M.I. schools were also streamed'; and that the larger the schools were the more likely they were to be streamed (for instance, 70 per cent of schools with 500 or more pupils were streamed, compared with 56 per cent of schools with from 351 to 500 pupils).

Since the move to non-streaming is a specific feature of the mid-late 1960s, and since it has important implications for the methodology and ethos of the school and classroom in terms of teaching procedures, it is worth pursuing this topic in greater detail.

Volume 2 contains an appendix (11) giving an abridged version of two reports submitted to the Plowden Committee by the National Foundation for Educational Research, which had been commissioned by the DES to carry through a study of the organization of junior schools and effects of streaming with the aim of reporting to the Committee. The full report was, of course, only finally published in 1970, but this is not here referred to.

The data in this appendix derive from a general survey of current practice conducted by questionnaire in 1963, sent to 2,290 schools (there was an 82 per cent response). From the figures presented it is concluded 'that a junior school pupil in 1963 was much more likely to be in a school using a form of homogeneous rather than heterogeneous ability grouping - in fact at least 56 per cent of all pupils were in schools using homogeneous ability grouping', though a note states that the figure is probably nearer 70 per cent. Once again, it is the large schools which are shown to use streaming most consistently - 65 per cent of them were streamed, only 6 per cent entirely unstreamed, and 5 per cent unstreamed except for one year group. Nevertheless a later statement says that '19 per cent of schools at present using homogeneous streaming intended to introduce non-streaming or to extend it beyond the first year'; this statement occurs in a section headed New Trends in Junior School Organisation. Similarly 36 per cent of schools using non-streaming 'streamed' their fourth

year pupils, but 24 per cent intended to change this and un-
stream them (Plowden Report, 2, pp. 550ff.).

In a section entitled The Characteristics and Attitudes of
Teachers in Streamed and Non-Streamed Schools, it is stated that
'the climate in the unstreamed school - if we are to judge by what
its teachers say about themselves, their methods and their attitudes - is more permissive and tolerant, less structured and
places less emphasis on the more traditional methods of class
teaching than its streamed counterpart'. An attempt was made to
dichotomize teachers answering the questionnaire according to
the types of lessons they gave, into those giving 'traditional
lessons' and those giving 'progressive lessons'. Item analysis
yielded versions containing the following items:

'Traditional' - writing class prepared compositions; learning
lists of spellings; formal grammar - understanding parts of
speech; saying and learning tables by rote.

'Progressive' - projects - in which the child does his own
'research'; pupils working or helping each other in groups;
practical arithmetic, e.g. measuring, apparatus work; free
activity.

It seems that these two types, or styles of teaching, related
to whether the school was streamed or unstreamed. Generally it
was also found that the younger teachers tended to have more
'progressive' opinions, particularly in their rejection of 11-plus
selection, their 'permissiveness' and their 'tolerance of noise'.
Those with two years' experience or less were the most hostile to
the 11-plus. On teaching methods it is said that teachers in
streamed schools, on average, tended to make more frequent use
of 'traditional lessons' and less frequent use of 'progressive
lessons' than teachers in non-streamed schools. Again it was in
the streamed schools that significantly more use was made of
tests of various kinds to check progress and diagnose difficulties.
However, analysis of the 'traditional and progressive scores' of
teachers in streamed and non-streamed schools shows that
'teachers in both types of school are fairly "traditional"' (my
italics - BS); the differences between them, it is said, would
seem to be 'nuances rather than marked divergences of opinion'.
This, I think, is an important and significant finding. Analysis
relating to the degree of permissiveness, attitudes to physical
punishment, etc., are used to support this statement. As already
indicated, the 'most discriminative statement between the two
sets of teachers (streamed and non-streamed) is "the 11 plus
examination is an entirely fair method of assessing a child's
abilities" '. 69 per cent of non-streamed teachers disagreed with
this, while 56 per cent of streamed teachers agreed. However, as
is then pointed out, this indicates that 'substantial proportions of
teachers in both groups are opposed to the system' (Plowden
Report, 2, pp. 557-65).

This interim report concludes with a short section on attitudes
of teachers to streaming and non-streaming. The conclusions given
are that 'substantial proportions of teachers are in favour of

streaming' and that 'since of all junior schools in the country
which are large enough to do so, at least 65 per cent stream and
only 11 per cent clearly do not, it seems reasonable to suppose
that the majority of junior school teachers in England and Wales
are in favour of the practice, that a substantial proportion are
undecided, and that only relatively few are firmly committed to
the opposing view', that is, to non-streaming. The researchers
continue, rather rashly, as things worked out, that 'this finding
must be stressed at a time when some writers suggest that the
death knell of streaming has already sounded'. They add that,
coupled with the finding concerning parents' views (parents
generally preferred streaming) the evidence suggests that 'any
universal change recommended may meet with considerable opposition - particularly since the attitudes for or against streaming
seem to form part of a whole syndrome of views, practices and
beliefs' (Plowden Report, 2, p. 571).

I have placed considerable emphasis on the data concerning the
move to unstreaming in primary schools because, in spite of the
researchers' predictions, in fact non-streaming took off with
astonishing rapidity during the mid to late 1960s, having the
expressed support of the Plowden Committee itself, which stated
its views moderately but firmly on this issue. We do have further
hard data which makes this clear beyond doubt. For instance,
Deanne Bealing, in a survey of two local authorities in the Midlands carried through in 1971, to which we will return shortly,
found that the vast majority of primary schools were, in fact,
unstreamed (Bealing 1972). Neville Bennett found much the same
thing in his survey of all primary schools in Lancashire and
Cumbria in 1975 - only 13 per cent of the schools which replied
to his questionnaire were streamed (Bennett 1976, p. 58).
Finally the HMI primary survey of 1978 found that only 4 per cent
of children in 9-year-old classes in the survey were streamed
(HMI Survey 1978, p. 28). Within fifteen years, then, the
position found in 1963 was totally reversed. While it can, of
course, be argued that fine streaming may have continued within
the non-streamed class, the swing to unstreaming as a principle
of school organization appears to be one chief characteristic of
the so-called 'primary school revolution' which cannot be gainsaid.
Its implications will be discussed later.

IV

The first systematic study of the actual organization of junior
school classrooms was that undertaken by Deanne Bealing in
1970, and published in 1972 (Bealing 1972). This was a questionnaire survey of a 10 per cent sample of teachers in two local
authority areas in the Midlands, one of which organized its
secondary education on a comprehensive basis, the other on a
selective basis. An 89 per cent response was achieved from 189
teachers in a carefully drawn representative sample of classes.

The survey results reflected, as the author puts it, the 'new ideas and trends in primary education [which] have resulted in the erosion of the traditional classroom layout with its rows of desks and static children'. It was found that 'the overwhelming majority of classrooms contained children of mixed abilities and attainments. With the exception of remedial classes, streaming was totally absent in the comprehensive authority schools and even under the selective authority less than one in five teachers had streamed classes.' It was also found that the system of grouping was widely popular. About four teachers in five adopted a group layout for their classrooms although only a small proportion were equipped with modern tables or table units. Again 'only about one fifth of the teachers reported that their desk was in the traditional centre front position', and about two-thirds of teachers split their time about equally between sitting at their desk and circulating amongst the children – the other one-third 'circulated most of the time'. The prevalence of group layout, teacher mobility and opportunities for pupils to work independently outside the classroom 'all suggest an informal approach to organisation'.

While the survey found that a considerable amount of mobility was permitted to pupils, it was also found 'that teachers still reserve a relatively tight measure of control'. Further about two-thirds of the teachers streamed within the class in terms of their grouping strategy, though grouping was also widely based on friendship patterns. Finally, as regards the organization of children's work, it appeared that class teaching was still quite widely used for all subjects except reading, but that the most striking feature relating to teaching methods was 'the predominance of individual work' – an outcome to which the whole thrust of the Plowden Report was directed. The evidence on the nature of group work was difficult to interpret, though this also was popular in all subjects, especially mathematics and art and craft. Bealing concludes as follows:

> Some of the results, if substantiated in follow-up work, question widely held beliefs about the 'primary school revolution'. Despite the relatively informal classroom layouts adopted by the vast majority of teachers there was so much evidence of tight teacher control over such matters as where children sit and move that it seems highly doubtful that there is much opportunity for children to choose or organise their own activities in most classrooms. There was widespread use of groupings based on similar abilities and attainments although the overwhelming majority of teachers were working with unstreamed classes (Bealing 1972, p. 235).

These conclusions are supported by another survey of a different character carried through by Moran a year earlier, and published in 1971. In this study, also carried through by questionnaire, Moran gained information about how teachers who specifically operated 'the integrated day' organized their classes. The subjects were members of a conference run on the topic a year or

two earlier. It is interesting to note that a main point which
emerged was similar to Bealing's; that is, that the bulk of
teachers organizing their classes in this way in fact normally
maintained a tight control over the children's activities. This is
worth bringing out here, because 'the integrated day' is generally
regarded as the most 'way-out' method of organizing children's
learning activities, though it should be quite evident that complex organizations of this kind, if they are to be carried through
successfully, do specifically require a high degree of teacher
control.

The next survey, which can claim to have a systematic character, was that carried through by Neville Bennett at the University of Lancaster, as a preliminary to his controversial study
published as 'Teaching Styles and Pupil Progress' (1976). This
was also a questionnaire survey, directed specifically to class
teachers in primary schools. It covered both teaching methods
adopted by the teachers (e.g. seating arrangements, classroom
organization, curriculum organization, discipline problems, etc.)
and elicited teachers' opinions about education, relating, for
instance, to aims, educational issues, and teaching methods. On
the basis of responses to this questionnaire, Bennett, using
cluster analysis, classified his teachers into twelve teacher types
or what he called teaching 'styles'. Only one of these styles, comprising just 9 per cent of the population studied (468 teachers)
was categorized as 'progressive' in the Plowden sense; that is,
met the Plowden criteria relating to progressive education. The
rest are described as either 'mixed' in their styles, or largely
'traditional'. Although the data on which Bennett's categorization was made can be criticized, nevertheless it is legitimate to
draw the conclusion that the 'primary school revolution' had only
marginally penetrated the north-west, and this, indeed, is one
of Bennett's own conclusions (1976, pp. 37ff.). Incidentally,
Bennett found that 83 per cent of his teachers held that 'pupils
should be told what to do and how to do it.'

Finally there is the evidence from the first large-scale observational study in primary schools, that carried through as part
of the ORACLE research programme, based at Leicester. This
focused on close observation both of pupils and teachers in over
100 primary school classrooms in three local authority areas in
the Midlands; the results of the first year's observation, carried
through in 1975-6, has recently been published (Galton et al.
1980). Briefly, it was found that the vast majority of these
classes were what is best called 'informally' organized, in Bealing's sense. Perhaps the most striking finding was the extent of
individualization both of work and of attention in the primary
classrooms. However, for our purposes, an important outcome was
the extent to which the teaching was found to be largely didactic
in character. The promotion of enquiry or discovery learning
appeared almost non-existent. Since this was a main prescription
of the Plowden Report, this finding is significant. Collaborative
group work or enquiry was also found to be seldom realized -

many teachers never used collaborative group work at all for
any subject. Further, as regards the content of education, a
major emphasis on 'the basics' was also found. One-third of normal teaching sessions was devoted to number work, or mathematics, one-third to language (the great bulk of which time was
spent on writing), and one-third to general subjects, topic and
project work, art and craft, and science (which hardly featured,
as the HMIs survey also found).[4] These findings concerning the
curriculum confirm Bassey's study (in Nottinghamshire), and
the HMI Primary Survey of 1978 (Bassey 1978; HMI Survey 1978).
Certainly there was little evidence there of any fundamental
shift either in the content of education or in the procedures of
teaching and learning, in the sense that didacticism still largely
prevails.

V

What can we conclude about all this? Perhaps it is too early, yet,
to conclude anything, but one general point may be made. It
seems that there has been a rather fundamental change in primary
schools (perhaps more in infant than in junior schools) in terms
of their internal structure, organization, and perhaps particularly in relationships. But whether it ever amounted to anything
which might be called a 'revolution' seems extremely doubtful.
Within the general change to non-streaming, which is symptomatic
of a transformation in attitudes and approach (and in objectives)
within the classroom, didacticism is the most general mode, or at
least so it appears from the evidence to hand. While pupils are
now given much greater responsibility in the organization of their
work, it does not seem that they have much opportunity to control
its content and direction, except, perhaps, in marginal cases. In
other words, the image of the way-out, 'progressive' teacher,
propagated by the media as a result of the Tyndale events, seems
very far indeed from actuality. If this is true, we are left with a
problem. Why did it all happen? What is it all about? How was it
that primary school methods became a national political issue
around 1975-6?

    It may, perhaps, be argued, that, as the Plowden Committee
reported and hoped, there was a definite 'trend' taking place
within the primary schools in the late 1950s and early 1960s which
had the potential of carrying all before it. Such concepts as enhanced pupil responsibility for their own studies, the promotion
of enquiry and of independent initiative on the part of pupils,
flexibility of organization which is a keynote of the report, allied
with wider contemporary phenomena or 'happenings', may have
been seen as a threat of a breakout developing also within
secondary schools and higher education implying that the so-
called control function of education was at risk. It was not only
the primary schools, of course, that were subjected to criticism
at the time of Callaghan's speech at Ruskin College in 1976. Wider

issues were also raised especially about the relations of education to industry. In fact the whole 'relatively autonomous' area of education was under attack, and a mobilization taking place of those elements in society that wished to see a strong reimposition of control. Such a tactic may have underlain the exaggeration of the rhetoric about primary education in a deliberate attempt to provide a rational basis for the reimposition of control. No one who visited a number of primary schools in an industrial area on the day after the publication of Bennett's book, as I had the opportunity of doing, can doubt its immediate deflationary effect on teachers in the schools. They saw it, or rather, its presentation by the media, as a denial of all the values they cherished. And this, of course, was only one of the elements in the situation.

Perhaps the explanation is simpler than that. As suggested earlier, the mid 1960s were the last expansionist period both in the economy and in education. Some kind of 'revolution' in education was then seen as appropriate by almost everyone. By the end of the 1960s this situation had changed radically, and was to change further for the worse in the early 1970s. An educational revolution was no longer seen as appropriate. Any such tendency, therefore, was no longer to be encouraged. The primary school revolution, perhaps it may be concluded, if it took place at all, was premature.

NOTES

1   See Gosden and Sharp (1978), pp. 197-200, for a description
     of Clegg's part in these developments.
2   This survey related to a sample of 171 schools, see Plowden
     Report, 2, Table 6, pp. 225, 278.
3   Plowden Report, 2, Table 7, pp. 226. The actual Table, as
     printed, gives 35 per cent and 45 per cent in the first two
     categories, but these statistical errors (repeated in the text,
     p. 225) must have evaded the proof readers.
4   Observations on which this analysis is based relate to 'nor-
     mal teaching sessions', i.e. those taking place in the class-
     room. They exclude physical education, dancing, singing,
     games, etc.

2 PRIMARY TEACHERS' AIMS, 1969-77

Patricia Ashton

In 1971 1,500 teachers completed a questionnaire on the Aims of Primary Education (Ashton et al. 1975). They were the full staff complement of 200 primary schools spread across England and Wales. In 1979, fifty-three of the sixty teachers involved in the first year of the ORACLE study completed the same questionnaire. The major section of the questionnaire asked teachers to indicate how important they thought each of seventy-two aims is for children in their school. The aims had originally been compiled from the deliberations of some 400 teachers working in discussion groups during 1969-70. This paper sets out the findings from the ORACLE survey and compares them with the national survey of eight years earlier.

The 1971 sample conformed closely to the national distribution of age and sex of primary teachers and of the types of school in which they worked. The ORACLE sample similarly conformed fairly closely to the national picture in the proportion of men to women teachers but the age distribution was a little different; teachers in their thirties were slightly over-represented and those in their fifties and over correspondingly under-represented. The ORACLE sample was confined to only three local authorities and to predominantly suburban schools within those. The 1971 national survey had involved teachers working with five- to eleven-year-olds in infants, junior or primary schools. The ORACLE teachers were confined to the eight-to-ten age group and were working in primary, first and middle schools. In summary, the major differences between the characteristics of the national and the ORACLE samples were that the latter was much smaller, roughly one-thirtieth of the size, involved no teachers of infants and very few teachers in rural schools.

Potentially the most significant difference, however, is that the ORACLE survey was conducted eight years later. The most recent of those eight years in particular have seen major events in the history of primary education. Callaghan's Ruskin College speech in the autumn of 1976 is frequently thought to have initiated the 'Great Debate'. Whether the Great Debate ever actually became such is in doubt but some pressure to reassess priorities in education was in the wind. The same period saw the establishment of the Assessment of Performance Unit and its selection of maths, language and science as the first areas for consideration. Despite all the disclaimers, the creation of a unit with the remit to monitor national standards could hardly fail to impinge on teachers' thoughts about their priorities. The Green Paper (DES

1977) bore a similar message and its emphasis on the skills required by modern industrial society provided a sharp contrast to
the Plowden philosophy published ten years earlier. Another
event was the publication of the Taylor Report which generated
greater community interest in the curriculum. Accountability
entered the vocabulary of education. Most unusually, a piece of
research made an impact during this period and it seemed that
few teachers had not encountered Bennett's (1976) findings in
favour of formal teaching methods as they were popularly represented. The core curriculum was another phrase which entered
teacher discourse. At the same time, economic stringency and
falling rolls brought about drastically reduced promotion opportunities, redeployment and early retirement. These became the
parameters within which teachers have come to view their personal career prospects. All this forms a necessary context within
which to compare teachers' aims in 1979 with 1971.

Two questions were posed to the teachers before they were
asked to rate each of the seventy-two aims for importance. The
first of these characterized two broad fundamental purposes of
primary education and asked the teachers to indicate the relative
weight they gave them by sharing five points between them. The
two purposes were identified and described following the sense
conveyed by the early aims discussion groups that teachers
seemed to operate from within one or other such orientation to
education. The 1971 survey showed that, while all but a very few
teachers subscribed to both purposes to some extent, the one
they favoured was a powerful predictor of the aims to which they
gave greater importance. The two purposes are as follows:

A   The purpose of primary education is to begin to equip
     the child with skills and attitudes which will enable him
     to take his place effectively and competently in society,
     fitting him to make a choice of an occupational role and
     to live harmoniously in his community.

B   The purpose of primary education is to foster the devel-
     opment of the child's individuality and independence
     enabling him to discover his own talents and interests,
     find a full enjoyment of life in his own way and arrive
     at his own attitudes towards society.

For brevity, these can be characterized as respectively a
societal and an individual purpose. The percentages of the 1971
and the 1979 teachers distributing five points in different ways
are given in Table 2.1. While the overall pattern is similar, there
is a perceptible change in the direction of emphasizing the
societal purpose. A very similar proportion, almost three-quarters,
opted for the most nearly balanced position of assigning three to
one purpose and two to the other. There is a reduction of about
5 per cent in those firmly emphasizing the individual purpose
by giving it a four or five and a complementary increase in the
percentage emphasizing the societal purpose.

Table 2.1   Teachers' evaluation of basic purposes of primary education

Societal	Individual	% of 1979 sample	% of 1971 sample
0	5	0	2.1
1	4	7.5	10.1
2	3	32.1	29.9
3	2	39.6	42.4
4	1	18.9	12.2
5	0	1.9	3.3
		100.0	100.0

The second question was designed to reveal teachers' general orientation in their work with children. They were asked to consider seven aspects of development and to indicate which they thought were the two of most importance in primary education and which two were of the least importance. The responses of the two samples are shown in Table 2.2.

Table 2.2   Teachers' perceptions of relative importance of different aspects of development

Aspect of development	Importance	% of 1979 sample	% of 1971 sample
Aesthetic	Most	1.9	6.2
	Least	56.6	15.6
Emotional/personal	Most	43.4	53.6
	Least	9.4	7.8
Intellectual	Most	67.9	52.9
	Least	3.8	12.7
Moral	Most	17.0	22.7
	Least	13.2	10.3
Physical	Most	1.9	3.6
	Least	43.4	51.0
Social	Most	13.2	7.5
	Least	66.0	61.9
Spiritual/religious	Most	13.2	7.5
	Least	66.0	61.9

Once again, the broad picture is similar in 1979 and 1971 with the aspects of development falling in almost exactly the same order in terms of the percentage of teachers considering each of them most important. Within that pattern, however, the shifts are substantial. Two-thirds of the ORACLE teachers rated intellectual development as most important as against half of the 1971 sample of teachers. For the 1971 sample, emotional/personal development

attracted the largest number of choices as most important. While
this aspect retained second place for the ORACLE sample, the
percentage of teachers choosing it fell from 53 to 43. Moral development held third place for both samples but with 5 per cent
fewer teachers selecting it in 1979. Spiritual/religious and social
development tied in fourth place in 1971 and again in 1979 but
6 per cent more teachers selected them as most important on the
latter occasion. Physical and aesthetic development were chosen
by the fewest teachers as most important in both surveys and in
both cases that percentage dropped. 40 per cent more teachers
rated aesthetic development as least important in 1979. This, together with the increase of 15 per cent in teachers selecting intellectual development as most important, constitutes the biggest
difference between the two samples of teachers.

The seventy-two aims named knowledge, skills and qualities
within the areas of intellectual, physical, aesthetic, spiritual/
religious, emotional/personal and social/moral development. The
teachers were asked to rate them for their importance for children
in their school, using the following scale:

5 I think that this aim is of the utmost importance in primary
   education.
4 I think that this aim is of major importance in primary education.
3 I think that this aim is important in primary education.
2 I think that this aim is of minor importance in primary education.
1 I think that this aim is of no importance in primary education.
0 I think that this should not be an aim of primary education.

Table 2.3 summarizes the importance given by the teachers on
the two occasions to those aims which have to do with the formal
curriculum.

It will be seen that the overall order is remarkably similar for
the two samples but that there are very marked differences.
Maths, writing and science have gained in importance and religious
knowledge has lost ground. There were three aims related to
maths. One referred to maths for everyday life, one to computation and one to a 'modern' definition of maths as concerned with
thought and problem solving using the appropriate concepts and
language. When the aims were ranked in the order of the average
score each was given, these three appeared fifteenth, twentieth
and thirty-fourth respectively in the rank order in 1971. Eight
years later, computation had leapt from twentieth place to second,
everyday maths from fifteenth to fifth and 'modern maths' from
thirty-fourth place to tenth.

Of the aims related to writing, spelling had moved from thirty-
third to seventeenth place, legible writing from twenty-fifth to
twenty-first, writing clear and meaningful English from forty-
fourth place to thirtieth and basic grammar from fifty-first to
thirty-fifth. Writing interestingly and with sensitivity retained
its fortieth place with a slightly reduced average score.

Table 2.3   Relative importance of curricular aims as perceived by teachers in 1971 and 1979

1971	1979
OF MAJOR IMPORTANCE Reading	OF MAJOR IMPORTANCE Reading Maths
VERY IMPORTANT Oracy Maths	VERY IMPORTANT Oracy Writing
IMPORTANT Writing Art and craft General knowledge Religious knowledge	IMPORTANT General knowledge Art and craft Science
OF MINOR IMPORTANCE Physical education Science Sex education Music	OF MINOR IMPORTANCE Physical education Sex education Music Religious knowledge
OF NO IMPORTANCE Second language	OF NO IMPORTANCE Second language

Clearly, the basic skills were substantially more important to the ORACLE teachers than to the national sample. Maths had become very nearly equivalent to reading in importance. Fluent and accurate reading actually slightly increased in average score, while reading with understanding marginally lost ground in comparison, these two aims taking first and third place respectively as against fourth and second in 1971. Though writing had slightly less importance than reading and maths for the ORACLE teachers, it followed these much more closely than it had done for the national survey teachers in 1971.

The change in the placing of science from sixty-second to fifty-first is less marked but 13 per cent more teachers did rate it as important. The average rating given to knowledge of the Bible and Christian beliefs dropped from important to minor importance and knowledge of the major world religions remained one of the four lowest-rated aims.

The importance given to oracy, the middling importance given to art and craft and general knowledge and the low importance given to physical education, sex education and music remained the same. A second language retained its position as last with a reduced average score.

These were the ways in which the opinions of the ORACLE teachers were akin to and different from those of the national sample. They were a different and much smaller group but it is difficult, given the educational history of the period, to resist the hypothesis that they do reflect a national trend.

Aims to do with personal and social behaviour were rated, on the whole, little differently by the ORACLE teachers than by those who took part in the national survey. These two sets of aims are listed in Tables 2.4 and 2.5 in the order of average scores given by the 1979 sample. The place in the total rank order is given for each aim together with the placing by the 1971 sample for comparison.

Table 2.4   Aims concerned with personal behaviour: positions in rank order of aims in 1979 and 1971

	1979	1971
OF MAJOR IMPORTANCE		
Enjoyment of school work	6=	5
Reasoned judgments and choices	8	23
Happiness	11	1
VERY IMPORTANT		
Obedience	20	17
Individuality	23	6=
Planning independent work	28=	32
Enthusiasm and eagerness	30=	10=
Questioning attitude	34	24
IMPORTANT		
Self-confidence	35=	18=
Industriousness	37	36
Inventiveness and creativity	41=	30=
Playing a part in own development	41=	55=
Self control	46=	22
Forming a considered opinion	48	50
Criticism and discrimination	50	57=
Adaptability and flexibility	52=	47
OF MINOR IMPORTANCE		
Understanding own emotions	56	54

Only one aim to do with personal behaviour gained appreciably in importance. The ability to make reasoned judgments and choices moved from twenty-third place to eighth in the rank order and attracted an average rating of major importance rather than importance. Four 'personal' aims lost importance to a noticeable degree. That the child should be 'happy, cheerful and well balanced' (listed on the Table as 'happiness') rated first in the national survey, fell to eleventh with the ORACLE teachers and only just received an average rating of major importance. Another priority in the national survey, that the child should be 'an individual, developing in his own way' ('individuality') fell further, from sixth to twenty-third for the ORACLE sample and lost its rating of major importance. Enthusiasm and eagerness lost ground from tenth to thirtieth place and self-control from twenty-second to forty-sixth.

Table 2.5 Aims concerned with social behaviour: positions in rank order of aims in 1979 and 1971

	1979	1971
OF MAJOR IMPORTANCE		
Moral values	4	3
Care of property	6=	6=
VERY IMPORTANT		
Tolerance	12=	9
Courtesy	16	8
Kindness and consideration	17=	13=
Ability to engage in discussion	26	37=
Community responsibility	27	26
Appropriate behaviour	28=	28=
IMPORTANT		
Good social mixing	46=	28=
Clear, fluent and appropriate speech	46=	49
OF MINOR IMPORTANCE		
Forming lasting relationships	61=	57=

In respect of social behaviour, aims were viewed remarkably similarly by the national sample and the ORACLE teachers. The emphasis remains upon behaviour which is responsible and generally thoughtful of others. The two aims to do with making personal relationships with others lost ground. 'Good social mixing, being able to make easy social contacts with other children and adults in work and play situations' lost eighteen places in the rank order. 'Forming lasting relationships' slipped to a rating of minor importance.

Together with the changes in rating of maths, writing and science, these slightly different views of desirable personal and social behaviour present a 'harder nosed', more cognitively oriented face to primary education. In 1971, infant school teachers tended significantly to rate aims to do with personal behaviour more highly than did the teachers of older children. While personal aims collectively have lost little ground, happiness, individuality, enthusiasm and eagerness may have suffered from the absence of teachers of younger children from the ORACLE sample. Nevertheless, that a sample of primary school teachers in 1979 define the ideal eleven-year-old as a comprehensively skilled and rational being rather more than a happy, co-operative reader, seems to

be in tune with the background of economic and educational
change. The emphasis on moral and social acceptability is unchanged.

Finally the teachers were asked to read through descriptions
of ways of teaching and to indicate which seemed to be closest to
their own approach. These descriptions, written by a group of
teachers as unemotively as possible, ranged from what might
loosely be called a very 'traditional' approach to a very 'progressive' one. The descriptions follow and the percentage of teachers
identifying themselves with each in 1971 and 1979 is shown.

MOST TRADITIONAL

There is an ordered body of knowledge and skills that should be
taught in the primary school. This is best taught in logical pro-
gression, and most economically to groups of children of roughly
equal ability in a quiet orderly atmosphere. The teacher's task is
to have full knowledge of what he wants his children to know, to
be capable, by analysis and experience, of presenting it to them
interestingly and in as well programmed a manner as possible,
and to set the pace of learning.
    1971:   8.9 per cent
    1979: 13.3 per cent

TRADITIONAL

There are certain basic language and number skills that should
be taught in the primary school. As well as those there are certain other areas of knowledge that should form part of the curriculum. The teacher's task is to present work in each area of
knowledge as stimulatingly as possible so that each child can
learn as much as he is capable of.
    1971: 20.3 per cent
    1979: 31.1 per cent

MODERATE

There are certain basic language and number skills that should
be learned through structured teaching. The remainder of the
children's learning can best be guided by a mixture of children's
and teacher's choice. The teacher's task is to teach the basic
skills as individually as possible and to encourage and stimulate
children to use them effectively and imaginatively in all other
work.
    1971: 45.6 per cent
    1979: 40.0 per cent

PROGRESSIVE

Children learn better when involved in individual work that
absorbs them and this is fostered by giving children as much
freedom of choice as possible in what they learn, when and how.
To enable effective choices to be made, certain skills have to be
mastered. The teacher's task is to provide stimulating opportunities to learn and practise the basic language and number skills
in order to have the tools to use in their self-chosen enquiries.
    1971: 17.1 per cent
    1979: 13.3 per cent

MOST PROGRESSIVE

Children learn only when they want to learn - when not knowing
becomes an obstacle to doing what they want to do. Learning,
therefore, takes place most effectively when children are involved in individual enquiries of their own choice; thus the children's interests and needs as they arise constitute the curriculum.
The teacher's task is to create a psychological environment in
which enquiry can arise and a physical environment rich and
stimulating enough to enable it to be pursued successfully at the
child's own pace.
    1971: 8.1 per cent
    1979: 2.3 per cent
    The greater preference for a more formal teaching role among
the ORACLE teachers is quite marked. 10 per cent fewer teachers
opted for the 'progressive' descriptions, 5 per cent fewer for the
'moderate' approach and 15 per cent more for the 'traditional' descriptions. Roughly 15 per cent of both samples chose the extremes
but while these were almost even in 1971, the balance had shifted
substantially to the formal extreme in 1979. Overall, in 1971, the
distribution of teachers' preferences for teaching role conformed
very closely to a normal curve. It would be very interesting to
know if the skewed curve illustrated by the ORACLE sample
would be repeated nationally at the beginning of the 1980s.
    To sum up the results of this enquiry, it seems that a primary
school child in the early 1980s is likely to have a broadly similar
but differently focused experience from his older brothers and
sisters in school at the beginning of the last decade. He is more
likely to meet teachers concerned to equip him with skills and
attitudes which they judge society to require. Probably more
attention will be given to his mathematical and formal language
competence. He is more likely to find science in the curriculum
and less likely to have very much religious education. His ac-
quaintance with general knowledge and the arts will continue as a
moderate priority. While required to be equally considerate and
well-behaved, his personal and social development will be tilted
more towards a reasoning than a feeling engagement with his
physical and social environment. All this is likely to be sought in

an atmosphere of greater formality with more overt teacher direction of his activities.

3 CLASSROOM ORGANIZATION, 1970-7

Deanne Boydell

Primary teachers are sometimes presented by their detractors, both inside and outside the profession, as keen to jump on to every educational bandwagon which presents itself and just as keen to abandon it when the going gets tough or some different innovation appears. Thus, in the years following the publication of the Plowden Report (1967), journalistic descriptions of the exciting changes which had undoubtedly taken place in some primary classrooms fed the popular view that primary teaching, as previously known, was being swept away. Terms like the 'integrated day' (which was not even mentioned in the Plowden Report) and 'family (or vertical) grouping' found their way into educational parlance and it was popularly supposed that a kind of revolution in both thinking and practice had taken place within all the nation's primary schools. Of course the supposed existence of such sudden and far-reaching changes evoked a widespread response from commentators of all kinds variously extolling, defending or criticizing the 'progressive' nature of primary schooling. Arguments and controversy about the merits or otherwise of Plowden-type education soon became intertwined with two other issues, the concern with pupils' 'standards' in the basic skills and the notion that teachers could or should be held 'accountable' in some way for their work. In due course a reactionary backlash appeared in some writing and the popular image of primary classrooms seemed to undergo another change. It was being suggested that teachers, disenchanted by their flirtations with modern methods, were returning on a large scale to the well-tried and proven techniques of conventional teaching. Teachers, it was implied, had returned to their senses.

Needless to say such an admittedly oversimplified account is not at all complimentary to primary teachers. It suggests that, far from being independent and professional judges of the great mass of ideas and advice with which they are bombarded, they are for the most part fickle followers of educational fashion. However, this issue, important though it is, begs another more fundamental question. In reality has the past decade actually seen at classroom level (and not just simply in the prevailing writings of educationists) a major swing both towards and away from 'progressive' type practices? Can the assumption of a revolution followed by a backlash be validated?

Surprisingly, until recently, there has been very little effort

to describe or monitor (let alone evaluate) 'new' classroom practices except in the writings of such innovating practitioners as
Brown and Precious (1968) and Ridgway and Lawton (1968). This
is perhaps understandable in view of the degree of autonomy primary teachers often possess and the grass-roots origins of many
innovative experiments. However, it is hardly conducive to a
widespread understanding of what is happening inside the schools.
To add to the confusion it very soon emerged that teachers themselves were often attaching very different meanings to the new
terms which came into use. Several years ago, for instance, one
study found that teachers who claimed to practise some form of
integrated day in their classrooms were using the term in a wide
variety of ways. The term simply referred to different types of
classroom organization in which children were engaged in several
ongoing activities at once. In other words at classroom level it
was found to imply nothing about the degree of children's choice
or the extent to which the day was characterized by uniform or
formalized breaks (Moran 1971).

Gradually, through the 1970s, questions started to be asked
about what was actually happening in the schools. Studies began
to suggest that something of a myth may have grown up about
the impact of Plowden-type thinking (Bealing 1972; Bennett 1976)
and classroom practices themselves became a focus of attention
(Bassey 1978; HMI Survey of Primary Education in England 1978;
Galton, Simon and Croll 1980). However none of these investigations were concerned with change, per se; in other words there
were no efforts to monitor what was really happening to teachers'
classroom practices in the immediate post-Plowden era. Did the
1970s see a period of development of Plowden-type thinking, a
consolidation of some changes or the abandoning of 'progressive'
practices? The purpose of the research described here was to
throw some light on these kinds of issues by returning to a
sample of schools whose teachers had reported on their methods
of classroom organization seven years earlier and asking the
teachers now working in them to report again.

The original 1970 survey involved approximately 10 per cent of
all the junior teachers working in two local authorities, one of
which was then operating a comprehensive system of education
and the other a selective system based on the 11-plus. Efforts
were made to make the sample representative of the number of
teachers working in the two authorities and in schools of different sizes. For example, 189 teachers in thirty-nine randomly
selected schools took part in the survey. This represented a very
high response rate of almost nine teachers in ten. Each teacher
completed a three-part questionnaire on the way their own classroom was organized. Part I dealt with organizational features such
as streaming which are primarily matters of school policy. Part II
looked at various 'geographical' features of the classroom like the
layout of furniture and children's locations and movements and
Part III was concerned with the organization of children's work
and activities. Full details of the 1970 survey and its findings

were reported at the time (Bealing 1972). The teachers' reports
revealed a very extensive range of practices although the overwhelming majority of teachers had unstreamed classes and adopted
a form of organization, if only for part of the time, which allowed
children to engage simultaneously in a variety of activities. The
findings highlighted the deficiencies of dichotomies like tradi-
tional-progressive to describe what was happening at classroom
level (a teacher might be 'progressive' in some aspects of her
organization and not in others). The study was also the first to
suggest, on the basis of objective information, that the so-called
primary revolution could be more of a fiction than a fact.

In 1974, four years after the original survey, local government
reorganization brought about the merger of the two LEAs which
had taken part and the adoption of a single policy of comprehensive education for all the secondary schools in the new authority.
Three years after this, in 1977, the thirty-nine schools which had
taken part in the original investigation were invited to take part
in a follow-up survey. This was the year which marked the tenth
anniversary of the publication of the Plowden Report.

In the seven-year period between the original and follow-up
surveys two of the original schools had closed but amongst the
remaining thirty-seven only two declined to take part in the follow-
up investigation. Overall 187 teachers reported. This represented
another high response rate, which was only slightly lower than
before, of more than eight teachers in ten. Almost a quarter of
the teachers had been teaching a junior class in the same school
at the time of the first survey and of these more than half remembered completing the original questionnaire. The questionnaire
used in the follow-up survey was a slightly modified version of
the original but its length, format and questions remained basically unchanged. A full description of the 1977 follow-up investigation and its results have been published elsewhere (Boydell
1980). The purpose of this article is not to repeat the comprehensive comparison of classroom organization in 1970 and 1977 which
the follow-up survey made possible but to summarize the main
findings and discuss their implications.

By 1977 streaming had totally disappeared. A few 'remedial'
children still found themselves in special permanent 'remedial'
classes but many were simply withdrawn from their normal unstreamed classes for regular extra help. Two other innovative
organizational practices mentioned in the Plowden Report, namely
vertical (or family) grouping and team teaching (in some form or
other), had not found the same success. Vertical grouping had
become a little more popular (even in large schools where mixed
ages within the same class was not an organizational necessity)
and was reported by almost a third of the teachers, but team
teaching was still extremely rare. Thus, in terms of the organizational features of the classroom which the teacher can influence
only in so far as she can influence school policy, it would appear
that the sole innovative practice to find universal appeal was
unstreaming.

The class teacher may have only an indirect or limited influence on some decisions which affect her work. However, with respect to the 'geographical' aspects of her classroom she frequently has a more or less free hand. In 1970 teachers in the survey schools adopted predominantly group layouts. These were still as popular in 1977 although there was a noticeable move toward the use of smaller seated groups. In 1970 the overwhelming majority of teachers had rejected the traditional centre position in front of the class for their own desk. By 1977 even fewer teachers were placing it here although teachers seemed to be doing more teaching from their desks than previously. Circulating round the classroom was still included in the repertoire of almost every teacher. However, fewer teachers reported that they circulated for most of the time, more reported that they divided their time about equally between circulating and seeing children at their desks and more reported that they spent most of their time sitting at their desks and getting children to come and see them. This latter practice was extremely rare seven years previously and although still uncommon it had increased considerably in popularity and was used by almost one teacher in eight in the follow-up survey.

Apart from the information on teacher location and movement there were further hints that the classrooms in 1977 were more static and tightly controlled than in 1970. There was less opportunity for children to engage in independent work either individually or in small groups outside the classroom. There was slightly less pupil choice of their special 'base' seats within the classroom. There was less probability that children would be allowed to change work places without the prior consent of their teacher. There was also considerably less likelihood that teachers would regularly move children to different places for work in one or more curricular areas. Finally there was a slight increase in the proportion of teachers who expected children to ask permission for temporary moves such as consulting them or collecting materials (although the overwhelming majority still allowed children to make this type of move on their own initiative). None of the observed changes was large or dramatic, indeed some were so small that they could be attributed to the chance factors of statistical error that characterize any research investigation. Nevertheless, the interesting thing about them was that they all pointed in the same direction, namely that the survey teachers in 1977 held an even firmer managerial command of children's location and movements than in 1970. In making this point it should be emphasized that their control in 1970 was also very tight.

Given this fact, it remains as important as ever to investigate teachers' rationales for assigning children to their places. For the great majority of children these places are exclusively or mainly in the social setting of a small seated group. The Plowden Report advocated groups because of the opportunities they provide for interaction, but even if the class teacher actively discourages contact between group members some is bound to take place: children can easily observe the work and rate of progress

of the other children at their table and hear the teacher's private
conversations with individual pupils. Although the size and composition of a group cannot guarantee that any given type of contact will occur amongst group members the available evidence
tends to suggest that these types of factors can be important
(Boydell 1975). Virtually every teacher in the sample found
occasion to direct children to places although they used different
numbers of policies in different combinations and for different
purposes. About three-fifths took into account their children's
abilities and attainments and used homogeneous or heterogeneous
ability grouping (or both at different times). However, this was
a marked drop since 1970. Nevertheless, similar ability/attainment
groups, although less common overall, were still the most popular
strategy and more than half the teachers found occasion to use
them. Placing children together who get on well remained the
second most popular strategy and was mentioned, as in the earlier
survey, by about half the teachers. Mixed ability groups had
decreased in popularity whilst mixed sex groups had increased.
Both types of grouping were used by about a quarter of the
teachers in the follow-up survey. Thus, in summary, it may be
said that as before teachers reported using a wide range of
rationales although they were now less likely to use their perceptions of children's abilities and attainments as a basis for assigning places.

The class teacher must not only organize her own locations and
movements and those of her class but, even in schools where
there is an agreed curriculum, she must also organize the children's work. The original survey found that despite the predominance of individual work, group work was also widely reported and
that classwork was still much in evidence for all subjects except
reading. In 1977 the overall picture remained rather similar although there had been some slight shifts in emphasis. Individual
work, except in reading, was no longer quite as popular. Group
work, defined in terms of different seated groups of children
having different tasks (not necessarily joint tasks) was still used
by most teachers although its popularity had fallen off in all
areas except English. Classwork had gained slightly in popularity;
it was now included in the repertoire of more teachers. However,
overall it seemed that the 1977 survey teachers were doing much
the same as their counterparts in 1970, namely still relying on a
mixture of methods for all curricular areas. In addition to asking
teachers about the type of work they set (classwork, individual
work, group work), the 1977 survey also collected information
(for the first time) on the type of teacher contact. For each separate curricular area teachers reported whether they used class
teaching (talking publicly to the whole class), group teaching
(talking privately to small groups) and individual attention (talking privately to individual children). Although individual attention was extremely popular for the three Rs, and class teaching
was included in the repertoire of almost every teacher (except
for reading), the main feature of the results was the extent to

which teachers were, once again, using a mixture of methods.

As the results of the follow-up survey are based on only a small sample of teachers in a small area of Britain they must be treated with caution. Moreover as indicators of change they also have their limitations. For instance, they say nothing directly about the classroom situation in the survey schools in the intervening years: there was a seven-year gap in the collection of reports and that period may have seen the emergence and disappearance of a number of organizational changes which would remain undetected. However, the exploratory nature of the investigation should not detract from one main point. In the immediate post-Plowden era the classroom organizational practices of a representative sample of teachers in thirty-nine schools in two LEAs could in no sense be described as 'revolutionary'. Some seven years later the reports of teachers from the same schools presented a very similar pattern. In brief, the original survey provided no evidence for a major swing to innovative methods. The follow-up survey provided no evidence for a wholesale return to traditional techniques. Although it would be dangerous to assume that an identical picture would have emerged had teachers' policies been monitored in the same way anywhere else in Britain it would be equally wrong to suggest that the survey schools were in any way 'peculiar'. It would seem reasonable to say that, far from being fickle followers of fashion, junior teachers, as a whole, are probably far more conservative and cautious in their approach than some commentators would suggest. It would seem very likely that, overall, the kinds of patterns of classroom organization which children encountered in 1977 were very similar to those which existed in 1970 although, if the survey was anything to go by, a number of changes had occurred.

Of prime importance here is the demise of streaming. In 1967 the authors of the Plowden Report noted that streaming was by far the most common way of organizing junior schools (para. 806) but they felt that teachers' views may have been moving faster than practice (para. 807). Even by 1970 the overwhelming majority of teachers in the survey schools had unstreamed classes so that in this respect they may not have been typical of teachers nationally. However, the fact that 1977 saw a complete absence of streaming suggests that the Plowden Report's assessment of professional opinion a decade earlier was correct. In addition the fact that unstreamed classes had stayed unstreamed suggests that teachers had come to terms with the opportunities and constraints such classes present. Interestingly enough streaming within the classroom, although still widely used, was less popular than before as, indeed, was deliberate mixed-ability grouping. If this were shown in other studies to be part of a more general decline in the importance attached to ability for any grouping purpose (heterogeneous or homogeneous) it would raise a number of interesting issues. If teachers no longer so freely use their judgments of children's abilities to group them, do they still attach the same importance to intelligence when assessing their pupils?

If not, how do they now tend to perceive their children? How do
they organize their impressions? What constructs do they use?

The Plowden Report put forward persuasive arguments in favour
of groups but gave little indication of how they might operate in
practice. The observed shift towards smaller seated groups may
be indicative of teachers' experiences: it is no easy matter to set
up 'workable' groups of children (any more than it is to establish
'workable' teams of adults). Teachers may have found that smaller
groups tend to work better. If so their experiences bear out the
results of a pioneering American study of natural groupings of
people, including children at play, which was conducted almost
thirty years ago (James 1951). This found that in many ordinary
situations people prefer the physical and psychological intimacy
of groups of two or, at most, three.

Although teachers' policies on children's locations and movements were broadly similar to 1970 the small shift towards an even
firmer control suggests that teachers' perceptions of their own
managerial role may have undergone a slight and subtle change.
As has been argued elsewhere (Sharp and Green 1975), the
major irony of any classroom requiring both informality and pupil
choice is that if all the children were interested, keen and individually teacher-directed the teacher's management problem would
be insuperable. Although the classrooms organized by the teachers
in the 1970 survey were not characterized by great informality or
a large degree of pupil choice, they were nevertheless structured
in complex ways. Perhaps the observed tightening of control since
then reflects teachers' classroom experiences and is an attempt
by them to simplify their managerial task and reduce the time
spent on ongoing classroom management. This would, in theory
at least, give them more opportunity to 'teach' and monitor individual children. This seems a plausible explanation in view of the
fact that teachers reported spending less time circulating and
more time seeing children at their desk. Seated at their desks,
teachers are less susceptible to the numerous short child-initiated
interruptions which characterize circulating (although this may
mean that children waste more time waiting to see the teacher). If
teachers have found a practical need to simplify their managerial
role this may also explain why the setting of individual work was
not quite so popular: quite apart from any other considerations
it is an extremely time-consuming practice.

To summarize the conclusions from the follow-up survey it
would appear that, despite the importance of some of the observed
changes, popular views about the organization of junior school
classrooms may have been based more on fiction than fact. Classroom organization is not, of course, the sole criterion for assessing change, nor is it necessarily the most important aspect of
classroom life. Teachers' attitudes and classroom behaviour provide two other obvious perspectives. However, classroom organization is important because, in the words of the Plowden Report,
it 'can reflect and reinforce attitudes' (para. 819) and attitudes
are themselves inextricably linked to practice.

4 GROUPING AND GROUP WORK

Sarah Tann

The ORACLE results, reported in 'Inside the Primary Classroom', showed two clear trends: the prevalence of 'grouping', and the near absence of 'group work'. For the purpose of this paper it is important to clarify these two terms. 'Grouping' refers to an organizational feature of the classroom, whereby, on average, four or five children are seated around a table, each usually working on an individual assignment. 'Group work' refers to a pedagogical feature of the classroom, whereby a small group of children work together, collaboratively, on the same problem or task. The ORACLE evidence for the common use of grouping, but not of group work, is confirmed by other research studies (Bealing 1972, Bennett 1976) and by the HMI Survey 'Primary Education in England' (1978). However, the two terms have sometimes been confused; for collaborative group work to take place there must, of course, be some form of grouping, but children can be seated in groups (grouping) without collaborative group work taking place.

Until recently classroom studies have tended to describe the general pattern in primary classrooms as one in which children work in groups, without distinguishing between grouping and group work. The nature and quality of teacher-pupil interaction, and so of teaching styles, differs in the two cases. These differences are, therefore, of interest to those concerned with relating teacher style to learner achievement.

The lack of knowledge about the nature of pupil interaction in group work led to the setting up of a small-scale research project to study discussion processes in small groups of pupils engaged in collaborative problem-solving exercises. By making such a study it was hoped to cast light on how pupils behave in this situation; on what gains they make, as well as to identify which pupils benefit most. Material of this kind about the way small groups operate would, it was believed, be of interest to teachers concerned with encouraging this learning environment.

In investigating how pupils behave in collaborative group work, the focus of attention was their verbal behaviour. In order to find out what gains the pupils made, two particular aspects were examined: first, whether there was an increase in the level of interest, motivation and satisfaction deriving from the group context, and second, whether cognitive and interaction skills relevant to problem-solving were developed. In the investigation as to which pupils benefited most, interest focused on different pupil types as distinguished largely by achievement and anxiety levels.[1]

Finally, as the groups were set up specifically for research purposes, interest focused also on the differential effects of a range
of grouping policies on group-work processes.

Before describing the details of the research, a brief summary
may be given of views expressed by educationalists concerning
the purposes of collaborative group work. Previous research[2]
has suggested that it has a unique potential as providing a specific context within which certain valued skills can be developed.
This is claimed to lie in the opportunity group work provides for
fostering autonomous learning and increasing the satisfaction
gained therefrom. Its distinctive processes include the sharing of
experiences and the expression, exchange, exploration and modification of ideas in a co-operative social context. It is also claimed
that group-work processes lead to an increase in reasoning power
and to the development of a critical attitude to evidence. This, in
turn, enhances the autonomy of the learner. Specific verbal skills
have been identified which researchers have concluded may promote these processes and so help to realize the potential of group
work.

In the current research, particular attention has been paid to
pupil strategies which seem successful, and those which seem to
fail. These strategies are related to the nature of the group and
the nature of the task in an attempt to find out how the structure
and functioning of such groups can be improved and form a more
positive learning environment.

The use of terms such as 'success' and 'fail' implies that some
form of evaluation has taken place. This needs to be made explicit.
For the purposes of this research project a discussion was considered a success if the group appeared to solve the problem as
they defined it, in a way which was felt to be satisfactory to that
group. Thus success depended on the quality of the solution and
on the degree of group satisfaction, both of which were heavily
dependent on the nature of the discussion process. In no way was
an ideal solution used as a yardstick of success. In this research,
four tasks were designed to be tackled by each of twenty-four
groups of pupils and in each case a wide range of solutions could
be (or were) appropriate. However, there were certain issues in
each task which were held to be important in the process of arriving at a solution, and which were thus regarded as integral to
the task. If a group chose to redefine the task boundaries and
made a deliberate decision to discount any such issues, this was
acceptable; but to be unaware of them or to ignore them usually
indicated a less thorough approach to the task. Further, as all
the tasks were designed for collaborative consideration, a discussion was not considered successful if a solution was forced on
the group by any one member, however good that solution seemed.
Thus participation and collaboration of members were important
aspects of the successful group. On the other hand, the discussion
was not considered successful if the group appeared easily satis-
fied, but the solution did not appear to be well thought out to
the researcher. The concept of success, as used in this instance,

assumes the importance of submitting ideas to rational analysis.
In attempting to solve the task problems the groups were expected
to identify the problem and define its boundaries, offer ideas and
give reasons to substantiate them, evaluate the alternative suggestions, choose one and follow it through to a satisfactory conclusion.

For the purposes of this investigation concern did not, therefore, focus so much on the content of the task as on the process
of the task discussion. Thus no systematic attempt was made to
assess the group solution itself. The tasks were not intended as
a means of instruction, nor of imparting 'facts', nor were they
designed to facilitate a specific 'discovery'. Instead, the group-
work situation provided an opportunity to investigate whether
the members did acquire, exercise or develop skills which were
relevant to problem-solving within a particular social context.
The intention behind the tasks was that the pupils would enjoy
working on them, and their function was to be a means toward
learning to learn in a group and developing skills which embraced
both the task and the interactional dimension - how to handle
the task and to operate effectively in a group context.

THE TASKS SET

The research was carried out with twenty-four groups, each of
four or five pupils, from two classes in a junior school aged ten
plus and from first-year pupils in a secondary school aged eleven
plus. Each of the twenty-four groups was set the same series of
four tasks. Each task was presented at a different session at
approximately one month intervals. (It took about one month to
complete one task with each of the twenty-four groups.) The
tasks were all 'creative', in that the product was not a single
discoverable or identifiable state but was open-ended in character. The type of difficulty encountered was particularly that of
'problem space' in which the boundaries of the problem had to be
established by the groups. The tasks differed in two main ways.
First, in the degree of ambiguity of the boundaries: thus the
tasks moved from a fairly closed situation where the problem was
closely defined to an open situation where the boundaries were as
broad as the group chose to make them. The second difference
was in the type of demands the task made; two of the tasks were
basically concrete and factual, requiring considerable reporting
and reasoning skills, the other two involved fantasy and required
more interpreting and imagining skills. Tasks 1 to 4 became increasingly open; while tasks 1 and 3 were concrete and tasks 2
and 4 fantasy based.

These task differences were designed to test whether such differences affected group processes, and whether distinct pupil
types responded differently to different task demands. Thus the
profiles of group dialogues were compared to ascertain if there
were any significant differences relating particularly to the fact-

fantasy dimension and its possibly differential effect on the proportion of reasoning and imagining utterances. Pupil-personality
profiles and dialogue-contribution patterns were also compared
to examine, for example, the relationship between academic self-
concept and social anxiety and rate of contributions in both
'closed' and 'open' tasks (or problems).

GROUP STRUCTURE VARIABLES

Apart from designing and setting up the tasks, it was also necessary to form the pupils into groups. Here, too, it was intended
to employ a range of variables and to monitor their possible effects
on the group processes. Half the groups were formed on the basis
of pupil choice and the other half were allocated to groups by the
researcher on the basis of sex and achievement. Some were formed of pupils of similar achievement levels, some of mixed achievement levels, some of both of these being of the same sex, and
some of mixed sex.
  In the free-choice groups the link between achievement and
sex was not, of course, controlled, though it was noted. It was
noticeable that boys tended to choose across a wider spectrum of
the achievement range than the girls. No mixed sex groups were
formed by free choice!

CATEGORY SYSTEM

To enable systematic analysis of the group discussions, which
were recorded and transcribed, a schedule or category system
was designed. Its purpose was to enable detailed analysis of the
verbal strategies used both by the groups as a whole and by
individuals within the groups. The main categories embodied in
the schedule concerned reporting, imagining, reasoning, evaluation and directing, while a second set of categories focused on
interactional relationships (initiating, challenging, accepting,
etc.).
  Analysis based on these categories made it possible to chart
the progress of the problem-solving process, to show the extent
to which the members collaborated and the relationships between
them, and to plot the direction and flow of the discussion in relation to each member. By this means it was possible to identify
the ways in which specific verbal strategies were used to meet
the group's task needs, and the manner in which the participants
operated as a group in relation to each other, as well as the
nature and extent of each member's role.[3]

DISCUSSION STAGES

By using such a system of analysis it was also possible to identify
the different stages in the discussions and to estimate the relative
importance of the separate utterance categories to each stage.
The first stage was that of 'orientation' - both to the task and to
other members of the group. During this stage the problem was
identified, overall interpretation of the task made, and the boundaries of the discussion outlined by focusing on the main issues
involved. It was very often the omission or foreshortening of
this stage that led to repetitions, contradictions and disputes
later in the discussion. The particular skills employed at this
stage were generally those of reporting and interpreting, and of
directing strategies which focused on the central task demands.
During this orientation stage the initial roles and relationships
of the participating members were established.

In the second, 'development', stage ideas were generated,
challenged or justified by reason or evidence, and often modified
and refined. This stage was the most variable one. Sometimes
the first ideas offered were accepted by the group unanimously
as good ideas. Sometimes they were accepted for more negative
reasons, for instance, for lack of alternatives. Conversely, the
development stage in some groups was lengthy because many ideas
were produced and considerable challenge and modification occurred
until a solution was found acceptable to the group. On the other
hand, some lengthy discussions were characterized by many ideas
being initiated and few being followed through, challenged or
modified, and no solution being found. In such groups the interaction strategies (that is, those concerning relationships) seemed
more important than the task strategies as a means of differentiat-
ing the groups; these groups frequently scored high on initiating
strategies and low on modifying, as they rarely listened to each
other's ideas or reacted to them, whereas consensus groups
scored high on accepting, as they were unlikely to challenge,
develop or modify other contributions. Of the task strategies, the
most useful during this stage were reasoning and evaluating.

The third, 'concluding', stage was characterized by an increasing proportion of evaluating and directing strategies. In the interactional categories, there was also often an increase in accepting
while few initiating and challenging strategies were used.

The discussions were analysed in two ways. First, the frequencies of each category were calculated. These were of interest in
that they showed the extent to which each category was used as
well as their distribution over time and between members of the
different groups. From this it was possible to assess the amount
and nature of the utterances and, by identifying the speakers,
their direction between members. Such frequencies were used to
form discussion profiles for each group which served two distinct
purposes. The distribution of utterances between members was
used to establish member roles and relate these to emerging
leadership patterns. The other purpose of the discussion profiles

was to help in quantifying the utterances and so to identify the
different stages of the discussion and the changing relative importance of different strategies in each of the stages. Second,
the systematic analysis of every utterance also made it possible
to examine sequences and to estimate the effects of particular
verbal strategies. This was important in identifying strategies
which appeared to make a positive contribution to the development
of the discussion.

RESULTS: ANALYSIS OF THE DISCUSSION

Two strategies, reasoning and challenging, were found to be
crucial in helping to develop a critical and thorough approach to
problem-solving. Where reasoning was conspicuous by its absence,
or at best was merely implicit, rather than explicit, discussions
were not successful. Challenging was also of particular interest;
it was a strategy used to seek reason or justification, or substantive evidence. Thus it could be singled out as particularly useful
in problem-solving. The incidence of these two strategies was
also found to be correlated positively.

Questioning in general, of which challenging was one specific
form, appeared also to be an important strategy, but one which
was not effectively employed in many of the discussions. The
lack of questioning often resulted in ideas being uncritically
accepted on their first presentation. This was important in each
of the stages of the discussion. In the orientation stage, lack of
questioning often resulted in the boundaries of the problem not
being well defined, and this caused difficulties in subsequent
stages. In the development stage, it resulted in fewer alternatives
being generated and tested, and thus in the final stage the evidence for specific suggestions, and the range of suggestions from
which to choose, was limited, and this hindered the process of
evaluation and reaching conclusions.

One possible reason why questioning was little used may be
derived from the ORACLE material, reported in 'Inside the Primary Classroom'. It was found that open-ended or higher order
questioning was in fact very little used by teachers. It follows,
therefore, that the example of teachers offered little experience
to pupils as to how to use questioning in a problem-solving situation. On average 12 per cent of all observed teacher-pupil interactions were of a questioning nature. Only 6.3 per cent were
task orientated and only 0.6 per cent were open-ended questions
of a 'higher cognitive order'. The study also concluded that
pupils in classes which were characterized by a high proportion
of questioning made greater gains than others. It may be that
such pupils learnt the skills - and value - of using questioning
strategies themselves, though no data was collected on this
issue. However, the teacher-based assessments in the ORACLE
study also indicated that children in these classes gained a higher
yield of information from the questions they asked than pupils

taught by other styles ('Progress and Performance in the Primary Classroom', p. 137).

Apart from reasoning and challenging, two further strategies appeared also to be of particular importance in the group context: listening and managing disputes. It was clear that some children found it hard to listen to others' ideas, and to assimilate and assess them when the ideas interrupted their own train of thought. Thus some groups talked at each other (scoring high on initiating and low on response categories); these discussions involved a lot of repetition and often competition in deciding which ideas belonged to whom. Thus personalities and status in the group were at stake, rather than the task problems.

Disputes within a group and ways of managing them were a further area of interest. Here sex differences were conspicuous. In boys' groups members seemed more willing to take risks, to offer ideas which might be rejected or ridiculed. But this was generally done in an atmosphere which involved neither loss of face nor ill-feeling. The boys usually threw themselves into the tasks with enthusiasm and thought the novelty of group work 'a good laugh'. Girls' groups, however, reacted very differently. The discussion was usually much more consensus orientated. The members were wary about the novel situation and felt uneasy about what was expected of them. The girls were more likely to accept ideas and let them go unchallenged. When difficult issues were raised they were often avoided and left unresolved. This sometimes led to a further characteristic, back-tracking, where the issue was re-introduced to the group later, often after other contributions had been made which helped to decide the original area of dispute. Another feature of the girls' groups was the seeming acceptance of a contribution which was then in the same breath challenged. The girls were less likely to reject outright. They preferred to sugar the pill. The boys, however, didn't bother with such niceties.

An examination of the discussion profiles shows the extent to which listening and conflict management were problems in any particular group. Groups comprising pupils who found it difficult to listen to each other, for example, scored high on initiating and much lower on modifying or on the other response categories. Groups in which disputes frequently occurred scored high on ignoring and rejecting, and low on modifying and accepting.

SUPPLEMENTARY DATA: WRITTEN FEEDBACK

While such observations of discussion processes tell us something about how pupils behave, it was also important to examine other variables that affect those processes. Thus other techniques of data collection were used to explore attitudes to group work. One of the supplementary techniques was the use of open-ended, written feedback from the participants concerning their views of the experience of group work and their own assessment of what they

had gained from this experience. The responses were particularly
revealing in that they indicated a wide divergence between the
pupils' attitude to group work and the potential that research
suggests exists in this mode of learning. Pupils in fact reported
that they did not feel that they were in a learning situation. Their
concept of learning seemed restricted to factual input and memor-
ization. In experimental group work it was not facts, but opinions
and interpretations which were exchanged and this, by the pupils'
criteria, was not 'learning'. The pupils seemed to be unaware of
what is involved in the process of learning, and how group work
might affect their learning, even by their own definitions. Similarly, there was little awareness of wider aspects of learning including, for instance, identifying, acquiring and practising cognitive skills necessary for problem-solving, or those interaction
skills specific to learning to learn in a group situation.

The majority of the pupils, when asked what they thought they
had learnt or gained from group work, replied that they gained
nothing. Yet all but five of the ninety-nine children involved who
gave this answer had given positive replies to a previous question
asking what they had enjoyed in the group work sessions. For
example, several pupils mentioned that they enjoyed the opportunity to share ideas and to work with their friends. Some also
mentioned that they had 'learnt how to communicate better' as
one pupil put it. Some held that they had 'enjoyed hearing other
people's ideas' and that it had 'helped them to come out of their
own shells'. Others suggested that they had 'enjoyed being given
the opportunity to manage their own affairs'. These were all aspects of group work which the pupils claimed to have enjoyed but
they were not things which the pupils considered that they had
gained from group work. It would seem, therefore, that if the
potential of group work is to be more fully exploited, pupils' attitudes to 'learning', both to what is learnt and how, needs more
careful attention.

SUPPLEMENTARY DATA: ACHIEVEMENT TESTS AND
PERSONALITY QUESTIONNAIRE

Despite the caution with which it is necessary to treat the data
derived from the personality questionnaire and achievement tests,
such data was useful in that it highlighted pupils who deviated
significantly from the mean scores. It was possible to examine the
behaviour of these pupils as they carried out group work and to
relate this to the personality and achievement profiles. Conversely, in the interpretation of deviant behaviour in the group work
context, it was possible to refer back to such data and note any
relationships.

The main findings derived from these data relate to the groups'
reactions to individual members who might be one of four kinds:
the silent child, the slow child (low achiever), the bright child
(high achiever) or 'bossy' child. A variety of responses was

noted. The slow child, if a girl, tended also to be silent and to opt out despite invitations, not to say desperate appeals, to participate in the quieter, more conformist, consensus-oriented, self-conscious girls' groups. In the boys' groups slower members joined in and were helped along to a considerable extent. Silent members, however, were generally ignored in the boys' groups amid the hubbub of voices.

The small group experience made a considerable difference to some members' behaviour. This was particularly so of low achievers who found writing a struggle and had difficulty in expressing themselves orally. In class such children rarely had the confidence to speak out and were rarely given the floor for long enough for their ideas to be conveyed. For this kind of child, the cosy atmosphere of the small group seemed very important. Conversely, some found the group context very inhibiting. This was the case with children who preferred to work alone either because they could get on faster and do things their own way, or because they were anxious and preferred to remain anonymous in the classroom. As already indicated, among the girls there was a tendency for the slow child to be silent, and for the bright child often to be the 'bossy' one. In the girls' groups there was usually a clear leader who was also the pupil accepted by the others as being the cleverest, as judged by the members' perceptions of the individual's achievements in formal school work. Among the boys, leadership was less clearly defined and the groups appeared more 'democratic'. However, in both groups, the brightest was not always the best in the group context. Often because the brightest child accepted the position granted by other members, such a child expected its suggestions to be accepted without challenge. This frequently led to brief, blunt contributions which were imprecise, unreasoned and substantiated by 'it *is* so'. Very often another member would unobtrusively take on the tasks which one might associate with a leadership role; for instance, that of monitoring the group discussion, focusing on specific issues and directing the task process. Such children were not recognized as leaders, as the role they actually played was not expected of them on the basis of school work. Thus group work for some children provided a valuable opportunity for different skills to be practised and different roles to be played.

There were, then, considerable differences relating to sex and achievement in the ways in which the children responded to the group situation. This indicates the importance of careful consideration of the composition of groups when formulating grouping policies. Apart from the consensus orientation of the girls referred to earlier, the most marked response was the high performance of low-achieving boys and the equal participation rates of the members in unstreamed or mixed-achievement groups. However, differences of behaviour relating to sex and achievement became more marked amongst the older pupils. This is possibly because of the mode of teaching prevalent in each of the schools. In the high school, where the children were more often taught as

a class, achievement differences were made more public and children responded to the expectations and demands made of them. Conversely, in the junior school where work was strongly individualized, achievement differences were less well noticed.
Low-achieving boys' groups tackled each task very thoroughly and were often more careful than the other groups to examine suggestions, to give more reasons and provide more evidence. They also used their own experience in support of their ideas, as well as information gained from out of school sources such as evening television programmes. In general boys seemed to refer to television more often than girls. Whether this was because they watched more or remembered more is not known. Nevertheless it was very interesting to see how much such low-achieving children learnt from this visual medium and how well they responded to the oral means of sharing their knowledge in the group situation. These two characteristics of groups of low-achieving boys - their careful and reasoned approach and their use of information sources based outside the school - were just as conspicuous amongst individual low-achieving boys in groups where the range of achievement was considerable. A particular feature of such groups, as mentioned earlier, was the equal rate of participation from each member despite the achievement range. Low-achieving members were rarely dominated by their high-achieving peers, and their contribution whether adding explanations or evidence, modifying others' utterances or challenging to evoke further clarification, all played a positive part in the discussion.
However, in the high school, low achievers' scores were likely to relate to low-level performance in the groups. This was particularly so among the girls, who remained silent despite appeals to participate.

EFFECTS OF TASK TYPE AND GROUP STRUCTURE

The research was designed to investigate the response of pupils to group work in general, but also to test the effects of differences in task type and group structure on the interaction process, at both the group and individual level. These effects could clearly be seen through the monitoring of group processes by the coding system already described. Not surprisingly, tasks 1 and 3, which were designed to stimulate reasoning, resulted in higher reasoning scores than tasks 2 and 4, and similarly tasks 2 and 4, which invited more imaginative responses, resulted in higher imagining scores, than tasks 1 and 3. But what was interesting was that, in spite of the different variables being tested, certain groups consistently scored higher in reasoning than other groups across both types of task.
At the individual level there were also interesting findings. A small number of pupils preferred the more factual, reasoning tasks than the fantasy, imaginative ones. In one case, a higher-achiever boy (who had plenty of facts at his fingertips) disliked

the imagining tasks as he considered them 'soppy'. One socially anxious child stated that he preferred the factual tasks, as the imagining ones were too personal and threatening in that they encouraged the criticism and scrutiny of his own opinions and ideas. On the other hand, an academically anxious child was more concerned about the factual tasks which might show her facts to be incorrect. Such responses highlight the complexities of the reaction to group work and indicate the care that must be taken in setting the tasks and structuring the groups in order to minimize any adverse effects due to individual member's sensitivities.

The most conspicuous finding resulting from an examination of the group work structure variables relates to the problems which occurred in mixed-sex groups. In these, the members at best tolerated each other and at worst swore at each other. Just as differences in the verbal behaviour relating to sex became increasingly acute amongst the older pupils, so too the problems in mixed groups became sharper with older pupils; indeed in only one instance was it possible to persuade a mixed-sex group, in the secondary school, to participate at all.

CONCLUSION

During the course of this research specific strategies were identified as important to the success of group work: questioning, listening and managing disputes. This suggests the need deliberately to develop the use of such strategies, particularly questioning, if co-operative group work is to be utilized in the classroom. The study also illustrated the complex effects of group composition on interaction processes and the need to consider the structure of such groups carefully in terms of desired educational outcomes. The study also highlighted the gap between pupils' expectations of group work and the theoretical value of such work as indicated by researchers. There is clearly a need, therefore, to clarify the purpose of such work and communicate these values (and attitudes to learning derived from them) to the pupils.

Nevertheless the study indicated that co-operative group work can provide a valuable alternative context for the practice of skills leading to such goals as collaborative learning, intellectual autonomy and enhanced oral communication. As yet, group work appears to be little utilized in the primary classroom. Greater understanding as to how pupils benefit most may be of assistance to those who wish to use this strategy for these particular goals, as one part of the pupil's total learning experience.

NOTES

1   The achievement levels were determined by the ORACLE tests
    already described in 'Inside the Primary Classroom', and a

Likert-type questionnaire to elicit personality traits (identified by previous research) found to be relevant to group work
performance.

2   The main research studies on group work by pupils and students in Britain are those carried through by Abercrombie
(1960), Barnes and Todd (1977), Rudduck (1978) and Tough
(1977); none of these, however, is concerned with junior
school children.

3   For a discussion of the limitations of any such verbal category
system see Chapter 12 by Ruth Jonathan in this volume.

5 PROJECT WORK:
an enigma

Sylvia Leith

Project or topic work, as it is often called, has an idiosyncratic meaning in the sense that there is no generally shared understanding of the term and its application to classroom teaching. Several definitions can be found in the literature but all essentially emphasize that project work allows children to develop their own methods of seeking, organizing and recording knowledge and often allows them to work co-operatively in groups on a common topic. Emphasis is frequently placed on an integrated approach to subject matter and sometimes a multi-media approach is encouraged. In some schools project work is believed to be an essential element of the primary curriculum.

A questionnaire was sent by the author to a random sample of thirty-three primary schools in a specific local authority area in the autumn of 1978 to determine the extent and type of project work in their classrooms. Twenty-two schools responded and completed questionnaires were received from 167 teachers. Nearly all stated that their pupils did project work in their classes. Recent reports of research studies confirm these findings and give estimates of the time spent on project-type work. Bassey (1978) reported from his survey of 900 primary school teachers that seven curriculum areas are definable: mathematics, language, thematic studies, art and craft, music, physical education, and integrated studies. For each of these areas teachers were asked to estimate the amount of time spent by a typical pupil during a typical week. Project and topic work time was placed in either the thematic or integrated-studies categories according to how the teacher perceived the children's work. In either case, a large proportion of the pupils' time was spent in these areas. In a typical week, 59 per cent of the pupils were reported to spend $2\frac{1}{4}$-5 hours on thematic studies, and 19 per cent of the pupils spent one quarter to 3 hours on integrated studies. The ORACLE study, based on actual classroom observations of teachers and pupils, reports that 15 per cent of pupils' curriculum time was spent on project or topic work (Galton et al. 1980, p. 192). Thus, both recent studies confirm that a substantial portion of the primary pupil's week is spent on this kind of activity.

The results obtained in these two large-scale researches are mirrored in the teachers' responses to the questionnaire. It seems that, in general, teachers do value project work and do spend a substantial portion of their time on this method.

It may be that teachers use project work because they believe they are encouraging individualization as well as the group work

stressed by the Plowden Committee in whose Report (1967) project and topics methods were advocated 'to make good use of the
interest and curiosity of children, to minimize the notion of subject matter being rigidly compartmental, and to allow the teacher
to adopt a consultative, guiding, stimulating role rather than a
purely didactic one' (p. 198). The aim was clearly to encourage
pupils' independent, individual and group work with active participation in learning.

It is, however, interesting to note that in the primary education
survey conducted ten years later (HMI Survey 1978) neither
topic nor project work received much emphasis. The survey quotes
from the Bullock Report (1975), which held that much of the writing done in the name of topic work amounts to 'no more than copying' (p. 393); and their own survey also suggests that this is
still happening extensively. Topic work is referred to by name
only six times, project work not at all, and the thematic approach
only once in this way:

> Many primary schools used a thematic approach to the work in
> social studies and a wide variety of topics were introduced at
> each age level. Often the environment of the school, or a place
> within easy reach of it, was the focus of this kind of work, al-
> though the children also studied other countries and other
> times (p. 70).

Topic work was said to occur in religious education, in an area
such as 'helping other people', in history with reference to a current event or a 'homes' or 'life on the farm' theme. It was stated
that science was infrequently taught and, when it was, it was
often in relation to other topics studied. A further indication of
the problems associated with topic work was the statement:

> In geography and history the work was reasonably matched to
> children's capabilities in less than half of the classes. Elements
> of these subjects were frequently taught as topics or projects
> which sometimes resulted in repetitive work rather than an
> extension of children's skills and knowledge (p. 82).

Thus the HMI Survey does not allot much space to project or
topic work and some of the authors' comments are not positive. If
this lack of comment reflects a negative evaluation of the time and
effort spent on project work, this seems in direct conflict both
with the statements of the teachers in the questionnaires and the
evidence of the Bassey and ORACLE studies.

It could be that the inspectors saw much evidence of project
work in the classrooms they visited but did not comment on it at
length because its value is intangible and difficult to assess. The
stated goal of the HMI Survey was to present a representative
picture of the organization of primary schools in England, the
range of work done by the children, and the extent to which the
work is matched to their abilities. Their recommendations reflect
their concern about the lack of assessment in all areas. They state
that teachers must be able to assess the performance of their
pupils in terms of what they next need to be taught, and recom-
mend that this be made a vital part of initial and in-service train-

ing (p. 123). A critical statement on assessment follows:
  Careful assessment of the children's progress has implications
  for the teacher's approach, too. It is not sensible for teachers
  to attempt to use a teaching technique that is clearly beyond
  their operational skill and is therefore inefficient . . . (p. 124).
This might be seen as an attempt to cast doubt on the value of
project work as a method, as well as a recognition of the difficulties of assessment.
  If project work is a valuable teaching method then it should
surely be assessed along with the other curriculum areas.
  The questionnaire probed the actual state of project assessment
in the primary schools today. In response to the statement: 'I
use a definite scheme for assessing children's work', 50 per cent
of the primary teachers said that they never used such a scheme,
and only 17 per cent stated that they often did. It might be concluded that assessment is not seen as an important aspect of project work by the majority of the teachers in the sample. Among
the reasons given for this approach was that cut and dried assessments are not really accurate - so much depends on the topic, the
type of child, the kind of help from home, materials at hand and
other related factors. Other teachers stated that projects vary
too much to allow a single rigid scheme for assessment to be of
any real value. Again, different expectations apply to different
children. A teacher of five year olds stated that she sometimes
used a definite scheme but felt that the best way of assessing a
project was by listening to the children's use of language, reading their information, and seeing how far they could relate the
information gained to other things at a later date.
  In reply to the questionnaire, about 40 per cent of teachers
said that they often encouraged their children to evaluate their
own projects, while less than 10 per cent said that they never
encouraged children to do so.
  If this is an accurate picture of project work in primary schools
today, a good deal of time is spent on the activity, as confirmed
by the Bassey and ORACLE studies, but few teachers use definite
schemes to assess it. It is of course possible that they use intui-
tive or subjective assessments rather than organized schemes
based on the objectives they set for the children.
  Very little is written about assessment of project work at the
primary school level. It appears that most teachers feel that they
know the children so well that appropriate comments on the success or failure of the project can be written or delivered to the
child in a short conference or within the context of the class presentation of the project. In many cases children do not have a
clear idea of what the teacher expects for the project. In a book
concerned with project work, Thier (1970) emphasizes that an
important aspect of meaningful project learning in science is the
evaluation of the results. Self-evaluation is suggested as being
an important element:
  the pupil should have some idea of the outcomes he expects
  from his investigations. He needs to acquire enough understand-

ing of the problem he is trying to solve to evaluate for himself
the success or failure of the investigation in regard to his objective. Your [the teacher's] evaluation of the quality of the
child's project should be based on his satisfaction that the problem he has stated is solved for him. It may be that he will feel
he has solved the problem while you feel that the evidence presented is inadequate. By asking questions and encouraging
further investigation, you can help the child to realize this,
but the best strategy is to refrain from arbitrarily evaluating
the child's work as a success or failure. Especially in the case
of individual projects where you want to encourage the child
to work at the limits of his capabilities and interests, it is not
usually valuable to give grades or comments based on some level
of performance by the group. Rather, evaluation should be
looked at as an opportunity for encouraging the child to look
at and analyze his own work (p. 200).

Thier's view of evaluation is interesting. The real problem, however, is the application of this theory to classroom practice.

Other writers present similar views but none has a classroom
example on which teachers can model their own assessment.
Haggitt (1975) suggests that the teacher keep records of the sequence of activities that the children move through, as well as of
the concepts they are acquiring. Progress sequences in the areas
of writing, mathematics and reading are given as examples (p. ix).
Kent (1968) firmly states that assessment of projects is an important component and that it is not enough for a teacher to survey
the results of several weeks' work with the vaguely approving,
'Well, that was fun, wasn't it?' (p. 31). He suggests that the
teacher keep records from which conclusions as to the success of
the children can be drawn and plans for further teaching developed. In a small book which Taylor (1974) has designed to help
students plan and carry out their own projects, a lesson on evaluation techniques is included. An evaluation sheet is provided as
a model from which it is suggested that the teacher and class
develop a modified version for each particular project.

A rather different view of assessment is presented by Rance
(1968) who suggests where a class as a whole works on a topic,
the finished topic book should be available for study by the class
for a while, and that then a test on the content should be given
to the children. Along with this revision process, it is suggested
that a short discussion be held to assess the quality of the end
product with a view to future improvement of standards of work.
During this discussion the teacher should present 'leading questions' to highlight what she considers to be the successful and
unsuccessful aspects of the work. For individual topics, the
teacher should be guided by the criterion that the work, when
completed, should show evidence that source material has been
carefully evaluated and that the resulting information has been
written in the child's own words.

Assessment of project work in the secondary school is a more
highly developed skill and one for which more precise information

is available to teachers. For example, in the Schools Council Examination Bulletins 31 (1975) and 32 (1975) both continuous and final assessment of project work are dealt with. Some of this information could apply as well, to projects in primary schools.
The assessment must be based on the reasons for giving project work to the children, or, in other words, must be related to the skills and abilities which it is hoped will be developed by this sort of activity. A complication is, however, introduced by the fact that, for many teachers, an important aspect of the project is that it allows individual children to pursue a particular topic in which they have an interest; the implication of this is that the subject-matter of the project is unlikely to be common to all the children's work and comparisons between one project and another become more difficult (p. 97).
The authors go on to suggest that assessment can be carried out through various headings: presentation, research, content, and conclusions. Another suggestion is to consider an oral conference with the pupil to help determine how much he has actually learned.
The authors of the Open University volume 'Curriculum Change and Organization III', Unit 16, 'Syllabus Building and Assessment' (1975) state that project assessment is a particularly difficult problem because of the diversity of project titles and content. They suggest that a list of assessable criteria be made and much weight should be given to continuous assessment. They also suggest that some criteria are specific to certain projects and others are more broad ranging. Another way of grading for project competence would be to list the constituent sub-skills for each criterion.
A specific attempt to assist the classroom teacher in project work assessment was made in 1975 when a group of teachers began to work with Dr Patricia Ashton on this particular problem. Part of the recently established ORACLE project consisted of working with different groups of teachers to devise appropriate ways of assessing children's progress in selected aspects of the curriculum, and Dr Ashton agreed to establish a group to study the assessment of project work.
The group's priorities were to define the nature and objectives of project work. It was decided that objectives which could be achieved only or mainly, through project work would be included. After several meetings and much discussion, a complete list of objectives was developed. Eight separate categories were recognized, with several subsections, representing stages in the progress of the child in achieving the objectives. In all, forty-seven criteria for the assessment of project work were developed under the following headings:

A   The personal choice of topic
B   The planning of the project
C   The selection of sources relevant to the project
D   The extraction of relevant information from the sources
E   The organization of information relevant to the project
F   The selection of appropriate ways of expressing information and ideas

G   The self-evaluation of the project
H   The self-motivation to carry out and complete the project
in accordance with the plans made.
From these criteria a project assessment sheet was developed.
On the back of the sheet, space was provided for the teacher to
record the projects done by the child during his time in the
school. A guide-sheet for the classroom teacher was also written.
An evaluation study of these project assessment sheets was
undertaken by the writer in the school year 1978/9. A meeting
was held with a teacher group early in the autumn term to enlist
their support and assistance, as well as to obtain an understanding of the background and rationale of the undertaking. The
major concern of the teachers was to assist in the improvement
of instruction and assessment within the classroom, and they felt
that the use of the project assessment sheets was one way to
further this. A few minor modifications were made to the sheet,
a copy of the final draft of which is included as Tables 5.1 and
5.2. It was agreed that the writer would contact a number of
primary schools to find out the extent of their involvement in
project work. From those who responded, a number of schools
would be selected with sufficient variety of type and locations in
which to try out the assessment checklists.
Thirty-eight primary schools were contacted in October 1978.
Twenty-two schools indicated that they did project work and sent
in a list of the teachers who used projects as part of their classroom teaching. From these, a selection was made of nine schools
in which teachers were interested in trying out the checklist.
Meetings with the teachers and heads were held during the lunch
hour or after school. A total of thirty teachers in the nine rural
and urban schools took class sets of the assessment sheets to use
during the autumn and Easter terms.
Several other heads were also contacted and the schools visited
with the aim of enlarging the sample, but no other teachers could
be encouraged to use the checklist.
When they were contacted again at the end of the Easter term,
none of the original sample of thirty teachers had actually used
the checklist with the children. The heads reported that the
teachers were too busy to use the checklist or that they had lost
interest in it. Many said that the idea itself was good but the
actual use of the list would have been too time consuming. Several
said that it had been useful to guide their thinking in planning
project work. Others stated that the checklist was valuable but
that they were too busy with other school activities. In several
cases, heads were leaving the school in June and had not pressed
the staff to carry out the evaluation scheme. Many expressed
the view that the January to March term (1979) had been very
difficult for all concerned, with storms, strikes and fuel shortages,
and teachers had been fully taxed purely in maintaining regular
activities. A few heads suggested contacting them in late June
to ascertain if the checklist had been used in the summer term.
This was done and the same negative results were obtained.

Several explanations might be offered for this state of affairs. The checklist itself might have been the source of the problem; perhaps it was too cumbersome and unmanageable, and perhaps it looked as if it would take too much of the teachers' time. Perhaps it was a very inopportune time to attempt this evaluation. It is, however, possible that there are deeper, more fundamental issues at stake.

Let us go back to the original issues raised. Why do most teachers assign project work? And why do they not find evaluation necessary? Here lies the basic enigma. Project work has long standing as a valued teaching method. If it is given time on the curriculum then why is it not assessed and used as a measure of pupil progress?

Without an attempt at assessment it is impossible to know what pupils gain from project work. They may or may not acquire the intellectual and social skills thought desirable by the teachers.

This being so, it seems appropriate to ask what the teachers themselves gain by using the project method. It could be that teachers do project work because they feel they should: it has a good aura about it, and is recognized by heads as being of merit. It could be no more than an attempt at individualization and group work, and without an attempt at assessment it easily satisfies on both these counts. A sceptic might be tempted to suggest that teachers use project work to help solve a management problem; it enables them to gain a breathing space within the very hectic setting of an overcrowded, demanding classroom. He might add that they fear assessment because assessment would reveal an unwelcome truth - namely that this respectable time-filler does little more than keep the children occupied while their teacher is busy with other duties.

The enigma remains. Individual teachers must make a personal evaluation of the use of projects as a teaching method. If, in the light of the foregoing argument, it is deemed an appropriate teaching method, then it is also a curriculum area which needs specific objectives and organized schemes of assessment as attempted by the teacher group described here. Perhaps the answer is that all teachers using the project method need to develop their own sets of goals including skill and content objectives for each project the children attempt, and then, based on these, develop a simple assessment scheme. This does not seem too much to ask for an endeavour which can take up as much as 15 per cent of pupil lesson time.

Table 5.1

PROJECT ASSESSMENT   CHILD'S NAME . . . .

Please tick the boxes in accordance with the following key:
1. child cannot do this at all
2. child has some capability – with help
3. child has some capability – independently
4. child appears to have mastered this skill

	1	2	3	4
A. The personal choice of a topic				
Does he spontaneously ask questions about things/people/events around him?				
Does he persist in asking questions until he is satisfied with the answers?				
Can he decide on a topic that he wants to pursue?				
B. The planning of the project				
Does he know what fields of knowledge are relevant to his chosen topic?				
Can he decide what questions he wants to ask, and thus what information to look for?				
Can he decide what sources of information he is going to use?				
C. The selection of sources relevant to the project				
Does he know that information and ideas can be obtained from people, books, the classroom, the wider environment etc?				
Can he decide which of these sources might be relevant to his project?				
Can he identify information relevant to his project from a variety of sources?				
D. The extraction of relevant information from the sources				
Can he formulate a sequence of questions to obtain the information that he wants?				
Can he read with understanding, recognising information relevant to his questions?				
Is he acquiring some of the following:				
book use skills – using a table of contents				
using an index				
using a catalogue				
using the library/resource centre				
observation skills – listening				
watching				
scanning				
reading skills – summarising				
note-taking				
survey and/or questionnaire techniques				

Please leave empty any box relating to a
skill which a child has no experience of.

1 2 3 4

E. The organisation of information relevant to the project
Can he express information and ideas in an appropriate sequence in whatever medium he is using, e.g. speech, drama, writing, pictures?

Can he relate information he has acquired to the question(s) he has asked?
Can he link together the different parts of the project and organise the information and ideas he has acquired in a suitably clear and precise way?

Is he acquiring some of the following:

information organising skills — classifying
ordering
analysing
synthesising

Please leave empty any box relating to a
skill which a child has no experience of.

F. The selection of appropriate ways of expressing information and ideas
Does he know that information and ideas can be expressed in a variety of ways?
Is he acquiring some of the following skills?

painting
model making
writing
sketching
map making
tape-recording
drawing diagrams
discussing
debating
verbal reporting

Please leave empty any box relating to a
skill which a child has no experience of.

Can he select a form of expression which most clearly conveys his information and ideas in relation to his question(s) using some of the above skills?

G. The self-evaluation of the project
Can he judge how adequate his project is in relation to the question(s) he has asked?
Does he recognise an improvement in the skills he is using?
Can he assess his approach, presentation and the general quality of his work?
Can he assess the criticisms of others?

H. The self-motivation to carry out and complete the project in accordance with the plans made
Are his skills adequate for what he wants to do?
Can he set criteria for his own achievement and assess it?
Does he value his achievements?

Table 5.2

	PROJECT TITLES	
Individual		Class
YEAR 1 (Age Group . . . . . .)		

Any notable strengths or weaknesses or significant regressions.

YEAR 2 (Age Group . . . . . .)		

Any notable strengths or weaknesses or significant regressions.

YEAR 3 (Age Group . . . . . .)		

Any notable strengths or weaknesses or significant regressions.

YEAR 4 (Age Group . . . . . .)		

Any notable strengths or weaknesses or significant regressions.

Part II
THE TEACHER
AND THE CHILD

6 PRIMARY TEACHERS' APPROACHES TO PERSONAL AND SOCIAL BEHAVIOUR

Patricia Ashton

Primary teachers have many aims for their stage of education. They seek to develop concepts, skills and capabilities in every area of a wide curriculum. At least as important to them, however, seems to be the way in which children learn to behave. Teachers aim for children to be cheerful and independent, self-confident, tolerant, enthusiastic, to develop their own moral values and to acquire a host of other attributes of this kind. Concerns like these emerged clearly from the Schools Councils' 'Aims of Primary Education' project (Ashton et al. 1975). Indeed, of the eight aims which teachers declared to be the most important, six were to do with personal and social development. Teachers involved in the ORACLE Project completed the same questionnaire about their aims. It was clear that they shared very largely the same concerns about personal and social development. When teachers are asked how they teach reading or maths or any other area of the curriculum, they usually give a fluent and detailed account of techniques, materials and organization. Asked how they develop specific kinds of behaviour they value, there is more often a lengthy pause followed by, 'Well, it depends . . '. In the light of the importance they give to personal and social development, this seems surprising. Is it more difficult to describe the techniques and strategies of catering for personal and social development, or do they tend not to exist? This chapter describes a small-scale exploration of the question.

A group of primary teachers agreed to help tackle the problem. They met on numerous occasions and discussed what they did to foster the behaviour they wanted. The intention was to try to find general approaches common to all the teachers. Did they talk and explain, or plan their classroom organization, or design children's tasks so that they would be helpd in learning the desired behaviour? If some such features could be found, they would provide a basis for putting questions to other teachers to gather more information. Repeatedly two features did emerge, but both were the opposite of a planned policy. One was that of taking action after the event. Rather than planning for the development of the behaviour they wanted, the teachers seemed to react when a child behaved in a way that they did not want. The other feature was that the action they took depended on the individual child. One child would be sharply reprimanded, another mildly punished and another quietly talked to for the same misdemeanour. Leaving teachers' stated aims aside, these two features are very understandable in terms of daily life in classrooms. No matter how

much teachers might like children to be enthusiastic or tolerant,
if they are not, the practical consequences may be negligible.
If, however, the children are actually apathetic or actively in-
tolerant, this may have important practical consequences. In coping with such behaviour, teachers are bound to take the action
they judge most likely to be effective with the individual.

At this point it was suggested that the study might focus more
profitably on how teachers deal with undesirable behaviour.
Patterns might emerge which had failed to do so in exploring
approaches to desirable behaviour. Rather than continuing to
try to see how teachers attempt to foster kindness, for example,
the approach would explore how teachers react to unkindness. An
enlarged group of teachers joined in to devise a way of making
this study.

The ten personal and social aims rated as most important in the
Schools Council survey were taken as a starting point. For each
aim, the group of teachers invented a classroom incident in which
children's behaviour was the opposite of what was wanted. These
incidents were given in booklet form to the sixty teachers who
had taken part in the first year of the classroom observation study
and who were thus teaching eight- to ten-year-olds. The teachers
were asked to write an answer to the question 'What would you
do?' for each incident. They were also asked to indicate how much
each incident would concern them using a five-point scale from
'A lot' to 'Not at all' and whether it happened in their classroom
'Frequently', 'Sometimes' or 'Never'. Thirty-nine of the teachers
completed and returned the booklets, and what they wrote about
each incident is described below. The incidents are given in the
order of their frequency in the classroom as reported by the
teachers. In each case the aim from which the incident was derived is given, although this was not available to the teachers.

1   You find that your new class tends to lack care of their belongings; for example, coats are knocked down and left lying
about, lost property is frequently unclaimed.
(Aim: The child should be careful with, and respectful of, both
his own and other people's property.)

There was no doubt of the familiarity of this incident. Only one
teacher reported that it never happend with children in her class;
twenty-two recognized it as an occasional event and sixteen as a
frequent one. Two-thirds of the teachers were very concerned
about this problem. As one wrote, 'I am concerned, but find it
an increasing battle to keep classroom and cloakroom tidy. They
are chased and fetched back to tidy up - but the results are no
better.' Another wrote, 'This is a common disease among my
children', and another, 'Problem is that our children really do
not seem to care about their belongings.' Even so, there appeared
to be no common way of dealing with the problem. The most usual
ways, shared by only a third of the teachers in each case, were
those of simply insisting on tidying up or explaining the principles

of care of property. Eleven teachers said that they would organize routines for cloakroom use or depute monitors to keep an eye on the others. The strategies of having a class discussion on the subject, persuading children to take responsibility for their possessions and 'telling them off' were each suggested by about one in four of the teachers. An appreciable minority would adopt two or all three of these devices. However, it is evident that this obviously common and apparently straightforward problem has not given rise to a way of dealing with it which has any real popular currency among teachers.

2   You are trying to encourage mixed-ability groups to work co-operatively in project work. You find that the more competent children tend to be impatient with the contributions of the less able and avoid making use of them.
(Aim: The child should be developing tolerance; respecting and appreciating others, their feelings, views and capabilities.)

Thirty-five of the thirty-nine teachers indicated that this 'sometimes' happened in their classrooms and it was generally of considerable concern. There were three main ways of dealing with this behaviour, and thirty-one of the teachers recommended one or other of them. Two of these ways consisted of talking to the children; about half of the teachers would encourage the less able children and in addition explain the situation to the more able in an attempt to persuade them to be patient. Roughly a third of the teachers would explain the principles of tolerance and appreciating the contributions of different children. The third main strategy suggested was that of managing the situation more carefully by organizing compatible groups, selecting more appropriate material for different children, and so on.

3   Several quite able and hard-working children in your class seek constant reassurance when tackling any new work and are generally reluctant to take initiative.
(Aim: The child should be self-confident; he should have a sense of personal adequacy and be able to cope with his environment at an appropriate level.)

Thirty-three of the teachers recognized this as something which sometimes occurs in their classrooms. A third of them claimed that they would feel a lot of concern about it and the remainder would be moderately concerned. Almost two-thirds of the teachers would talk to these children giving them encouragement and support. Half of the teachers would take action by organizing friendship groups, making certain that the work was at an appropriate level and giving clearer instructions for new work. Ten of the teachers recommended the use of praise, rather more than for any other of the incidents.

4   In situations in which children have opportunities to choose

how they will approach their work, the completed books of each
child are often very similar in content and presentation across
the whole class.
(Aim: The child should be an individual developing in his own
way.)

Twenty-four of the teachers indicated that this was an occasional
event in their classrooms and five, a frequent one. Most claimed
that they would be moderately concerned by it. The most popular
way of dealing with this, shared by two-thirds of the teachers,
was to take action by changing seating, organizing more individual
assignment work and rearranging the content and timing of the
work so that opportunities to copy would be minimized. A third of
the teachers indicated that in certain circumstances they would
accept such a situation. They pointed out that if the quality of
the work was satisfactory, then the less able children would
benefit. A number wrote that if the work was satisfactory then
they saw no great problem about it all being rather similar. About
a quarter of the teachers suggested reassuring those children
who felt the need to copy and generally giving them extra attention.

5   Although numbers of children in your class work conscientiously, they only ever seem to find satisfaction in finishing work.
(Aim: The child should find enjoyment in a variety of aspects of
school work and gain satisfaction from his own achievements.)

Almost two-thirds of the teachers experienced this with their
classes. They varied very much in the amount of concern that
they would feel about it, though with the greater number not
greatly concerned. Half the teachers said that they would not
only accept the situation but would welcome children finding satisfaction in completing their work. The teachers who would take
action suggested trying to make the work more interesting, providing alternative tasks and trying to train children gradually
to devote more time to a task.

6   On several occasions children in your class insist that they
have washed their hands; the dinner-lady knows that they have
not, but they refuse to do as she tells them.
(Aim: The child should be generally obedient to parents, teachers
and all reasonable authority.)

Twenty-one teachers had experienced this incident from time to
time, and two, frequently. No one would be unconcerned about
it but some regarded it much more seriously than others. Most
teachers did view this incident as an issue about obedience. However, eleven teachers were equally concerned, or in some cases
concerned only about the hygiene aspect of the incident. There
seemed to be three main ways of dealing with it. The most common
suggestion was that of simply insisting that children do as they

are told. Almost half the teachers would explain the principles of hygiene and also of courtesy to dinner-ladies. The third most frequently suggested strategy was that of making rules about hand-washing and checking on their observance. Seven teachers recommended reprimand or punishment.

7   For the third time in a fortnight, money has gone missing from children's desks during playtime.
(Aim: The children should be beginning to acquire a set of moral values on which to base their own behaviour; for example, honesty, sincerity, personal responsibility).

This was clearly one of the most worrying incidents with twenty-four teachers giving it a top score of concern to them. Twenty-one teachers reported that it did sometimes happen in their classrooms although seventeen said that it never happened. Most teachers suggested taking steps to find out who was responsible. After that there were three strategies recommended by about half of the teachers. Organizing routines and procedures for care of money, for regulating entry to the classroom and for surveillance were most frequently suggested. Other than that, teachers would discuss the problem with the children and make rules about the keeping of money. Nine teachers would enlist the help of the Headteacher, more than for any other incident.

8   One child in your class has a severe stammer; some children make fun of her and others ignore her.
(Aim: The child should be kind and considerate; he should, for example, be willing to give personal help to younger and new children, to consider the elderly, the disabled.)

The teachers split roughly half and half on whether they ever experienced this kind of incident in their own classrooms. Almost all of them would be very concerned about it. The most frequently recommended way of dealing with this was that of talk. Most teachers would support and encourage the child concerned and try to elicit help and sympathy from the others. Just under half would discuss the incident in terms of the principles of kindness and mutual tolerance of defects. Just over a third recommended referral to a speech therapist and were clearly more concerned about the child's speech problems than about the behaviour of the other children.

9   Because a teacher left and has not been replaced, a class has been split and six children have been taken into your class. After two weeks these children still seem unsettled: they seem to need a lot of individual attention and are generally reluctant to join in with the rest of the children. You find, on looking through their books, that their work has deteriorated.
(Aim: The child should be happy, cheerful and well balanced.)

While fewer than a third of the teachers ever experienced this
kind of incident, almost all of them said that they would be most
concerned about it. There was the greatest measure of consensus
in regard to this incident with twenty-five of the teachers recom-
mending taking action by rearranging the groups and planning
the work carefully so as to integrate the newcomers. Half of the
teachers would give extra attention to the children concerned,
talking to and generally encouraging them. A third most frequently suggested device was for the teachers to try to find out
what the children's previous experience had been, whether they
differed from the previous teacher in any particularly upsetting
way, and what specific cause there might be for the children's
failure to settle.

10   Complaints have been received about the behaviour of children in your class on the way home from school: large groups
obstruct the pavement and seem unaware of people trying to get
past.
(Aim: The child should know how to behave with courtesy and
good manners both in and out of school.)

Only ten of the teachers claimed any familiarity with this incident
although it attracted quite a high level of concern. Talk was the
predominant means recommended for dealing with this problem.
About half the teachers would discuss the situation in a general
way and about half would try to explain the principles of consideration for others.

In this discussion of teachers' recommendations for dealing with
the incidents, eleven strategies have been identified. Six of
these were fairly common and were suggested by at least two-
thirds of the teachers for one or more of the incidents. By way
of a summary, these were as follows:

A   Talking with the children concerned. 38 teachers.
e.g: 'Use gentle persuasion and encouragement.'

B   Taking action with method, organization, etc. 37 teachers.
e.g: 'Work allowing a more individual approach should be ming-
led with the more basic everyday activities.'

C   Investigating. 31 teachers.
e.g: 'Question the children concerned with the incident.'

D   Having a discussion or lesson with the whole class. 30 teachers.
e.g: 'Discuss their thoughtlessness.'

E   Explaining principles. 29 teachers.
e.g: 'I would explain in more detail to the class about honesty and also
explain that sometimes we have to be sorry for people who perhaps
are not given money of their own and want to be the same as the rest.'

F Telling, insisting. 29 teachers.
e.g: 'Have yet another nag about it.'

G Making rules. 24 teachers.
e.g: 'Remind them that they are always asked to do this.'

H Involving others, Head, parents, specialist help. 22 teachers.
e.g: 'I should get the Head to deal with it.'

I Reprimanding, punishing. 21 teachers.
e.g: 'Possibly keep them in one playtime tidying up the cloakroom.'

J Praising. 17 teachers.
e.g: 'Praise like mad when they get it right.'

K Giving children responsibility. 13 teachers.
e.g: 'It is the class's job to help the child by being sympathetic
and patient.'

Four additional strategies were suggested by a third or fewer of
the teachers:

L Setting an example. 13 teachers.
e.g: 'Most important of all, the teacher most show the way by
being the perfect example.'

M Making a personal appeal. 11 teachers.
e.g: 'I should also tell them that I personally feel let down and
that my pride in my class has been shaken.'

N Threatening. 8 teachers.
e.g: 'Let them know that I would be on the lookout for such behaviour and that if it continued the offenders would face reper-
cussions at school.'

O Ignoring. 5 teachers.
e.g: 'I would show that I was not prepared to waste valuable
school work time in searching for missing items - in other words,
I had lost interest.'

On the basis of the teachers' responses to these ten varied incidents there appear to be fifteen distinguishable strategies for
dealing with undesirable behaviour. Some of them, as shown
above, are much more widely used than others. Two were almost
universal among this group. One of these, the strategy of talking to, persuading, encouraging children in trouble of one kind
or another, accords very much with the impression gained from
the original study group of teachers. It can occur only after
the event and it is likely to be adjusted to what are perceived to
be the needs of the individual child. The other very common

strategy is that of taking action with method or organization as a means of changing behaviour in desirable directions.

This raises an interesting question which bears on the one posed at the beginning of the chapter. If teachers tend to be so aware of the potency of using method and organization to remedy undesirable behaviour, why do they tend not to report using it in an anticipatory way to foster the behaviour they aim for in the first place? The solution may be, as suggested earlier, that undesirable behaviour has more practical consequences than desirable behaviour and thus constitutes a stronger motivation to action.

Most of the teachers had a preferred strategy which they suggested markedly more than any other as they wrote about each incident in turn. Five of the teachers were distinctively principle-givers. While they used other strategies for dealing with undesirable behaviour, they gave particular emphasis to the explanation of principles underlying the behaviour they wanted. Eight of the teachers were 'talkers'. They most often reacted to untoward incidents in the classroom by talking to the children concerned. Mostly it was supportive, encouraging talk but sometimes it was a 'telling off'. This seems to be a coping device, something immediate which deals with the incident at the time and which may or may not have any long-term implications. Fifteen of the teachers were 'managers', people who took action with the situation by changing their methods or their organization. They seemed to take greater responsibility for the children's behaviour and to view unfortunate incidents in the classroom more as a consequence of their own activity as a teacher. The action they recommended seems to have obvious longer-term implications. They most commonly suggested changes which would influence the children's behaviour in a continuing way. They more often suggested helping the children to take responsibility themselves, a strategy which seems to bear out a longer-term view of personal development. They also more often suggested using praise to encourage desirable behaviour, another indication of a concept of shaping behaviour. Generally, the 'managers' seemed to be more versatile, suggesting more strategies and more varied ones. Table 6.1 shows the differences between 'managers' and 'talkers' in their response to each incident. A strategy has been listed if it was suggested by more than half the group.

'Managers' seem to be prepared to do more about undesirable behaviour; while they will often use the strategy of talking to the individuals concerned, they seem to be prepared to do much more besides and to take action with the class as a whole. In keeping with this greater inclination to action, it is interesting that they consistently indicated that they would be rather more concerned about all but one of the incidents than the 'talkers'. The one which would worry them rather less was disobedience. In particular, the 'managers' indicated substantially more concern about lack of satisfaction in work, lack of self-confidence and unhappiness. It might be worth considering whether these are the attributes which would bear most adversely on the children's

Table 6.1 *Responses of managers and talkers to classroom incidents*

Incident	'Managers'	'Talkers'
1. Carelessness with belongings	Devise routines for cloakroom, etc. Try to imbue children with sense of responsibility.	No shared strategy.
2. Intolerance	Change groups round and alter work set. Encourage less able, persuade more able to be patient.	Change groups round and alter work set. Encourage less able, persuade more able to be patient.
3. Lack of confidence	Check suitability of work, give clearer instructions. Encourage.	Encourage.
4. Lack of individuality	Change organization and timing of work.	Change organization and timing of work. Encourage.
5. Lack of satisfaction in work	Change tasks, try to develop concentration.	Accept.
6. Disobedience	Explain principles. Make rules.	Insist.
7. Stealing	Investigate. Institute new classroom routines. Discuss with class. Make rules.	Investigate. Discuss with class.
8. Unkindness	Encourage sympathy. Support 'victim'. Explain principles of kindness. Seek specialist help for child concerned.	Encourage sympathy. Support 'victim'.
9. Unhappiness	Change organization. Investigate causes. Give extra attention.	Give extra attention.
10. Discourtesy	Discuss with class. Explain principles of consideration for others.	Discuss with class.

learning. It might be that the concern of 'managers' for personal
and social behaviour has its origins in a concern for cognitive
development.

So far in this discussion it has been taken for granted that
teachers think that some behaviour is desirable and other behaviour is not. Most teachers, for example, think that children
should be kind or, at least, should not be unkind. Why do they
think that? Do different teachers have different reasons for
thinking it? If they have different reasons, does that make a difference to how they go about encouraging kindness and discouraging unkindness?

This was a small-scale, exploratory study but an attempt was
made to begin to open up these questions. Forty-two of the
sixty teachers involved in the classroom observation study were
interviewed; most of them had completed the booklet discussed
earlier in this paper.

Despite the generous co-operation of Heads and teachers, circumstances could not always be ideal. Sometimes teachers had to
be interviewed in classrooms, and teachers could not be expected
to give their undivided attention to the questions. The time that
could be given varied considerably. For these reasons, no attempt
has been made to analyse the interviews systematically, but
rather to draw impressions from numerous re-readings of the ver-
batim records made at the time.

The teachers were asked to select, from a list, three kinds of
'good' classroom behaviour and three kinds of 'bad' behaviour
that they thought particularly important. They were then asked
to talk about why they especially liked and disliked that behaviour. Six clear types of reason emerged. First, teachers talked
about what they thought society should be like and argued that
children should be helped to behave in accordance with the
social ideals of teachers. For example, one teacher said children
should be helpful, because 'This is my whole concept of society -
we should strive to help one another the best way we can.' In
talking about the value of social awareness, another teacher
said, 'It's a more general view of society than something specifically for children.' A second reason, though still taking adult
life in society as the criterion for encouraging certain classroom
behaviour, emphasized what would be functional rather than
what was ideal. One teacher gave as a reason for encouraging
children to take responsibility for their own time: 'It's important
because children are going in future years to live in an age when
they will have a great deal of time on their hands - if they can
learn in school to use time, it will be useful much later on.' Another teacher argued that children need to take pride in their
work, because 'It's what people need throughout life - not just
in school - in a job, to get on in life socially - to set themselves
standards.'

The next two reasons for encouraging certain classroom behaviour relate to children's present experience, their education.
Education is talked about almost as if it is an end in itself. No

doubt what these teachers thought education should be about
has its roots in their views of society and adult life, but this
was not made explicit. Just as the two reasons related to views
of society represented the ideal and the functional, so too do
the reasons related to what education is about. In the first case,
the teachers' ideals for education provide the justification for
encouraging certain behaviour. 'I always aim for autonomy –
it's what education is all about – self-discipline.' In the second
case, behaviour is valued because it is functional for education.
'It is important that children take responsibility for their own
work because in the last analysis it's down to them – we can
help, talk, make possibilities but eventually they have to accept
that only they can do it.'

A fifth reason for encouraging certain behaviour was again
because it is functional, but this time at a practical classroom
level. 'Obedience is paramount,' said one teacher. 'Unless children will do what the teacher wants, there's not much point in
going on.' Another said that children should be socially aware,
because 'If you get children thinking of this you can run the
class happily with all working together. If they don't – you get
snatching and quarrelling – it's chaos, especially with group
work.'

The sixth reason related to the way the teacher felt about the
behaviour personally and was often, though not always, given
as a justification for objecting to, rather than favouring, certain
behaviour. Teachers said things such as: 'I can't stand impu-
dence, it sets the hairs on the back of my neck'; 'I personally
dislike to see bullying and aggressiveness. I would dislike it if
they happened to me'; 'I take disobedience as a personal affront';
'I can't stand bullying, it's an emotional thing inside me' and,
'Children should be purposeful; I like to see my class busy all
the time.'

In summary, teachers seemed to give six types of reason for
encouraging or discouraging certain classroom behaviour:
1 Accordance with the teacher's social ideals.
2 Accordance with what the teacher thinks will be functional
   in adult society.
3 Accordance with the teacher's educational ideals.
4 Accordance with what the teacher thinks is functional for
   education.
5 Accordance with what the teacher thinks is functional in the
   classroom at a practical level.
6 Accordance with the teacher's personal feelings.

The teachers were then asked what they actually did about the
kinds of behaviour they want to encourage or discourage.
Specifically, they were asked what they did with a new class to
enable children to behave in what the teachers considered to be
an appropriate way. It was observed at the beginning of this
chapter that teachers seem to find difficulty in explaining what
they do in relation to developing specific qualities such as kindness and independence. However, when they were presented with

a more general question about 'behaviour they want to encourage', the teachers were much more fluent. Moreover, what they said, and that they were able to say so much more in response to the general question, seemed to provide a clue to the difficulty in relation to specific behaviour. These impressions are presented tentatively as possible directions for a more extended study.

The abounding impression was that personal and social behaviour is not viewed by teachers with the same detachment as they view progress in reading or maths or any other area of the curriculum. Cognitive skills and concepts can be regarded as rather impersonal entities, and teaching techniques and learning materials can be considered dispassionately. Not so, it appeared, with personal and social behaviour, which seemed to be viewed by many teachers as cause and consequence of their continuing relationship with the children. If this is so, then it would explain their greater ease in talking about general behaviour which bears on the inter-personal relationship with the teacher rather than the separate components.

The quality of the teacher-children relationship seems to be of immense importance to the teachers, and, they imply, to the children. As one teacher said, 'It's our class, I want us to be happy, it's our home – it's a wonderful relationship', and another, 'I want a give and take relationship. I want to please them and them to please me. I want them to be happy in school, I want to be happy myself.' Because of its importance, it matters to the teachers that children behave in a way that sustains the relationship. Another teacher reported that he says to children, 'We'll get on very well if you work hard and behave yourselves. I like people to work hard and behave themselves. If you do this, we'll get on very well – if you don't, we won't.' As this quotation further shows, the relationship is used as a lever for encouraging the desired behaviour.

Teachers have less detachment from children's personal and social behaviour than from any other area of their learning. It is obviously much more difficult to plan for learning which is involved to so much greater a degree in the inter-personal relationship between teacher and children. Moreover, standards and expectations seem to be rather more variable for personal and social development than for other areas of learning. While teachers consider personality and personal circumstances in relation to learning to read and progress in maths, for instance, these things bear much more closely on personal and social learning, and expectations vary accordingly. Furthermore, it seems plausible that the absence of desirable behaviour is less of a motivator to action than the presence of undesirable behaviour, and that therefore teachers consider means for dealing with the latter rather than the former. Thus, while teachers may indeed value certain kinds of behaviour in the classroom, they may see it as a bonus rather than a positive goal to be planned for.

Having said that, much of the way in which children behave in the classroom does bear importantly on other areas of their learning. Many of the teachers remarked that children who can work harmoniously together, who are self-confident and purposeful, able to concentrate and to take responsibility for a task, are likely to cope more effectively with their classroom work. If this is so, then perhaps it might be expected that teachers would plan for the development of these characteristics. They have a variety of remedial strategies to hand which they do use deliberately to deal with undesirable behaviour. Perhaps more thought needs to be given to using these strategies in a more consistent, anticipatory way.

7 TEACHERS' PERCEPTIONS OF THEIR PUPILS' ANXIETY

John Willcocks

Towards the end of the 1960s Sargant (1969) inaugurated a symposium of the World Psychiatric Association by describing anxiety
as 'still perhaps our major psychiatric problem at the present
time', and as 'an immense world problem'. There are no signs
that either its importance or its incidence have abated since then.
In countless books and articles, at all levels from the most technical to the most popular, the view has been repeatedly expressed
that people today are far more anxious than ever before.

The argument is developed in psychological terms by Keen
(1970), who suggests that the religious and other institutional
values of earlier times not only imposed restraints but also provided a guidance for decision-making. Now that these values have
broken down, man is faced with a kind of ambiguity which has not
been his usual lot. He cannot avoid constantly making decisions,
yet has no unambiguous set of principles or beliefs by which to
make them; and his concrete experience of this paradox produces
anxiety.

Writing from a sociological standpoint, Just (1974) draws attention to the enormous difficulties of substantiating comparisons
of mental well-being between different societies and periods, and
concludes that it would be presumptuous to maintain that there
is a higher level of anxiety in our present culture than in other
times and places. Nevertheless she emphasizes that the anxiety
itself is undeniable and that its symptoms can scarcely be overlooked. In her view it is the social structures of modern life
which make it 'painful for many people to cope'.

At a more popular level writers have greater freedom to speculate boldly without worrying too much about the problems of substantiating their arguments. In a persuasive recent article Tubiana
(1978) blames scientific enquiry for the breakdown of the comfort-
ing myths and values of yester-year, and sees in that breakdown
the explanation both of the current high levels of anxiety and of
the widespread mistrust and even hatred of science. Even so,
he argues that only the knowledge derived from scientific enquiry
will ever lead to an understanding and consequent alleviation of
anxiety.

The justification for such an enquiry into the anxiety of primary
school children is not hard to find. If the problem is endemic in
our culture as a whole, then since the primary school classroom is
a part of that culture there might be strong grounds for supposing
that anxiety will play a major part in it. Further, the breaking
down of traditional dogmas and values in the greater world outside

has been mirrored in the move towards informality in the educational system. It is convincingly argued by Simon, in Chapter 1 of this volume, that the so-called primary school revolution has been not nearly so profound and far-reaching as is generally supposed. Nevertheless, that there has been a persistent questioning of values and a deliberate loosening of structures is not a point of contention. It might therefore be reasonable to expect that the emphasis placed on self-directed study and the absence of rigid authoritarian structure will have generated considerable anxiety in pupils and teachers alike.

The first task involved in an enquiry of this nature is one of definition, and with anxiety this certainly constitutes a major problem since theoreticians have presented so many conflicting conceptualizations. In a detailed analysis of all the major and some idiosyncratic theoretical formulations, Fischer (1970) describes the orthodox Freudian, neo-Freudian and ego-psychological approaches, and the accounts derived from physiology, learning-theory and existential philosophy, as well as the independent approaches of Schachtel (1963) and Goldstein (1939). Against the background of such a bewildering array of theories it is scarcely surprising that there is no simple definition which is universally acceptable, although this is a somewhat paradoxical state of affairs in view of the general consensus about the central position and importance of anxiety in our current way of life.

In view of the difficulty of reaching a satisfactory definition of the concept, the starting point of the present study was an examination of what teachers themselves mean when they describe pupils as anxious; and it is that aspect of the enquiry which is presented here.

The first year of the ORACLE research programme provided a favourable opportunity to carry out the task. A full account of the techniques of observation and assessment used in the programme has been given elsewhere (Galton et al. 1980; Galton and Simon (eds) 1980); here it is enough to say that ORACLE observers were already working in fifty-eight primary classrooms, and had already had the opportunity of establishing close contact with the teachers. A mass of data was being collected, including measures from the systematic observation of behaviour, achievement scores and pupils' responses to an attitude questionnaire which included two anxiety scales, one relating to anxiety about the teachers and the other to anxiety about fellow pupils. This seemed an ideal setting in which to collect teachers' opinions about the anxiety of their pupils.

A popular method for this kind of exercise is a series of ratings on a five- or seven-point scale. In appraising the child's anxiety (or creativity or helpfulness or whatever), the teacher places a tick somewhere in a series of boxes. A tick in either the first or the seventh box indicates that in the teacher's view the child is unusually well endowed or unusually lacking in the quality under investigation, while a tick in one of the central boxes indicates a position nearer the normal or average. Among the attractions of the technique are its simplicity and the fact that the resulting ticks can easily be converted to numerical values (which is helpful if one is hoping to correlate the teachers' ratings with something else). However, it is not free from drawbacks. If it is to be used by a number of teachers, as would have been the case here, great care must be taken to see that they all use the scale in the same way, and that they are in broad agreement about the nature of the quality they are assessing. To take creativity as an example, if some of them consider that it is normally distributed, while some believe that all but a few children are innately creative, and yet others believe that only a Leonardo can really be termed creative in the true sense of the word, it is clear that lumping together their ratings as though they were equivalent will be quite unjustified. Before the exercise can sensibly take place, participating teachers will need either to take part in extended discussions to agree on definitions and criteria for scoring, or at the very least be instructed to follow a set of ready-made criteria. The former procedure renders the whole enterprise extremely cumbersome, especially if the teachers come from widely scattered geographical areas; the latter procedure calls into question the value and precise nature of the ratings. If, to continue with the example, a teacher rates the creativity of her pupils according to a definition quite different from her own understanding of the term, we are left with a series of scores which in no way reflect the teacher's own opinions about the creativity of her pupils.

Anxiety, in common with some other constructs, presents an additional level of difficulty, since in relation to some children it will seem to the teachers an inappropriate concept. There will be anxious pupils and perhaps very anxious pupils; but there will be many others to whom the term seems not to apply. If a child has never behaved in a way which has made the teacher think of him as anxious he will simply seem not anxious, and the task of placing him on a seven-point scale for anxiety will consequently seem entirely artificial.

Because of these problems the technique of rating on a points scale was rejected in the present enquiry. Instead, the teachers were simply asked to list the names of any children in their classes who struck them as being unduly or unusually anxious. However, since the main point of the enquiry was to gain an understanding of how teachers use the concept, they were also invited to give a brief indication of the sorts of behaviour which had in each case led them to attribute anxiety to the child. The request for this information was made informally by the classroom observers during the course of their visits to each teacher, and a small printed sheet was provided for the list of names and signs of anxiety. The use of this personal approach rather than a postal questionnaire led to a 100 per cent response rate.

An examination of the teachers' comments about the sorts of behaviour which had led them to nominate particular children as anxious revealed marked differences between teachers. Some

briefly indicated only one sign of anxiety beside a child's name;
others wrote at greater length, in some cases producing what
amounted to a short essay on the child in question. As a first
step towards categorizing the aspects of anxiety perceived by
the teachers, their comments on each child were broken down into
separate statements or thought units, which varied from single
words such as 'disruptive', 'giggly', 'spiteful' and so on, to
quite long comments such as that the child 'hides so that other
children cannot see his glasses', or that he 'delays the task about
which he is anxious for as long as possible.'

On average three separate indicators of anxiety were given for
each child; but a fifth of the children were described by a single
statement, while the number of separate statements for an individual child rose as high as fourteen.

Not all the teachers' responses referred to specific examples
of overt behaviour. Some were scarcely more than alternative
terms for anxious, such as 'nervous' or 'highly strung', while
others described mental states or character traits which are not
in themselves at all synonymous with anxiety but which had led
the teacher to infer it, such as 'excitable' or 'very meticulous'.
Yet other statements pointed to the child's history or family
background, and seemed to be hinting at the aetiology rather
than the symptomatology of the supposed anxiety. However, a
large number of the statements related specifically to observable
aspects of the children's behaviour, and included such disparate
items as blinking, nail-biting, making rude noises, and avoiding
the teacher's eye.

The classification of all these statements into categories was not
made on the basis of a theoretical taxonomy of anxiety but was
derived empirically from the data, since it was essential in attempting to reach an understanding of teachers' perceptions of anxiety
that the categories should be the result of what they themselves
were explicating. Statements which seemed to belong together
were put together, so that the separate categories emerged rather
than being predetermined. There were seven of these relating to
different types of explanation:

  i   personality traits within the child himself
  ii   his abilities and achievement
  iii   his relationship with the teacher
  iv   his physical problems
  v   his family background
  vi   his difficulties with other children
  vii   his relationship to the school as an institution.

We have already seen that on average three separate statements
were made about each child, and frequently the statements belonged to separate categories. In relation to 70 per cent of the
children the teachers' comments included statements which fell
into more than one category, and 10 per cent of the children were
described as showing anxiety in four categories simultaneously.

The most-used category was that which related to personality
traits, and 50 per cent of the children nominated were said to

show characteristics which fell under this heading. However, its frequency of use should not be taken to imply an importance over and above that of the other categories. Of necessity a high proportion of the single-word and short-phrase responses went into this large category because they made no reference to specific symptoms or the settings in which the anxiety was apparent. For example, the responses 'nervous' and 'nuisance' were both categorized as personality traits even though either of them might have been reworded in such a way as to make it clear that some other category, such as physical problems or difficulties with other children, would have been more appropriate. Thus, in this sense, the largest category of responses may be taken as underlying the others, and as differing from them principally though not entirely in its lack of specificity. It included five subcategories which are listed below, together with a specimen statement from each:

   i   Withdrawal, e.g. lives in a world of his own.
  ii   Aggression/Antisocial behaviour, e.g. spiteful.
 iii   Feelings of inadequacy, e.g. lacks self-confidence.
 iv   Fears, e.g. timid.
   v   Miscellaneous/Ambiguous, e.g. mixed up.

The largest category relating to a specific area concerned the children's ability and achievement. It was used in 42 per cent of the nominations, and it could be divided into five subcategories:

   i   General ability, e.g. aware he cannot keep up.
  ii   Effort, e.g. needs to be kept at it.
 iii   Reaction to tests, e.g. cries during tests.
 iv   General achievement, e.g. worried about performance.
   v   Achievement in specific subjects, e.g. very poor reading.

Not all the teachers' responses in this category suggested low ability or poor achievement. Indeed a few of them indicated considerable success, and within the category as a whole there appeared such responses as: capable, bright, very good reader, communicates well through drawings, and so on. Clearly these were not intended in themselves as indicators of anxiety, but rather as qualifying factors in comments which consisted of more than one statement, as for example in the following response: 'Hypochondriac. Very good reader but poor written work, which worries her a lot. Frequently comes to teacher to tell her she's trying her best.'

The second largest category relating to a specific area concerned the children's relationships with the teacher. It was used in 36 per cent of the nominations, and the responses in it fell into six subcategories:

   i   Avoidance, e.g. reluctant to approach teacher.
  ii   Seeking reassurance, e.g. desires praise.
 iii   Seeking attention, e.g. must have optimum teacher attention.
 iv   Efforts to please, e.g. gives the answer he thinks the teacher wants.
   v   Defiance, e.g. refuses instructions.

vi   Miscellaneous/ambiguous, e.g. demands emotional commitment from the teacher.

The category relating to physical symptoms of anxiety was used
in 31 per cent of the nominations and consisted of five commonly
used subcategories together with a large number of unique responses referring to a very wide range of problems, grouped here
as a sixth miscellaneous subcategory:

i   Speech, e.g. stammers.
ii   Motor Co-ordination/Movement, e.g. clumsy.
iii   Tics/Mannerisms, e.g. twitch.
iv   Digestion/Elimination, e.g. tummy trouble.
v   Sport/Physical activity, e.g. does not join in PE.
vi   Miscellaneous, e.g. sleeping difficulties; worried about
weight; wears glasses; asthma; eczema; abdominal; mi-
graine; blushes; badly burned when a child; hypochondria.

Comments about a child's family were made in connection with
22 per cent of the nominations. As with statements about ability
and achievement these were not all unfavourable; they included
statements that every help was given at home, that the mother
visited the school to discuss the child's worries, and so on. Responses fell into four major subcategories:

i   Siblings, e.g. very clever elder brother.
ii   Parents, e.g. mother fusses over him.
iii   Family history, e.g. family background of nervous trouble.
iv   Miscellaneous, e.g. home problems.

Difficulties with fellow pupils featured in only 19 per cent of
the nominations, and fell into six subcategories:

i   Isolation, e.g. doesn't mix.
ii   Aggression, e.g. bullies infants.
iii   Competitiveness, e.g. anxiety geared towards competition.
iv   Rejection, e.g. other children tease him.
v   Inconsistency, e.g. friendly one minute and not the next.
vi   Miscellaneous, e.g. anxious about other children's affairs.

The final category was the smallest, and related in the main to
the children's difficulties in coping with the school as an institution, although it also included two responses relating to outside
organizations, namely a hospital and a school psychological service.
Out of the nominations, 11 per cent included statements in this
category, and it was not subdivided. Examples of statements
made under this heading are as follows: dislikes school, runs
away from school, difficulty with authority figures.

At one level, the problem of the validity of all these statements
does not arise. We have already seen that there is no standard
definition of anxiety against which they can be evaluated. From
a phenomenological viewpoint, if we ask teachers to indicate the
sorts of pupil behaviour which lead them to infer anxiety, then
whatever responses they make are 'the right answer', whether
they seem sensible to an outsider or whether they seem to miss
the point. At another level, however, it seems reasonable to look
for validity. Since the kinds of behaviour noted had led to an
inference that certain pupils were unduly or unusually anxious,

it is appropriate to ascertain whether there are any other criteria
by which the nominated children appear more anxious than their
school fellows, or whether there are systematic differences between teachers which would suggest that different groups of
them are more or less likely to attribute anxiety to their pupils.

The fifty-eight teachers nominated a total of 109 children of
whom 53 per cent were girls (as against 51 per cent in the total
sample). This constituted an average of about two children to a
class (with a mean class size of thirty children). However there
were wide differences between teachers in the number of children
nominated. Fourteen of them either stated that no children were
anxious or at least listed no names, while at the other extreme
two teachers listed seven children, and two teachers listed eight.
Among those teachers who gave no names there was a range of
comments suggesting that some may have spent considerably more
time thinking about the task than others. One teacher's response
was, 'None of the children are sufficiently with it to be unduly
anxious', and another remarked, 'They are all a funny bunch.'
On the other hand one teacher wrote the following:

> After due thought, I really don't think I have any who fall
> into the above categories. If it is of any help I will outline
> the signs I would consider as showing someone to be unduly
> or unusually anxious:
>
> i   reticence to approach for help or advice
> ii constant seeking of reassurance, even with simple tasks,
>   commands, etc.
> iii marked unwillingness to 'volunteer', e.g. work, speech,
>   etc.
> iv physical symptoms, i.e. frequent tummy aches, trips to
>   toilet, associated with tasks being undertaken
> v   confused reaction when talked to - i.e. the anxiety of
>   the discussion or explanation setting up 'bow waves'
>   and making logical thought difficult
> vi a marked deterioration in work when under some (even
>   mild) stress.

The wide range of types of response raised the possibility that
the exercise was yielding information about the teachers rather
than about the pupils. Whereas it seemed quite possible that
among fifty-eight ordinary classes chosen essentially at random
there were fourteen with no very anxious children and four with
as many as seven or eight, it now seemed at least a possibility
that among the teachers were some who were simply insensitive to
anxiety in their pupils, and others who, perhaps because of their
own anxiety, were seeing it where it didn't exist. No preliminary
hypotheses had been set up along these lines, and indeed if they
had been it is difficult to see what realistic procedures could have
been followed to test them properly. However, the analysis of the
first year's observational data from the ORACLE programme had
yielded a number of different teaching styles (Galton et al. 1980,
chapter 6); and it was a simple matter to examine the data retro-
spectively to see whether there were systematic differences in

the numbers of children nominated by teachers who favoured different teaching styles on the assumption that perhaps individual monitors might have been in closer touch with the peculiarities of specific children than, say, class enquirers or group instructors). No such differences were found. Nor were there significant differences in the numbers nominated by men and women teachers, nor by teachers of different ages.

The next step was to look at the relationship between the number of children nominated in each class and the mean score of that class on the anxiety questionnaire completed by the children. If the large number of teachers who listed no names were simply insensitive to anxiety in their pupils, then the questionnaire scores of their classes might be expected not to differ significantly from those of other classes where the teachers were aware of their pupils' anxiety. Indeed it might even be the case that teachers who were insensitive to pupil anxiety would exacerbate it through inappropriate treatment of anxious pupils, whereas teachers who were alert to it might alleviate it by making allowance for it. In that case, there might even be a negative correlation between the numbers of children nominated and the mean questionnaire anxiety scores of the class. In fact, there was a positive correlation of 0.37 which was statistically significant beyond the 0.001 level, suggesting that the teachers' nominations were indeed reflecting differences in the children and not simply differences in the teachers. However, this analysis was concerned with the mean questionnaire scores of classes as a whole, and did not discriminate between the nominated children and the rest. In a separate analysis the children were considered not in classes but in two separate groups; here the mean questionnaire scores of the nominated children were compared with those of all children who were not listed as anxious by their teachers, and the results are set out in Table 7.1. It will be seen that on both teacher-oriented and pupil-oriented anxiety the nominated children scored higher than the rest, and again the differences were statistically significant.

Table 7.1 Mean anxiety questionnaire scores of pupils nominated as anxious and all other pupils

	Nominated pupils			All other pupils			Significance of difference
Questionnaire category	*n*	*score*	*%*	*n*	*score*	*%*	
Pupil-oriented anxiety	87	13.5	54.0	1,109	11.0	44.0	*
Teacher-oriented anxiety	84	14.9	59.6	1,109	12.7	50.8	*
Overall anxiety	82	28.4	56.8	1,109	23.7	47.4	*

* Significant beyond the 1 per cent level.

A different approach was to examine the relevant data from the

systematic observation of pupils in their classrooms to discover
whether there were marked differences in behaviour between the
two groups. It must be emphasized that the observation instrument had not been specifically devised to monitor signs of anxiety,
and that as Jonathan points out in Chapter 12 of this volume,
aspects of behaviour which are not categorized in such a schedule
go unrecorded even though they may occur.

Among the kinds of behaviour mentioned by the teachers were
some which fell outside the normal repertoire of most children
within the age range under investigation (such as stuttering and
enuresis), and whose very presence had been seen as a sign of
anxiety. No comparisons were possible here, since the observation
schedule did not include such categories, and consequently no
record had been made of their incidence in the total sample. There
were, however, other kinds of behaviour which were noted because
of their intensity rather than their simple presence. A child who
was described as attention-seeking or as inhibited in group situations, for example, was merely showing ordinary behaviour to an
unusual degree, since most children seek attention occasionally,
or sometimes feel shy in a group. With such kinds of behaviour a
comparison between the two groups was possible. Of the 489 children who had been systematically observed over the year, 41 were
nominated as anxious by their teachers: thus the analysis which
follows involves a random sub-sample of just over a third of the
nominated children.

The analysis was restricted to those categories on the observation schedule where differences between the two groups might be
predicted on the basis of the teachers' comments. Since many of
them had mentioned difficulties in relation to work and achievement, and to interaction with the teacher and other pupils, the
following categories were included from the Pupil Record:

   i   full involvement and co-operation on approved task work
       (COOP TK)
  ii   non-involvement and total distraction from all work (DSTR)
 iii   general interaction with the teacher (all subcategories
       combined)
  iv   attempts to become the focus of the teacher's attention
       (INIT)
   v   teacher gives the child private individual attention (IND AT)
  vi   teacher makes the child the focus of her attention in a group
       or whole-class interaction (STAR)
 vii   teacher interacts with child specifically about task work
       (TK WK)
viii   general interaction with other pupils (All subcategories
       combined).

A persistent feature of the teachers' comments was that for
many aspects of behaviour both extremes tended to be mentioned.
One child might be described as timid and another as violent, one
as reluctant to approach the teacher and another as constantly
coming out to have her work checked. It is clear that in any consideration of mean group scores such extremes will be likely to

cancel each other out. The mean incidence of the behaviour may
be remarkably similar for the two groups, yet in one group the
individual children may all be close to the mean while in the other
there may be a large number of children at the extremes. In view
of this, the analysis was not restricted to a consideration of differences between group means, but also included an examination
of the differences between the variances of the two groups –
the variance being a measure of how much variability, or scatter,
is shown by the individuals in a group.

The means and variances of the two groups are shown in Table
7.2. It will be seen that for none of the categories examined was
there a statistically significant difference between the mean scores
of the two sets of children, and thus there is no evidence here
that children who are perceived as anxious by their teachers are
as a group more likely (or less likely) to stick at their work or
to be distracted from it, to seek or unwittingly attract the
teacher's attention, or to interact with other pupils.

*Table 7.2 Mean and variance scores on selected observation categories of target pupils
nominated as anxious and all other target pupils*

Observation category	Nominated target pupils (n = 41)		All other target pupils (n = 448)		F ratio*
	Mean	Variance	Mean	Variance	
COOP TK	56.12	131.17	58.27	117.47	1.12
DSTR	16.28	63.23	15.84	71.99	1.14
All pupil-teacher interaction	13.61	85.54	16.08	103.06	1.20
INIT	1.23	2.09	1.22	1.46	1.44**
IND AT	2.63	5.77	2.21	4.75	1.21
STAR	1.77	4.06	1.58	3.42	1.19
TK WK	10.82	72.41	13.40	93.65	1.29
All pupil-pupil interaction	18.23	112.43	18.45	64.30	1.75***

* It should be noted that in this particular use of F probability levels must be doubled
because of the arbitrary placing of the larger variance in the numerator (Guilford 1973).
Hence the levels indicated are 0.10 and 0.02, and only the latter has been termed
significant in the text.
** Significant between 2 and 10 per cent levels.
*** Significant beyond 2 per cent level.

An examination of variances, however, revealed one statistically significant difference between the two groups, and one near
miss. On these two categories the nominated children showed more
extreme behaviour than other children. Although in overall pupil-
teacher interaction there was no significant difference between

the variances of the groups, the nominated children showed more extreme behaviour in attempting to become the focus of the teacher's attention, a relatively high proportion of them either doing it very often or avoiding it as much as possible. More strikingly their overall amount of interaction with other pupils showed the same pattern, some of them persistently seeking it and others avoiding it.

While these findings can in no sense prove that the teachers were 'right' in their nominations, they are quite consistent with teachers' comments on the behaviour of the pupils they considered anxious, as well as supporting the view that in relation to personal interaction the characteristics of anxious behaviour are to be found at both extremes of the normal range rather than at one extreme only.

In relation to time spent working on or distracted from approved tasks, however, no such pattern emerged. Here there were no significant differences between the two groups. This was an interesting result in view of the common finding, in other studies, of negative correlations between anxiety and achievement levels (Cowen et al. 1965, Gaudry and Spielberger 1971, McGroskey 1977). Indeed, an earlier analysis of data from the present sample, as part of the ORACLE programme, had revealed precisely this kind of statistically significant negative relationship between anxiety questionnaire responses and scores on tests of basic skills (Croll and Willcocks 1980). That analysis, however, had been in no way concerned with teachers' perceptions of anxiety, and had not discriminated between the nominated children and the rest.

Table 7.3   Mean achievement scores of pupils nominated as anxious and all other pupils

| Achievement category | Nominated pupils | | All other pupils | | Significance of |
	n	score	n	score	difference
Mathematics	92	13.30	1,118	17.06	*
Language skills	92	10.93	1,111	13.20	*
Reading	93	15.84	1,125	19.11	*
Total	90	40.07	1,111	49.37	*

* Significant beyond the 1 per cent level.

An examination of the mean achievement scores of these two groups was now undertaken, and a summary is presented in Table 7.3. On all three of the curricular areas tested, the nominated children scored significantly lower, the difference being greatest in mathematics, somewhat less in reading and least of all in such formal language skills as grammar, punctuation, and spelling. Thus the situation was that although the two groups did not differ substantially in the amount of time they spent working at their tasks in the classroom, the children whose teachers found them anxious showed considerably lower levels of achievement. This may have been partly a function of the anxiety generated by the tests themselves, although the great emphasis given in the teachers' comments to difficulties with work and achievement within the classroom suggests that the problem was more than a simple matter of test-anxiety. It is not at all unreasonable to suppose that although the nominated children did not neglect their everyday classwork, their high levels of anxiety tended to interfere with whatever mental processes were necessary to carry it out efficiently.

However, it must be emphasized that the children were allocated to the two groups not on the basis of any pure or absolute measure of anxiety (for such a thing does not exist), but rather in accordance with their teachers' opinions. It was hypothesized that teachers' awareness of anxiety in their pupils would be triggered by such an occurrence as low achievement, and that consequently among children, who were by other criteria equally anxious, it would be those whose achievement was lower who would be more likely to be nominated as anxious by their teachers. To test this hypothesis and to penetrate further into the influence of pupil achievement on the teachers' awareness of pupil anxiety, each of the nominated children upon whom questionnaire data was available was matched with a child whose age group and questionnaire score were as nearly the same as possible, but who had not been nominated as anxious. Where the match for an individual pair could not be exact a subsequent match was adjusted so that the mean scores of the two groups remained the same. These two groups, then, had identical levels of anxiety in terms of their own questionnaire responses, but whereas one group consisted entirely of children whose teachers found them highly anxious there were no such children at all in the other group. Since there was a control for age, with which achievement levels are related, it could be assumed that any differences in test scores on basic skills would be directly related to the teachers' being aware of anxiety in the pupils, rather than to anxiety itself as measured by the questionnaire.

Table 7.4 Mean achievement scores of pupils nominated as anxious and matched pupils of equal W-questionnaire anxiety levels

	Nominated pupils		Matched pupils		Significance of difference	All pupils	
	n	*score*	*n*	*score*		*n*	*score*
Mathematics	81	12.8	81	16.4	**	1,210	16.8
Language skills	81	11.0	81	13.0		1,203	13.0
Reading	82	15.5	82	18.2	*	1,218	18.8
Total	80	39.3	80	47.6	*	1,201	48.6

* Significant between 1 and 5 per cent levels.
* Significant beyond 1 per cent level.

It will be seen from Table 7.4 that the group of nominated children made significantly lower scores than the others on maths and reading, the difference being greater for maths. On formal English skills the same pattern was repeated, though here the difference was not statistically significant, reflecting perhaps the lower priority many teachers said they gave to this aspect of the curriculum. This finding offers a clue to what happens when teachers attribute anxiety to a child. It would be fanciful to suppose that they go into the classroom armed with a paradigm of anxiety and then set about looking for children to fit it. Anxiety at some level is a normal feature of every child's make-up, and is unlikely to be of much concern to the teacher, or even to the child himself, so long as it does not lead to extraordinary or extreme behaviour, or interfere with the efficient performance of everyday tasks and duties.

In the analysis considered above the task in question was the acquisition of basic skills. Although the two groups saw themselves as equally anxious, it was those children who were performing the task less efficiently who tended to cause their teachers concern. One may suppose that the teachers, noticing low achievement, asked themselves why; and recalling other aspects of the child's behaviour which seemed to go along with the low achievement to form a pattern, they saw in anxiety a convincing explanation. Anxiety was not attributed to the other group because they were performing the task more efficiently. It will be seen from the fourth and seventh columns of Table 7.4 that on average their scores in all three curricular areas were very close to those of pupils as a whole. From the teachers' point of view there was no problem to solve, and hence no need to look for explanations.

The general conclusions which can be drawn from this enquiry are several. It seems that, as a group, primary school teachers make use of a wide range of criteria in reaching the opinion that particular children are unduly or unusually anxious. Foremost among these are difficulties with work and achievement, extremes of behaviour in interpersonal relations in the classroom, and certain types of physical or behavioural response which are rare or anomalous in the age group. Most teachers use some combination of these factors rather than a single one of them in attributing anxiety to a child.

The children who are seen as anxious differ from their classmates in various ways. As a group they score higher on a self-report anxiety questionnaire and lower on tests of maths, reading and formal language skills. Systematic observation in the classroom confirms that the frequency with which they interact with their fellow pupils, or attempt to attract the teacher's attention, tends more to the extremes than is the case with other children. All these findings are consistent with traditional theoretical formulations and provide strong grounds for supposing that primary school teachers generally recognize a high level of anxiety when they see it.

On average, they see it in about 7 per cent of their pupils.

While this figure gives no cause for complacency, it is well below the level which might have been predicted from a reading of the mass of literature mentioned at the outset. If we do live in an age of anxiety, we must be thankful that the typical primary school classroom seems to provide a relatively secure base in which our children can set about the task of learning to cope with it.

8 EXPECTANCY EFFECTS IN PRIMARY CLASSROOMS

Maurice Galton and Angela Delafield

It is quite commonplace to hear someone saying of another person's behaviour, 'It was just what I would have expected of him', or 'I didn't think she would behave like that.' In all walks of life we are often forced to make judgments about people on the flimsiest of evidence and a sensible person will tend to keep an open mind in such circumstances, being prepared to be proved wrong on occasions.

There is no reason to think that teachers should be any different in this respect in their dealings with pupils. The problem for a teacher, however, is that these judgments are often of crucial importance in determining the direction of a child's future development. In particular, a teacher's view about a child's level of attainment can have far-reaching consequences within an educational system where success is still mainly defined in terms of academic performance. Teachers caught up in the daily drama of the classroom, however, cannot always be expected to keep these long-term consequences in mind. For example, a study by Budd-Rowe (1974) which looked at the amount of time pupils were given to answer the teacher's question found that below-average pupils were allowed less time to respond than children who regularly came top of the class on various tests of attainment. It is not difficult to think of an explanation of why the teachers may have behaved in this way. When bright children failed to respond immediately to the question, the teacher would naturally enough assume that they were thinking about the answer and therefore gave them more time. When the exchange involved one of the slower pupils, however, it would be assumed that the child was silent because he did not know the answer. To spare the pupil further embarrassment the teacher would pass on quickly to the next child or rephrase the question. When the time came to write the end of term reports such a teacher might well comment of this slow child, 'Has difficulty in taking part in discussion or answering questions. Tends to remain silent rather than offering a response.'

On the basis of the evidence which the teacher had obtained during the course of the previous lessons this would appear to be a fair assessment. It would, in the case of the pupils in Budd-Rowe's study, have been an invalid one since she discovered that when the teachers allowed slower pupils more time they began to answer more questions. This example illustrates quite vividly the manner in which certain expectations become self-fulfilling prophecies. The teacher comes to a judgment about the pupil on the basis of the behaviour observed, but this behaviour is largely determined by the initial expectations that the teacher has of the pupil.

EARLY STUDIES OF EXPECTANCY EFFECTS

The existence of the self-fulfilling prophecy inside the classroom was perhaps most dramatically illustrated in the research of Rosenthal and Jacobson (1968). They told teachers that they would give pupils a test to predict which children in the class would suddenly begin to 'bloom' intellectually during the following six months. This statement was untrue, since the test was, in fact, one of general ability, very similar to those normally used to determine a child's intelligence quotient. After giving the test Rosenthal and Jacobson picked a number of children at random and told the teachers that these were the 'bloomers'. They then gave the original test again at the end of the year and found that those pupils who quite arbitrarily had been classified as 'bloomers' made greatest progress during the year. Rosenthal and Jacobson's explanation of this phenomenon was that because the teachers had come to expect that these children were going to do better, they gave them some special treatment in comparison to the rest of the class and that this subsequently was reflected in improved examination performance. Just what this special treatment was remained a mystery, since no one visited the teachers and the children in between the first and second test administration.

The study has been severely criticized both for the methods of statistical analysis employed and also on the more damaging ground that the teachers could not recall the names of the 'bloomers' when asked to do so (Grieger 1971). A number of studies have tried, with mixed results, to repeat the original work of Rosenthal and Jacobson (Goldsmith and Fry 1970; Schrank 1970; Fielder et al. 1971). In some cases teachers, when questioned, told the researchers that they had regarded some of the information given about potential 'bloomers' as erroneous and had rejected it. Yet another complicating factor was pointed out by Garner and Bing (1973), who argued that the very act of presenting information about selected children caused the teacher to respond to these pupils in a way which they would not have done if left to make up their own minds about the child's potential. A more important weakness of these experimental studies, however, is that, even if the existence of the self-fulfilling prophecy is accepted, there is no clear understanding of the mechanisms by which the improvement in the pupil's performance was achieved. Such information can only be obtained through the direct observation of teachers and pupils in the classroom.

OBSERVATION STUDIES OF EXPECTANCY EFFECTS

Most studies which have sought to observe the effects of teacher
expectations have been carried out in naturalistic settings.
Generally the researcher has asked the teacher to arrive at some
judgment of a pupil's general ability or potential and then pupils
have been observed to see if those labelled 'bright' received a
different kind of treatment from those labelled 'dull'. In the sim-
plest procedure, adopted by Brophy and Good (1970), teachers
ranked pupils according to school achievement. There are, however, a number of alternatives based on the use of rating scales.
Nash (1973) used the repertory grid technique developed by
Kelly (1955) to elicit teachers' constructs about individual pupils.
The constructs which teachers had in common were then used to
rank individual pupils in each class. Garner and Bing (1973)
asked teachers to rate pupils on a series of bi-polar scales including temperament, intellectual potential and conduct, while Silberman (1969), in a more elaborate method, identified attitudes which
teachers held towards pupils from an analysis of their descriptions
of particular children. He identified four attitude groups: attachment, concern, indifference and rejection, and asked teachers to
place three children into each of these groups by answering the
following questions:
Attachment
If you could keep one of your students for another year for
the sheer joy of it, whom would you pick?
Concern
If you could devote all your attention to a child who concerns
you a great deal, whom would you pick?
Indifference
If a parent were to drop in, unannounced, for a conference,
whose child would you be least prepared to talk about?
Rejection
If your class was to be reduced by one child, whom would you
be relieved to have removed?
Once the pupils were labelled or had been identified in various
ways they were observed in class during lessons. Both Nash
(1973) and Rist (1970) as well as Silberman (1969) all used some
form of participant observation in which a series of case studies
were compiled, involving pupils about whom the teacher had
different expectations. These studies tended to concentrate on
the tone of the teachers' statements and to distinguish between
pupils receiving positive and negative feedback in the form of
praise or criticism. The general claim has been that pupils labelled as poor students tend to receive more criticism and less praise
than pupils who are perceived as 'good' students. Systematic
observation has also been used in a number of studies (Jackson
and Lahaderne 1967; Garner and Bing 1973). Interactions were
coded either as primarily instructional, managerial or disciplinary.
Garner and Bing also coded the interactions as either work-

oriented or procedural (dealing with routine tasks) as well as assessing the positive or negative tone of the communication in these categories. These studies tend to show that pupils in the top achievement group had more frequent contact with the teacher. Brophy and Good (1970) extended this approach by recording what they termed 'dyadic interactions'. They noted the correctness of a pupil's response to the teacher's question and then the subsequent response of the teacher to that pupil. Their results showed that even when low-achieving pupils gave a correct answer they tended to get less praise whereas if they got the answer wrong they came in for a greater amount of criticism. More recent research has tended to confirm these findings (Dusek 1975; Hillman and Davenport 1978).

THE NEED FOR FURTHER STUDIES

These results, however, do not completely explain how the expectancy effect operates in the classroom. None of the observational studies tested the children. Indeed to have done so would have alerted the teachers to the nature of the study. It would, for example, have seemed somewhat strange to ask teachers to rank their pupils in order of ability and then to give a pre- and post-test while observing the children in between. In such circumstances teachers might have been tempted to give extra attention to pupils they had singled out either as bright or dull.

It is also possible to offer alternative explanations to account for the differential treatment received by pupils in, for example, Brophy and Good's study. It may be that the teachers asked the bright pupils more difficult questions and so felt that they deserved more praise whenever they gave a satisfactory reply. Similarly, they may have asked the slow pupils easier questions and therefore criticized them more often when they got the answers wrong. It could be that the teachers in the study estimated the children's potential correctly and were responding to their behaviour rather than initiating it. Indeed Brophy and Good distinguish between *proactive* teachers whose expectations are generally accurate, who 'keep in touch with changes in their students' behaviour and plan the work accordingly' and *overreactive* teachers who make inaccurate judgments about pupils, and 'not only allow themselves to be conditioned by student differences but exacerbate them by treating the pupils as even more different than they really are.' These latter teachers are the ones most likely to engage in the kinds of behaviour which will produce self-fulfilling prophecy effects.

To attempt to test these ideas it is necessary to seek comparisons between two groups of pupils. One group, the experimental group, would consist of pupils nominated by their teachers either as bright or dull. The second group, the control group, would consist of pupils who, although not labelled by their teachers, obtained similar scores on appropriate achievement tests. It is then possible to try to decide whether the teacher's behaviour is primarily a response to the pupil's, which in turn is dependent on his or her achievement level, or whether it arises chiefly because the teacher has a certain expectancy about the child's performance. If the latter hypothesis is true then there should be observable differences in teacher and pupil interactions between labelled and unlabelled children of similar achievement levels.

THE PRESENT STUDY

As already stated, however, this hypothesis is difficult to test in practice since by asking teachers to label children and then administering attainment tests, one may cue the teacher as to the purpose of the observations. However, in the context of the ORACLE project, it was possible to carry out such a study without alerting the teachers in this way. As part of the main process-product study, all children were given abbreviated forms of the Richmond Tests at the beginning of the school year. One of the main purposes of the first test administration was to identify pupils in the top, middle and bottom quartiles of the class in order to select a random sample of eight target pupils for subsequent observation.

In some classes, however, the researcher simply explained to the teacher that the computer analysis was not available at the time when she wished to begin her observations. She explained to the teacher that she was anxious to get a representative sample of pupils to observe. To this end she would be grateful if the teacher could identify the top three and bottom three pupils in the class so that not all of them would be observed, and thus the observation sample would not be biased in favour of a particular achievement level. It was explained to teachers that even in a randomly selected sample there was always a chance that certain types of pupils might be over-represented but that by naming pupils we could guard against this possibility by not including too many from the extremes. The actual targets in the main ORACLE study were, in fact, selected at random on the basis of their pre-test scores. It, therefore, became possible to study the interactions of pupils nominated by the teacher and to compare both their behaviour and their performance with other target pupils in the top and bottom quartiles. This procedure made it possible to overcome the criticism of earlier studies that, by asking teachers to nominate pupils, the researcher inevitably indicated which pupils would be the subject of observation.

To demonstrate a possible link between a teacher's expectations and the self-fulfilling prophecy, the following sequence of results must be established:

1   The teacher must make inaccurate judgments about the nominated pupils' achievement. For example, pupils nominated as low achievers must not score lower than the remaining target pupils in the bottom quartile of scores on the Richmond pre-test.

2 The nominated pupils must differ in the amount of progress they make over the year by comparison with the equivalent group of target pupils in a manner which is consistent with the self-fulfilling prophecy. In the previous example the nominated low achievers should make less progress than the equivalent group of target pupils.

3 Differences must be found in the interaction patterns between both nominated groups of pupils and their equivalent target pupils and between the nominated, high- and low-achieving pupils themselves. The nature and direction of such differences should correspond with the findings from previous studies and offer a reasonable explanation of how the self-fulfilling prophecy comes about.

Each of these matters will now be considered in turn.

PROACTIVE AND OVERREACTIVE TEACHERS

Table 8.1 provides a breakdown of the pre-test achievement levels for both the nominated and the remaining equivalent groups of pupils. The data were collected in ten classrooms within two schools. Five of the classes were made up entirely of nine-year-old pupils, four contained ten year olds and one class contained both age groups. For completeness, results for the target pupils from the middle quartiles, the average ones, are included on the bottom row of Table 8.1 by way of comparison. The ten classrooms provided ten boys and girls in the top and bottom groups respectively and twenty boys and girls in the average group, since selection of the pupils for observation involved deliberate matching of the sexes within each achievement level. In Table 8.1 the number of pupils nominated in each group is also broken down by sex. In the ORACLE sample, these ten classrooms would have contained twenty boy and twenty girl target pupils in the average group. It follows that six girls and five boys must have been nominated either as above or below average even though their pre-test scores put them in the middle quartiles of the achievement range within the class. In both cases there is a tendency to nominate more boys as high and low achievers, although none of the differences reached statistical significance.

Turning to the pre-test means derived from each pupil's combined score on all three Richmond Tests (reading, language skills and mathematics), the differences between the nominated and other pupils were relatively small and did not reach statistical significance. Nominated highs have almost the same pre-test mean as the remaining target pupils from the high-achievement quartile. Teachers, however, seemed to make more accurate nominations of slow-learning pupils from their classes. The nominated low group were on average two marks below the other targets in the bottom quartile who were unnamed by the teachers. These results were based on the average scores for the 110 pupils in the ten classrooms studied.

Table 8.1   *Breakdown of pre-test achievement level for 'nominated' and 'other' pupils*

Achievement level	Pre-test mean	Pre-test SD	No. of boys	No. of girls	Total sample
Nominated high	39.07	10.84	11	18	29
Other high	39.77	10.12	5	4	9
Nominated low	14.17	7.18	13	16	29
Other low	16.36	6.51	7	7	14
Remaining targets average	28.58	8.19	15	14	29

Labelling in itself need not be detrimental to a pupil's well-being. It is an essential first step in the diagnosis of pupils' difficulties. In studies of expectancy it seems important, therefore, to distinguish between teachers who can label accurately and those who cannot. For the low-achieving group in this study a teacher who made accurate judgments (a proactive teacher in Brophy and Good's terminology) would be one where the nominated lows had a lower pre-test mean than the remaining target pupils in the bottom quartile. In this case the teacher's nomination would be consistent with the information available about the pupil's performance. A teacher who made inaccurate judgments (an overreactive teacher) would be one where the nominated pupils of low achievement had a higher pre-test mean than the other pupils in the bottom quartile. In the high-achieving group the reverse would hold. Proactive teachers would nominate a group having a higher pre-test mean than the remaining pupils within the top quartile, whereas overreactive teachers would nominate a group of pupils as high achievers who enjoyed no overall superiority in terms of their pre-test scores. Of the ten teachers, five were proactive and five overreactive when nominating low-achieving pupils, while the corresponding figures for the high achievers were seven and three respectively. Only one teacher was overreactive in both his nominations, while no teacher was proactive in the selection of the two groups.

PUPIL PROGRESS AND THE SELF-FULFILLING PROPHECY

In Table 8.2 the performance of the different groups of pupils on the post-test is examined. The items used in the pre-test were again administered in the June of the year during which the observations were carried out. For each pupil a residual change score was calculated as described in 'Progress and Performance in the Primary Classroom' (pp. 58-60). This score is a measure of the extent to which a pupil performs better or worse on the post-test than would be predicted by his performance on the pre-test. Pupils with negative residual changes have done worse. In Table

8.2 the nominated high-achieving pupils are compared with the nominated low ones, using the remaining groups in the sample as a control. Scores on both the pre-test and post-test were available for only 95 of the 110 pupils. Nevertheless, in spite of the reduced size, the difference in the residual gains of the nominated low-achieving pupils differed significantly from that of

Table 8.2 *Residual change scores for nominated high and low achievers*

	Nomina-ted highs	Other highs	Control group	Other lows	Nomina-ted lows	Significance level and sample size
All teachers	+1.68		+1.68		−5.56	*
n	25		48		22	93
Proactive high	+3.41	+0.48	−1.46			NS
n	18	3	43			64
Overreactive	+1.95	+6.23	−2.64			NS
n	7	5	7			29
Proactive low			0.57	−0.05	−1.87	NS
n			37	7	11	55
Overreactive			+1.54	+4.86	−4.99	*
n			23	4	11	38

* Statistically significant at 5 per cent level: the control group consists of all pupils other than those in the two other groups being compared.

either the nominated highs or the control group of unnominated children at the 5 per cent significance level. On average, pupils who were nominated as poor achievers by their teachers performed nearly 6 marks below that which would be expected if they were judged solely on the results of their pre-tests. The progress of pupils in both the nominated high-achieving and the unnominated groups was the same, so that for this sample of pupils, at least, the teacher's nominations of bright pupils did not become a self-fulfilling prophecy. The results from Table 8.2 suggest that it is low achievers, in particular, who were at risk in the junior classrooms studied.

Further support for the view that it is below-average pupils who are more likely to be affected by the teacher's expectations comes from an examination of the residual change scores for proactive and overreactive teachers. This data is also included in Table 8.2. Although splitting the groups of pupils now means that the numbers involved in the comparisons are extremely small, the results for teachers who were overreactive when nominating low-achieving pupils still reached statistical significance at the 5 per cent level, whereas for the proactive teachers both the nominated and other low-achieving target pupils did less well than their scores on the pre-test predicted. The pupils nominated by

the overreactive teachers, however, made the least progress of
all while the group of target pupils who were not mentioned by
the teachers, although their pre-test scores were actually lower,
did much better than expected. The magnitude of their positive
gain was the same as the negative change recorded for the nominated group of low-achievers. This result provides a dramatic
illustration of the self-fulfilling prophecy. These overreactive
teachers were wrong in their judgment of these pupils' attainment
level at the start of the year, since the pre-test scores showed
that the nominated pupils outperformed the remaining targets in
the bottom quartile. Yet by the end of the school year the position
was reversed and nominated pupils had underachieved in comparison with the equivalent group of children.

The same effect was not found with pupils whose pre-test scores
were in the top quartile. None of the differences between children
taught by proactive and overreactive teachers was statistically
significant and the trend was in the opposite direction from that
predicted by Brophy and Good (1974). Here the nominated pupils
made less progress when taught by overreactive teachers.

It appears, therefore, that in junior school classrooms it is the
least able children who are most likely to be affected by a
teacher's incorrect judgments and the false expectations that are
formed as a result. In the previous section it was shown that
more teachers were overreactive when judging low-achieving
pupils than when nominating high achievers. When this fact is
coupled with the large difference in progress that was found between the nominated and their equivalent target pupils, particularly when they were taught by overreactive teachers, it would
seem that special attention should be paid to the observational
data obtained for these two groups.

TEACHER-PUPIL INTERACTIONS AND EXPECTANCY EFFECTS

The original observation schedules used in the ORACLE study
were not suitable for examining the effects of teacher expectations
since when recording feedback they did not code whether this
was in response to a correct or an incorrect answer to the
teacher's question. Accordingly a new observation schedule based
partly on the ORACLE categories and partly on those used by
Brophy and Good (1970) was developed. The categories are presented in Table 8.3. During the course of the lesson, whenever
an interaction involving either a target pupil or one of the nominated non-targets took place the appropriate person was identified in the audience category. The activity category was coded
according to the ORACLE classifications and the nature of the
utterance was then determined by the use of the next four categories, so that the observer decided whether the exchange was
about task work, task supervision, routine or distraction. The
next three categories assessed the tone of the utterance, which
was coded either as praise, criticism or a neutral statement.

Table 8.3   Delafield observation categories for coding 'dyadic' interactions between teachers and pupils

Categories	Comment
Audience	Identity of pupil (nominated high, low, etc.)
Initiator	Teacher or pupil initiates exchange
Activity	Curriculum area (coded as for Pupil Record)
Task work	Exchange is about set task
Task supervision	involves supervision of task, concerns
Routine	materials or results in a comment about
Distraction	a distraction or disruption
Praise	Tone of the exchange is positive (well done!)
Negative (criticism)	Negative (critical) or neutral
Neutral	
Response opportunities	
Correct	Coded only when the teacher asks
Incorrect	a question for which a target is
Part correct	expected to reply
Incomplete	
No response	
Feedback	
Praise	Coded when response opportunity
Criticism	categories have been used or when
Supplementary answer	an exchange is initiated by a pupil
Repeat question	and the teacher responds
Rephrase question	
Giving clue	
No feedback	
Neutral	

Table 8.4   Total amount of interaction (mean number of interactions per group)

	Mean	SD	n
Nominated high	22.17	13.94	29
Other high	20.44	6.77	9
Remaining average targets	19.96	13.68	29
Other low	20.50	12.82	14
Nominated low	18.24	11.34	29
Total sample	20.20	12.65	110

If the utterance was a question, then the nature of the pupil's response opportunity was recorded under the next five categories.

When a pupil made a response or initiated an exchange and the teacher in turn replied, this was coded under the eight feedback categories.

Table 8.4 shows the average number of interactions for each group. Although with such small sample sizes the results do not reach statistical significance, the trend was for high achievers to be involved in a greater number of interactions than average achievers, who in turn were involved in more exchanges than the low-achieving group. Nominated high achievers were involved in the greatest number of these contacts, while nominated low ones received the lowest.

Table 8.5 takes the analysis further by breaking down the total amount of interaction for each group into its constituent parts. Here, however, each category total is expressed as a percentage of the total number of interactions observed. From the previous discussion of the data in Table 8.2 it has been shown that the self-fulfilling prophecy operates only for the nominated low-achieving children. Differences in levels of interaction should therefore show the greatest disparity between low- rather than high-achieving groups. The data in Table 8.5 can be seen to offer some support for the suggestion that the original nominations of low-achieving pupils were related to the nature of the teachers' interactions with these children.

Looking at differences between groups, for example, nominated low-achieving pupils receive the greatest number of teacher initiated contacts while the other low-achieving target pupils receive the fewest. Presumably, since the order is then reversed for interactions about task work, this latter group of pupils must initiate more interactions about work than do the nominated-lows. As predicted from earlier studies, nominated low-achievers also have the highest number of disciplinary contacts while the nominated-highs have the fewest. Apart from these features no discernible trend emerges. It would seem that the nominated-lows receive more teacher attention than other groups, that the exchanges are more likely to concern disciplinary matters and that such pupils are less likely to initiate interactions. The pattern of results in the category of disciplinary interactions is in itself revealing. Whereas the nominated-lows have a higher percentage of this type of interaction than the other lows, the reverse is true of nominated-highs. This suggests that the teacher tends to nominate low-achieving children according to the frequency of disciplinary exchanges, whereas when asked to nominate high-achieving children she omits those who have caused a certain amount of trouble, nominating instead quiet, well-behaved pupils.

This suggestion receives some support when the data concerning praise and criticism are examined. In general the use of praise and criticism in these junior school classrooms appears to be less frequent than suggested by some of the early American studies involving the use of FIAC (Flanders 1960). The same appears to be true in comparison with American teachers in Brophy and Good's (1970) study, although the actual amounts of praise and criticism used are not easy to calculate from their tables of results. However, Brophy and Good suggest that a more useful index is the ratio between the proportion of criticism used and the combined proportions of praise and criticism. They noticed a tendency among teachers, who used criticism more often than their colleagues, to indulge in praise also to a greater extent. Although the variations are small in the data presented in Table 8.5, nevertheless there is a trend for those groups of pupils who receive more criticism also to receive more praise. For comparison with Brophy and Good's data, the ratio between criticism and the combined amounts of praise and criticism has also been included in the table. The range here is smaller than that found in the American study. Brophy and Good found that the high-achievers' ratio was 53 per cent compared to 85 per cent for the lows. In Table 8.5 the nominated-highs have a ratio of 58.7 per cent compared with that of 60.7 per cent for the nominated-lows. The nominated-lows have a higher ratio than the other low-achieving target pupils, and this is consistent with the idea that the pupils were nominated because they were more troublesome. The ratios for the high-achieving groups are the reverse to those predicted. The remaining high-achieving target pupils receive more disciplinary contacts than do the nominated ones, but their criticism ratio is the lowest of all the five groups in the table. Perhaps, because of their achievements, they are seen as 'high spirited' rather than as naughty.

The next section of Table 8.5 deals with the frequency of response opportunities. In Garner and Bing's (1973) study it was found that the average number of such opportunities came to 13.9 per cent of the total number of interactions. The figure of 15.4 per cent in Table 8.5 is quite comparable with this earlier finding. Examining the different categories of response opportunities, however, there are few consistent trends that explain the workings of the expectancy effects. For a start the nominated low-achieving pupils received a higher proportion of response opportunities than did the other low-achieving targets. They too made more correct responses, although they also tended to offer incomplete or partially correct answers more often or made no response. There were no similar patterns with the nominated-high pupils. Although, overall, they had the highest percentage of response opportunities they got fewer correct answers than the remaining high-achieving targets and were more likely to make no response. Among low-achieving children it may be that the nominated pupils were more likely to proffer an answer to a question, either because the teacher picked on them as a device to keep them involved, or because they themselves were in search of attention. Although nominated low achievers managed to answer a number of these questions correctly they were also prone to make incorrect answers too. The two nominated groups also had the highest proportions of no responses.

Budd-Rowe argues that what teachers do when children make no response is a key factor in translating teachers' expectations into

Table 8.5 Percentage use of the interaction categories (as a proportion of the total interaction) for nominated and other pupils

Variable	High achievers		Average achievers	Low achievers		All pupils
	Nominated (n =29)	Others (n = 9)	(n = 29)	Others (n = 14)	Nominated (n = 29)	(n = 110)
1 Source of interaction						
Teacher initiated	52.7	51.8	50.2	42.9	54.2	51.1
Pupil initiated	47.3	48.2	49.8	57.1	45.8	48.9
2 Activity categories						
Task	69.0	71.4	67.4	67.4	62.1	66.7
Task supervision	1.3	0.0	1.8	0.6	1.5	1.6
Routine	22.1	16.2	20.0	21.5	23.1	21.0
Disciplinary	7.3	12.4	10.6	10.5	13.3	10.6
Other	0.3	0.0	0.2	0.0	0.0	0.1
Total	100.0	100.0	100.0	100.0	100.0	100.0
3 Tone of teacher utterance						
Praise	4.5	3.6	3.3	5.2	4.2	4.1
Criticism	6.4	4.4	4.6	6.8	6.5	5.9
$\frac{\text{Criticism}}{\text{(Praise + criticism)}}$	58.7	55.0	58.2	56.7	60.7	59.0
4 Types of response opportunities						
Correct	11.7	13.2	8.2	4.7	8.3	9.1
Incorrect	1.7	1.4	1.9	2.0	4.5	2.6
Part correct	2.8	1.2	3.4	2.0	1.4	2.4
Incomplete	0.1	0.4	0.4	0.2	0.3	0.3
No response	1.2	0.4	1.1	0.2	1.2	1.0
Total % of response opportunities	17.5	16.6	15.0	9.1	15.7	15.4
5 Types of feedback						
Praise	2.6	5.0	1.5	1.6	2.0	2.2
Criticism	0.6	1.0	1.0	0.8	1.3	0.9
Supplementary answer	0.7	0.0	0.2	1.1	1.4	0.7
Repeat question	0.2	0.4	0.4	0.3	1.3	0.6
Re-phrased	1.0	0.4	1.5	0.3	0.4	0.9
Giving clue	1.1	1.4	2.6	0.7	1.6	1.6
No feedback	1.8	0.0	0.5	0.1	0.5	0.7
Neutral	9.2	8.3	7.0	4.3	7.8	7.6
Total % of feedback	17.2	16.5	14.7	9.2	16.3	15.2
% of feedback following response opportunity	82.2	77.8	71.3	78.5	65.5	74.1

self-fulfilling prophecy. In her study, when low achievers failed
to answer the question, the teacher tended to assume that they
did not know the answer and passed on to another child, while
in a similar situation involving a high-achiever the teacher tended
to assume the pupil was thinking out a solution and left him to do
this.

Some evidence in support of this can also be found in section
five of Table 8.5, which relates to teacher feedback following
either teacher questions or pupil-initiated exchanges. It has already been shown that the nominated low-achieving pupils had
nearly twice as many response opportunities as other low achieving target pupils. In Table 8.5, the ratio for the percentage of
response opportunities between these two groups came to 1.7
(15.7 per cent for nominated low achievers against 9.1 per cent
for the other low-achieving targets). Almost the same ratio was
obtained for the percentage of teacher feedback received by these
two groups (16.3 per cent against 9.0 per cent).

Nominated low achievers were, therefore, given more response
opportunities and received more feedback than other low-achieving
targets, a finding which appears contrary to Budd-Rowe's experience. However, when the percentage of feedback following on
immediately from a response opportunity is tabulated in the final
row of Table 8.5, an altogether different situation is revealed.
Now the nominated low-achieving pupils have the lowest number
of such exchanges, while the remaining low-achieving targets
have the second highest amount overall. As in Budd-Rowe's study,
when these nominated low achievers make a response they are less
likely to receive a follow-up comment from the teacher.

A similar if less dramatic result is obtained from the data for
the high-achieving pupils. Although both the nominated-highs and
the other high-achieving target pupils have approximately the
same percentage of feedback, the nominated pupils are more likely
to receive this feedback immediately following a response opportunity. The evidence presented here strongly supports Budd-
Rowe's view that the manner in which teachers converse with
their pupils is largely dependent upon their initial concept of the
child's ability.

THE OPERATION OF THE EXPECTANCY EFFECT

Although the conclusions to be derived from the data in Table
8.5 must of necessity be tentative - given that with the small
numbers of pupils involved none of the F ratios for the categories
reach statistical significance - it is possible to suggest a mechanism by which the self-fulfilling prophecy begins to operate.
Initially teachers make judgments about the 'ability' of pupils with
similar attainment levels largely on the basis of their behaviour in
class. In 'Inside the Primary Classroom' it was shown that for more
than 70 per cent of the time when a teacher is interacting, she is
dealing with individual pupils. For this system of individualization

to work efficiently in classes of an average size of thirty, it is necessary for an air of activity to prevail and for pupils to get on with their work when the teacher is engaged elsewhere. It has been shown that this is what typically happens in the modern primary classroom, but there will be some pupils who cause a certain amount of disruption. If these pupils are thought of as 'slow' learners, they are likely to be singled out as being less able than others who may perform no differently at their tasks. Conversely, if such pupils come from among the more successful pupils in the class, they are likely to be recognized as 'less able' than those who continue to work conscientiously when left to themselves.

Once these expectancies have been established, their effect is communicated to the pupil largely through the medium of teacher questions, and the resulting feedback following the pupil's reply. Even though the nominated low-achieving pupils gave a higher proportion of correct answers, they received less immediate feedback, whereas nominated high-achieving pupils were likely to receive a comment in response to an answer on four occasions out of every five. The data on the types of feedback seem to support Budd-Rowe's conclusion since the nominated high-achievers were more likely to have questions re-phrased by the teacher, whereas the nominated lows were more likely to have it repeated or be given a clue and to receive less praise and more criticism for their answer, a finding echoed in Brophy and Good's (1970) study.

This differential treatment in turn causes nominated low-achieving pupils to respond in one of two ways each of which is calculated to reinforce the teacher's initial assumptions about their 'ability'. First, a pupil might attempt to initiate more exchanges requiring feedback from the teacher. Such a strategy would explain why such pupils obtain almost twice as much feedback as other low-achieving targets while at the same time receiving less of this feedback immediately following a response opportunity. If these initiations are trivial or repetitive, then they are likely to receive a neutral or critical comment from the teacher, whereas timely initiation by a 'bright' pupil is likely to receive praise.

The second strategy open to nominated low-achieving pupils is to force a teacher to give them more attention, as instanced by the higher levels of teacher-initiated interactions which such pupils received in this study compared with the other low-achieving target pupils. These interactions will tend to be either disciplinary, following disruptive behaviour which could be interpreted as a cry for attention, or involve routine matters where the pupil asks where to find this item of equipment or what work to do next. Such exchanges will tend once again to reinforce the teacher's feeling that the child has difficulty in planning and managing the work, thus lending further support to the view that he is amongst the less effective members of the class.

This explanation is wholly consistent with other findings in the ORACLE series. In 'Progress and Performance in the Primary

Classroom' it was demonstrated that poorly motivated pupils were particularly at risk in classrooms favouring individualization of the learning process. Teachers who belonged to these styles (individual monitors, rotating and habitual changers) were among the most unsuccessful in terms of their pupils' progress. Seven out of the ten teachers whose behaviour has been described here came from these styles and if the proposed mechanism through which the self-fulfilling prophecy operates is indeed valid, then it is easy to see how the differential treatment which pupils receive at the hands of such teachers could lower their levels of application. If this were to happen it would be but a short step to a falling-off in their performance.

9 SOCIAL CLASS, PUPIL ACHIEVEMENT AND CLASSROOM INTERACTION

Paul Croll

One of the most important areas of educational research over the previous thirty years, in particular of research based in the sociology of education, has been the investigation of the achievement of pupils from different social backgrounds. Such investigations have almost invariably found that pupils from working-class backgrounds (that is, in general, pupils whose fathers were in manual occupations) achieved less well at school and in intelligence tests than pupils from middle-class backgrounds. Within these very broad categories of social class it was also usually found that pupils whose fathers were in unskilled manual occupations performed less well than those whose fathers were in skilled manual work, and pupils from families in clerical or other lower middle-class occupations less well than those from professional and managerial backgrounds.

The most dramatic consequence of these differences was the relative performance of children from different backgrounds in the 11-plus examination which selected children for different types of secondary education. Children from working-class families scored, on average, less well on the IQ tests on which selection was largely based. But, in addition to this disadvantage, working-class children secured fewer grammar school places than selection simply on their IQ scores would have implied. This double disadvantage in selection at 11-plus has been most recently documented in one of the reports of the Oxford Social Mobility Project. This large-scale study of a cohort of men born between 1913 and 1952 shows the powerful effects of social class on selection for different types of secondary schooling and how this operates, in part, through differences in IQ test scores, but also independently of such differences. The authors of this report write:

> Making the contentious assumption that measured intelligence indicates meritocracy and is an attribute of individuals independent of their class origins, it still turns out that meritocracy has been modified by class bias throughout the expansion of secondary-school opportunity (Halsey, Heath and Ridge 1980, p. 71).

This disadvantage for working-class pupils is maintained for all the age cohorts in the sample, and the youngest men in the study, who were selected for secondary education in the early 1960s, experienced approximately the same class bias as the older men.

The Oxford study is a recent documentation of relative class chances in education as part of a much more general study of social mobility. The class differences which emerged were well

known in the 1950s and were described in articles such as these by
Floud and Halsey (1957) and Halsey and Gardner (1953). These
findings also informed criticisms of the related practices of intelligence testing and selection for secondary education, partly on
the grounds that such tests 'are bound sharply to discriminate
against the working class' (Simon 1953, p. 81).

Another influential study of primary education, Douglas's
'The Home and the School' (1964) describes similar differences
between children from different backgrounds and also finds that
children from middle-class homes make more progress in the primary school than pupils from working-class homes:

> By the time he is eleven the clever manual working-class child
> has fallen behind the middle-class child of similar ability at
> eight years and equally the backward manual working-class
> child shows less improvement between eight and eleven years
> than the backward middle-class child (Douglas 1964, pp. 46-7).

These results were found both for scores on intelligence tests
and on tests of achievement. Like the Oxford study, Douglas
also found that the better scores on achievement tests of the
middle-class children and their better performance at 11-plus
selection were not explained by their better IQ test scores
(Douglas 1964, p. 48).

This discrepancy between IQ scores and school achievement is
important because it means that whatever views are taken on
what is measured by intelligence tests, there are still aspects of
working-class underachievement which need to be explained.
Extreme proponents of IQ tests have claimed that they measure
innate intelligence in a way that is fair to all children taking the
test, while critics have pointed to the circularity of the relationship between IQ tests and the notion of intelligence and have
claimed that such tests are inherently biased against working-class
children (e.g. Simon 1953). However, the discrepancy between
IQ test scores and achievement tests means that, even if IQ
results are taken at their face value, they cannot wholly account
for working-class underachievement. If the claim that such tests
measure innate ability is rejected, then the poorer performance
of working-class pupils becomes another aspect of working-class
underachievement at school.

Explanations for this underachievement have conventionally
been sought in terms of the contribution which the pupil's home
circumstances make to his capacity to take advantage of schooling
or as it is sometimes put, to his 'educability'. The most obvious
influences of home background are the material disadvantages
associated with poverty. Poor levels of health and nutrition, and
overcrowded or otherwise unsatisfactory homes effectively exclude
a number of children from educational success (Donnison 1972).
However, the lower average performance of children from working-
class families cannot be entirely accounted for in this fashion.
Pupils from families in skilled working-class occupations still
achieve less well than those from middle-class homes.

A number of authors have suggested that attitudinal factors as well as, or sometimes rather than, material circumstances adversely affect the performance of working-class pupils. Douglas, discussing the superior achievement of middle-class pupils writes:

> The reason for these differences may lie in the personal qualities of the pupils (their industry and behaviour in class) or in the attitudes of their parents, who may give them much or little encouragement in their work (1964, p. 48).

This emphasis on parental attitudes also emerges strongly in the influential report of the Plowden Committee, 'Children and their Primary Schools'. The research undertaken for the Committee compared the influence upon educational performance of parental attitudes (including the age parents wanted their children to leave school, the extent to which they visited the school, the extent of the help they gave their children with school work and the number of books in the home), home circumstances (including occupation, income, size of family and physical amenities in the home) and school factors (including size of class and experience of staff). From this analysis it emerged that parental attitudes were the most important of the three factors (Plowden, Chapter 3).

However, parental attitudes are closely linked with the material circumstances of the home, and it seems likely that measures such as the age at which it is intended that children should leave school and the numbers of books in the home do not adequately indicate parental attitude independently of the material circumstances of the home. The Plowden Report does also recognize the importance of material deprivation and suggests that special school provision may be necessary to overcome it.

Another explanation for the difference in school performance of middle-class and working-class children is found in the socio-linguistic work of Bernstein (1974). He argues that the linguistic patterns of working-class children (or perhaps of some working-class children) provides a crucial handicap to success at school. In particular he argues that there are 'entirely different modes of speech found within the middle class and the lower working class' (1974, p. 61). These are the famous elaborated and restricted codes. The first, the code of the middle class and of the school, is formal, explicit and logical. The second, the restricted code of lower working-class speech, is personalized and stereotyped and less able to convey logical arguments and complex messages.

All the above explanations for class differences in school achievement concentrate on characteristics of the pupils (favourable material circumstances, parental help and encouragement, appropriate linguistic skills) which enable them to take more or less advantage of schooling. There are, though, quite different explanations which focus not on differences in what children from different backgrounds 'bring with them to school', but on differences in what schools offer to pupils from different social backgrounds. Such explanations reject the question, 'What is it about

working-class children which makes them fail?' and ask instead,
'What is it about schools which leads to working-class children
doing badly?'

One approach to this question consists of examining the levels
of resources devoted to the education of different social groups.
To some extent this approach was contained in the Plowden Report
where it was recognized that deprived neighbourhoods often had
deprived schools. This led to the recommendation that such neighbourhoods should become Educational Priority Areas and should
receive additional resources (Plowden, Chapter 5). However, the
association between deprived neighbourhoods and deprived
schools, and the implication that this led to poor educational performance, were based on the impressions of the Committee rather
than on research, and elsewhere in the Report parental attitudes
are held to be more important for achievement than either material circumstances or school conditions (Plowden, pp. 34-6).

A more systematic attempt to relate resource provision to educational performance has considered the relationship between
social class, resource provision and school attainment by compar-
ing local education authorities in terms of these variables. This
analysis takes the local authority, rather than the individual
pupil, as the unit of analysis and relates the social class composition of the authority to average educational outcomes and the
educational policy and levels of resources and provision within
the LEA. On this basis it is claimed that much of the association
between social class and educational attainment can be accounted
for by superior levels of provision in more middle-class authorities (Byrne and Williamson 1972; Byrne, Williamson and Fletcher
1973). These studies have been heavily criticized on methodological grounds (Pyle 1975a; 1975b), but quite apart from inade-
quacies of the analysis, even on their own terms such studies can
offer only a very partial account of the relationship between social
class and achievement. This is because a comparison of the
average achievement and average social class composition of local
authority areas takes no account of variations in social class and
in achievement within these areas. In so far as LEAs are heterogeneous with regard to achievement and social class, and in so
far as these variables are related within particular local authorities, both of which are clearly the case, then the model of local
authority resource provision cannot account for the relationship.

An analysis of the relationship between resources, social class
and attainment within a local authority area has been conducted
by King (1974). In this analysis, individual schools were used as
the unit of analysis and were compared in terms of their social
class composition, average levels of attainment and levels of resources - measured by variables such as teacher-pupil ratio,
stability of staff and the number of subjects offered. This study
resulted in opposite conclusions to the analyses of local authorities.
The schools with a higher proportion of working-class pupils had
higher levels of provision but still produced lower levels of attainment.

It is probably fair to say that the relationship between school provision, social class and attainment is particularly susceptible to local circumstances and to historical factors, and that a study carried out in a single local authority in one particular year cannot be regarded as conclusive. However, the same general point applies to the study of schools as applies to the study of local authorities; any explanations of the relationship between class and achievement which arise from such studies refer only to the level of analysis at which the research is conducted. It may be possible to account for differences between local authorities or between schools in terms of relative levels of provision (although the analysis of local authorities by Byrne et al. is unsatisfactory and that of schools by King actually failed to support such an explanation) but this does not account for differences between individuals. To the extent that LEAs and schools are heterogeneous with regard to their class composition and their levels of attainment, it is still possible for class and attainment to be associated within them in a way that cannot be accounted for by differing levels of school or LEA provision. Many studies of individual schools have shown that this association does indeed hold within as well as between schools. The present study confirms these results, as reported below.

The possibility of investigating these processes at the level of individual children has, however, come about as a result of the relatively recent emergence of a style of educational research which concentrates on processes within the classroom. This type of research involves observation of pupils and teachers, looking at patterns of behaviour and interactions in considerable detail (see, for example, Chanan and Delamont 1975). Such an analysis of classroom behaviour and interactions, whether by rigorous, systematic and quantifiable methods, as in the ORACLE study, or by more impressionistic, ethnographic techniques, makes it possible to look for differences in the ways in which pupils behave and are treated by the teacher and other pupils which might be related to their levels of attainment. In principle, this makes it possible to account for the performance of children from different social backgrounds by reference to the different treatments such children receive in class. This view has been proposed by Nash (1973, p. 88):

It is no use saying that children from low social class backgrounds do poorly at school because they are from poor backgrounds until it is known that teachers behave to them in the same way that they behave to children from higher social class backgrounds. This is an assumption that is always made and never tested. It is an assumption that there is less and less reason to accept.

Possible support for such an argument comes from a variety of sources; from results which show that teacher expectancies of how pupils will perform are strongly related to actual performance (e.g. Nash 1973, 1976; US Office of Education 1970); from results which show that teachers expect the social backgrounds of their pupils to affect their school performance (e.g. Keddie 1971; Sharp and Green 1975; Goodacre 1968); from studies which show that the amount of teacher attention different pupils receive in the same class can differ dramatically (Sharp and Green 1975; Garner and Bing 1973; Good 1970); and from studies which claim that teacher expectations, induced experimentally, affect the progress made by pupils (Rosenthal and Jacobson 1968).

These results are of varying relevance to the question of the relationship between social class and achievement. To show that teachers' expectations of how pupils will progress in school are closely related to actual progress does not mean that these expectations cause the progress. Such a result is quite compatible with teachers making accurate assessments of their pupils and does not mean that they have made their own predictions come true. Similarly, if teachers have different expectations of pupils from different backgrounds, these could also be realistic expectations and need not mean that pupils from differing backgrounds are treated differently. Claims that pupils from different social backgrounds do indeed receive different treatments provide rather stronger evidence for the school or the teacher creating social class effects on achievement, but even here the implications of such findings must be treated with caution. To say that different pupils receive different treatment and progress at different rates leaves open the question of whether the treatment causes the progress or whether it has been accurately matched to levels of attainment. This is particularly so of studies which compare classes of children, for example, top and bottom streams in a school, rather than children within the same class. Finally, studies which experimentally induce teacher-expectancy effects have not dealt explicitly with social class. Even if such effects are real, their implications for social class differences can only be inferred and are not directly demonstrated.

Before considering the studies in this area three further points should be noted. First, much of the relevant research has been conducted in America and does not necessarily apply to British schools and classrooms. Second, a number of the relevant studies which give data on the behaviours and interactions of teachers and pupils in classrooms have not used systematic observation methods which can provide exact measures of these variables but have relied on unstructured - sometimes called ethnographic or anthropological - observation methods which result in accounts based on personal impressions and anecdotes. It seems ironic that studies concerned with the effects of expectancy and of unconscious bias on the part of teachers should use research methods which are themselves so vulnerable to just these processes on the part of researchers. Third, most research on classrooms has involved observation of a very small number of classes. Some of the best-known and most widely quoted of such studies have involved research on only one class or in only one school. For example, Rist (1970) observed one class over two years; Keddie (1971) an 'A' stream class and a 'C' stream class in one school; Sharp and

Green (1975) three classes in one school. Such studies may show
that the processes they describe can happen, but they cannot be
used as the basis of generalizations to other schools and classes.
Not surprisingly the less contentious of the arguments discussed
above are the best-established. Teachers' assessments of their
pupils' ability and predictions as to how they will perform are
quite well related to ability and performance as measured in tests.
An American study reported 'an extraordinarily consistent relationship between teacher expectations and the reading achievement
gains of pupils' (US Office of Education 1970). In a British school,
Nash found that teachers' estimations of ability correlated with
test results (1973, p. 31) and Barker Lunn in a large survey of
primary schools obtained similar results (1970, p. 69). In Chapter
11 of this volume Anne Jasman shows how teachers' assessments
of pupils on a variety of skills are related to performance in
achievement tests. Although there is room for debate about the
magnitude of these correlations and the sources of discrepancies
in assessment, the basic association is well established and it
would be very surprising if this were otherwise.
    Also relatively well established is the conclusion that teachers
expect that, on average, children from middle-class homes will
have superior attainment to children from working-class homes
and that, in general, pupils' home background (including their
parents' occupations) will influence their achievement. This has
been characterized as a 'social pathology' model in which teachers
explain pupils' failure in terms of factors such as home background
which are outside the school's control. Nash found that teachers'
assessments of pupils' abilities and their ratings of home background were correlated (1973). Keddie (1971) and Sharp and
Green (1975) present a good deal of qualitative data which suggest that social class is expected to be related to achievement.
These are small-scale studies in single schools, but Douglas reports similar findings in the large-scale survey on which 'The
Home and the School' is based (1964, Chapter 5). Again these
results are not surprising. The association of social background
with school success and in particular the relatively poor performance of working-class children has been a major theme of research
on education since the 1940s.
    A less clear cut argument relates to the claims that middle-class
pupils are rated more highly in assessments of ability by teachers
than their scores on tests of IQ and of achievement justify. This
was suggested in connection with the 11-plus examination by Floud
and Halsey. They found that when pupils were allocated to secondary education on the basis of their schools' assessments, working-
class pupils achieved fewer grammar school places than when they
were allocated in accordance with test results (Floud and Halsey
1957). Another study found that teacher assessments of reading
ability resulted in greater social class differences than did standardized tests of reading (Goodacre 1968). These results lend support to Keddie's assertion that teachers' 'categorizations on the
grounds of ability derive largely from social class judgments of

pupils' social, moral and intellectual behaviour' (Keddie 1971, p. 155). However, this is made more complicated by Nash's findings, which suggest that teachers are not very accurate in their perceptions of their pupils' home backgrounds. Nash found that there was no correlation between the teachers' assessment of the home background of their pupils and their actual home background. In this study actual social class did not correlate with achievement but the teacher's perceptions of a pupil's background did (Nash 1973). It is possible for teachers to believe in the effects of social class but be mistaken in their judgments of pupils' backgrounds, but if they are to mistake middle-class attributes for ability, to the systematic detriment of working-class children, it is necessary that their social class judgments of their pupils be accurate. However, this result is based on four teachers assessing a total of 117 children and clearly must be treated with caution.

One of the key issues in the question of whether schools and teachers help create social class differences in educational achievement is whether pupils from different backgrounds receive different kinds of treatment from teachers in a way that discriminates against working-class pupils. Some researchers have claimed that children from different backgrounds are treated differently and that it is through this process that social class differences in society are reproduced in the classroom. Two relevant American studies are those of Good (1970) and Rist (1970). Good was not concerned directly with social class but with the different treatments accorded to pupils of different levels of achievement. In the classrooms he studied he found that high-achieving children are given far more opportunities to contribute in class than low achievers. Good argues that this separates low achievers from other children and 'militates against their educational progress'. This last point, however, is an inference from the interaction patterns and is not itself a research finding. Rist's study found a direct relationship between social class and the treatment children received in class. A new kindergarten class of black pupils was almost immediately divided into groups on the basis of assumed ability. This assumption was strongly related to the social backgrounds of the children. From then on the groups characterized as of low ability received very much less attention from the teacher and much less help and support than did the supposed high-ability pupils.

These two studies present a clear picture of low-achieving pupils being effectively discriminated against in class. In Rist's research the initial categorization of pupils into high and low ability seems to have been made, at least in part, on social class grounds. However, these are both relatively small-scale studies, Rist's being of only one school class. Also, the evidence which is presented about this class is mainly qualitative and not based on systematic observation. The small amount of data in this study which is based on systematic methods gives a very much less clear cut picture of the differences between the treatment given to the different achievement groups than do the anecdotes and quotations (Rist 1970, p. 439).

Some English studies have also claimed that pupils of different social backgrounds and at different levels of achievement receive more or less favourable treatment, although, unfortunately, these are also based on ethnographic or 'participant observation' methods. A study of five primary classrooms which did use systematic observation found differences in the amount of teacher-interaction received by different pupils, but could not convincingly relate this to other characteristics of the pupils (Garner and Bing 1973). Keddie (1971) in the study of two-streamed secondary-school classes mentioned above claims that teachers had very different expectations of the 'A' and 'C' streams, in which notions of ability and of social class were confused. The different treatments of the two classes effectively prevented the 'C' stream pupils from challenging the teachers' characterization of them as being of low ability, while tending to confirm the favourable view of the 'A' stream. Unfortunately, Keddie does not have information about the social class composition of the two streams or about the process by which pupils were allocated to them.

Finally a well-known study of three English primary classrooms also claims that teachers do not distribute their time and other resources equally between children. Sharp and Green (1975, p. 115), claim that

there was a marked degree of differentiation between the pupils in terms of the amounts and kinds of interaction they had with their teachers . . . those pupils whom their teachers regarded as more successful tended to be given far greater attention than the others. The teachers interacted with them more frequently, paid closer attention to their activities, subtly structuring and directing their efforts in ways that were noticeably different from the relationship with other pupils less favourably categorized.

The favourably categorized pupils were those who fit 'the teacher's ideal for children "from a good area" or a "middle class district"' (p. 123).

None of these studies provides direct evidence of the effects of different teacher expectations or treatments on pupils' achievement. The classic attempt to show such effects is Rosenthal and Jacobson's (1968) 'Pygmalion in the Classroom' study. Here, teacher expectations of pupils were manipulated by means of faked test results supposedly predicting the progress pupils would make. In fact the predictions were allocated at random. These investigators found that the random predictions actually came true, strongly suggesting an expectancy effect. However, the study has been criticized on methodological grounds, and attempts to replicate the results have generally failed (see Boydell 1978 for a review of this study and its replications).

THE RELEVANCE OF THE 'ORACLE' RESEARCH

The studies reviewed above have suggested that the superior school attainment of middle-class children can, at least in part, be explained by the fact that teachers expect these children to have higher levels of performance, confuse middle-class attributes with ability and give preferential treatment (with regard to the amount and type of teacher interaction) to higher achieving and middle-class pupils. However, the evidence for these claims is not particularly strong. The relevant studies have been conducted on a very small number of classrooms and have relied on impressionistic and anecdotal accounts rather than on precise measurements of the amounts and types of interactions received by different children. The studies of Sharp and Green (1975) and Keddie (1971), which are most relevant to English schools, do not have measures of social class which are independent of the teachers' perceptions. Thus, these authors are themselves caught in the confusion between class and ability which they claim to be characteristic of the teachers.

The ORACLE research has a number of sources of data which are relevant to this issue. Detailed information is available on 489 pupils in fifty-eight primary and primary/middle school classrooms. This includes test data from the beginning and end of the school year; measures of attitude towards school; systematic observational data on the classroom activities and teacher-pupil and pupil-pupil interactions of these pupils; and teacher assessments of their abilities in a number of areas. The research design and details of data collection procedures have been presented in detail in 'Inside the Primary Classroom' and in 'Progress and Performance in the Primary Classroom'.

In addition to the observational data, attitude data and test and assessment data, a limited amount of data on the social backgrounds of pupils was also collected. This data is from only one of the local authority areas in the study but this was the authority in which the largest numbers of classrooms and pupils were observed. In this area details of father's or guardian's occupation were obtained for each of the eight target pupils in the twenty-nine classrooms in the study. For 188 of these 240 pupils this information could be used to place the pupils in one of four social class groupings. The four occupational groupings were: (i) professional and managerial (11.2 per cent of pupils), (ii) other non-manual (24.5 per cent of pupils), (iii) skilled manual (35.6 per cent of pupils) and (iv) other manual (28.7 per cent of pupils). The analysis which follows compares pupils in these four groups and also compares all pupils from the two non-manual groups with all pupils from the two manual groups.

With two exceptions the analysis will use data obtained during the first year of the study, as it is from this first year that the widest range of material is available. The variables which will be used are:
    (a) Observational variables (time on task, pupil-teacher inter-

action etc.) derived from one year of observation with the
Pupil Record.

(b)   The results of tests of achievement in the basic skills (the
abbreviated Richmond Tests) administered at the beginning
and end of the school year.

(c)   Measures of motivation, anxiety and adjustment to school
taken from a questionnaire administered at the beginning
of the school year.

(d)   Teacher assessments of pupils' abilities in a variety of
cognitive areas other than those included in the tests of
basic skills.

(e)   Exercises designed to monitor these cognitive areas.

(f)   Teacher assessments of mathematical abilities.

(g)   Exercises designed to measure these mathematical abilities.

(h)   Information from school records on the occupation of a
pupil's father or guardian.

Information about variables (f) and (g) were obtained during
the second year of the study. All other data was collected during
the first year.

Before proceeding to the analysis, there is one further point
to consider. The possibility that teacher time and attention is un-
equally distributed between pupils from different backgrounds
depends in part on the social composition of school classes. If,
because of the social location of school catchment areas or other
factors, school classes are homogeneous with regard to the social
background of their pupils, then there is no way that the teacher's
time can be distributed unevenly between pupils from different
backgrounds. Such an argument requires that classes be relatively
heterogeneous. In contrast, arguments about the effects of different levels of resources and provision on the school attainment of
pupils from different backgrounds depend on schools and classes
being relatively homogeneous with regard to social background.

In order to examine the degree of social homogeneity or hetero-
geneity in the school classrooms in the present study, each of
the twenty-nine classrooms was classified according to the proportion of pupils coming from homes in which the father was in a
manual occupation. For the sample as a whole the figure was 64.3
per cent and this was used as an average against which to compare the classrooms. Of the twenty-nine classes, fifteen (51.7
per cent) were fairly close to this average, having between 50
and 80 per cent of pupils from manual occupational backgrounds.
Of these fifteen, seven (24.1 per cent of the total) were very
close to the average, having between 60 and 70 per cent of
working-class pupils. The remaining fourteen classrooms were
evenly divided between those which were mainly working-class,
having 80 per cent or more of pupils from manual backgrounds,
and those in which the working class were under-represented,
having fewer than 50 per cent of pupils from such backgrounds.
However, in only three of the classrooms were there fewer than
30 per cent of working-class pupils and no classroom was entirely
homogeneous with regard to social composition.[1]

SOCIAL CLASS AND ACHIEVEMENT

Table 9.1 presents the scores on the tests of basic skills for the
158 children who took these tests both at the beginning and end
of the year, and for whom there is social class data. The results
are presented for the four occupational groupings and then for
the two non-manual groups combined, and similarly the two manual
groups. The table shows that the differences in achievement between pupils from different backgrounds noted in virtually all
previous studies in this area are repeated in the ORACLE study.
Pupils from non-manual occupational backgrounds do considerably
better in the tests than pupils from manual backgrounds, both at
the beginning and end of the school year. Pupils from professional
and managerial backgrounds score higher than pupils from other
non-manual backgrounds, who, in turn, score higher than pupils
from manual backgrounds. However, pupils from skilled manual
backgrounds do not have better scores than those from families
in other manual occupations.

Table 9.1   Social class and achievement on basic skills

	Profes-sional and managerial (n = 17)	Other non-manual (n = 39)	Skilled manual (n = 55)	Other manual (n = 47)		All non-manual (n = 56)	All manual (n = 102)	
Pre-test score	37.6	33.9	27.4	28.0	*	35.1	27.7	*
Post-test score	54.6	50.4	42.4	45.7	*	51.7	43.9	*
Residual change score	2.56	−0.14	−1.19	0.57	NS	0.64	−0.35	NS

Scores on abbreviated Richmond Tests; possible maximum 90.
* Statistically significant at or beyond 1 per cent level.

The amount of progress which pupils from different groups
have made over the year can be measured by taking the difference between their pre-test and post-test scores. However, this
procedure has a number of weaknesses and a better measure of
progress is given by an analysis of co-variance.[2] This analysis
compares the groups not in terms of their raw score gains over
the year but in terms of how their post-test scores differ from
what would have been expected on the basis of their pre-test.
These residual change scores are also presented in Table 9.1.
This shows that there is only a small difference between the manual and non-manual groups in terms of the progress they have
made over the year. A comparison of all four groups shows that
this difference comes about because the pupils from professional
and managerial backgrounds have made rather more progress than
would have been expected on the basis of their pre-tests. However,

pupils from other manual backgrounds have also made slightly better than expected progress. Unlike the results for the pre- and post-tests none of the differences in residual gains are statistically significant.

Another measure of differences in attainment between the different occupational groups is given by the achievement quartiles into which they fall in the ORACLE sampling scheme. The ORACLE research design involved selecting eight pupils for observation in each classroom to be studied. These pupils were selected by dividing the class into three groups on the basis of their scores on the pre-test, those in the top quarter, those in the bottom quarter and those in the middle half. One boy and one girl were then selected at random from each of the top and bottom quarters, and two boys and two girls selected from the middle group. The relationship between social class and achievement can therefore be seen as it operates within school classes. This is related to the question of the homogeneity or otherwise of school classes with relation to social class. In so far as school classes are homogeneous, then an overall relationship between social class and achievement as shown in Table 9.1 will not be apparent in individual classrooms. However, as Table 9.2 shows, there is a clear relationship between achievement quartile and social class within the classrooms studied. Pupils from non-manual backgrounds are heavily over-represented in the top quarter of the classes and heavily under-represented in the bottom quarter. The representation of pupils from manual backgrounds is, correspondingly, in the opposite direction. This contrasts with Nash's assertion that while large samples may show a correlation between social class and achievement, such a relationship is not apparent in actual classrooms (Nash 1973, p. 31). The ORACLE study shows that there are noticeable within classroom differences; children from non-manual occupational backgrounds are more than two and a half times as likely to be in the top quarter of the class than are pupils from manual backgrounds.

Table 9.2 *Percentages of pupils from each social class in each achievement quartile*

	Professional and managerial (n = 21)	Other non-manual (n = 46)	Skilled manual (n = 67)	Other manual (n = 54)	All non-manual (n = 67)	All manual (n = 121)
Top quartile	38.1	43.5	17.9	13.0	41.8	15.7
Middle two quartiles	57.1	45.7	53.7	51.9	49.3	52.9
Bottom quartile	4.8	10 9	28.4	35.2	8.9	31.4
	100.0	100.0	100.0	100.0	100.0	100.0

chi^2 = 22.81; P < 0.01   chi^2 = 21.14; P < 0.01

SOCIAL CLASS AND PUPIL ATTITUDES

Pupil attitudes were measured by means of a short questionnaire designed to gauge levels of anxiety, motivation and adjustment to school. Average levels of these variables, expressed as percentages of the maximum possible level for each, are presented in Table 9.3. The different groups vary little in terms of their measures of attitude towards school. There is a slight tendency for pupils from non-manual backgrounds to express higher levels of motivation and also higher levels of adjustment or contentment, but these differences are not statistically significant. In general all pupils expressed high levels of motivation and of adjustment / contentment and moderate levels of anxiety.[3]

Table 9.3   Social class and attitudes to school (percentages of maximum possible score)

	Profes-sional and managerial (n = 21)	Other non-manual (n = 46)	Skilled manual (n = 67)	Other manual (n = 54)	All non-manual (n = 67)	All manual (n = 121)
Motivation	81	84	80	77	83	79
Anxiety	53	50	50	52	51	51
Adjustment/ contentment	79	78	75	71	78	73

SOCIAL CLASS AND CLASSROOM ACTIVITIES

The kinds of data presented so far do not differ from those available in a number of other studies of social class and school achievement. However, the ORACLE study does differ from previous research in having a large body of data based on systematic observation of the classroom activities and interactions of teachers and pupils. It is this data that enables us to investigate the possibility that differences in the attainment of specific groups are a reflection of differences in the treatment they receive in class.

The figures in Table 9.4 show some aspects of the classroom activities of the four social class groups. The top row gives the average percentage of time totally involved in their task, the second row gives the average percentage of time involved in routine supportive activities such as ruling lines or fetching materials and the third row gives the average percentage of time spent waiting to interact with the teacher. These three rows add up to the fourth row, which is 'total involved time'. As can be seen in Table 9.4, the four social class groups are very similar both in terms of their total involved time and of the various activities which constitute it. Pupils in the professional and managerial group have slightly higher levels both for time directly on task and for total involved time, but the differences are not large and in no case are statistically significant. A major conclusion of the observation study was that children spend a very high proportion of their time involved in their work (see 'Inside the Primary Classroom', Chapter 4), and this conclusion holds good for all four of the occupational groups.

Table 9.4   Social class and classroom activity (percentages of total observations)

	Professional and managerial (n = 21)	Other non-manual (n = 46)	Skilled manual (n = 67)	Other manual (n = 54)	All non-manual (n = 67)	All manual (n = 121)
Working on task	58.4	55.5	53.9	56.1	56.4	54.9
Working on routine	11.1	12.6	13.1	12.1	12.1	12.7
Waiting for teacher	4.6	4.8	5.8	4.7	4.7	5.3
Total 'involved' time	74.1	72.9	72.8	72.9	73.2	72.9

SOCIAL CLASS AND TEACHER-PUPIL INTERACTION

The question of teacher-pupil interaction is a central issue in arguments such as those of Sharp and Green and the various other studies discussed above. These studies have claimed that middle-class and higher achieving children are systematically advantaged in terms of the amount and type of attention which they receive from the teacher. The results presented in the first report on the ORACLE project, 'Inside the Primary Classroom', cast some doubt on these assertions. It was shown that the only difference in the amount of teacher attention received by high, medium and low achievers was a tendency for low-achieving pupils to receive more individual attention than the other two groups, and it concluded: 'There is no evidence here that there is any discrimination either in favour or against any particular group of pupils according to their achievement level' (see 'Inside the Primary Classroom', p. 64). This analysis is repeated in Table 9.5 for the social class groupings in the study. The picture that emerges suggests the same conclusion that was made for achievement level; there is no evidence that any of the social groups were advantaged or disadvantaged in respect of teacher attention. In particular, there are no differences between the four social groups or between the two broader categories of manual and non-manual occupations with respect to the total amount of teacher attention they receive, the amount of this attention which is directly concerned with their task (rather than discipline or classroom management) or to the amount of this attention which is personal or individual. The fourth and fifth rows of Table 9.5 distinguish between those interactions initiated by the pupil and those initiated by the teacher. Here there are differences in patterns of interaction. Pupils from professional and managerial backgrounds are rather more likely than other pupils to initiate interaction with the teacher themselves, while a higher proportion of the interaction received by the other pupils comes about as a result of the teacher's initiative. These differences, however, do not reach statistical significance.[4] The implications of these results and their relationship to the findings of other studies will be considered in the conclusion of this chapter.

Table 9.5 Social class and pupil-teacher interaction (percentages of total observations)

	Professional and managerial (n = 21)	Other non-manual (n = 46)	Skilled manual (n = 67)	Other manual (n = 54)	All non-manual (n = 67)	All manual (n = 121)
Total pupil-teacher interaction	14.7	15.1	15.0	14.8	14.7	14.9
Interaction directly on task	9.1	10.5	10.2	10.5	10.1	10.3
Individual interaction	2.3	2.2	2.5	2.3	2.2	2.4
Interaction initiated by pupil	1.5	1.0	1.1	0.8	1.1	1.0
Interaction initiated by teacher	1.4	1.6	1.7	1.9	1.5	1.8

SOCIAL CLASS AND TEACHER ASSESSMENTS

The final area to be considered is that of teacher assessments of pupils and the extent to which these are affected by the pupils' occupational background. A number of the studies discussed above have claimed that teachers have higher expectations of pupils from middle-class backgrounds and that they confuse the sorts of attributes which go with coming from a middle-class home with achievement and ability. One of the earliest studies in this area showed that when selection for selective secondary schooling was based on school assessments, working-class pupils did less well than when they were based on test results.

The ORACLE study obtained teacher assessments of pupils in a variety of areas, as explained in Anne Jasman's chapter 11 in this volume. These were not, in general, directed towards the basic skills but were part of an experimental procedure to measure pupil accomplishment in cognitive areas usually ignored in conventional tests. However, the assessments of abilities in mathematics were rather closer to the areas normally covered in mathematics tests. In addition to these, a number of exercises were devised to provide independent measures of the abilities assessed by the teachers. Full details of the assessments and exercises are given in Chapter 11.

The purpose of the analysis reported here is to compare pupils from different social backgrounds in terms of the assessments which teachers make of them and then to see if any differences in teacher assessments can be explained by differences in actual levels of achievement. The procedure adopted is, first, to compare the average raw assessment scores received from their teachers by the various groups of pupils. Analysis of covariance is then used to compare the groups, not for their raw assessment scores, but for the extent to which the teacher assessments were higher or lower than would have been predicted on the basis of the pupils' performance in the tests of basic skills. Another analysis of covariance is then conducted to compare the groups in terms of the difference between actual teacher assessments and those which would have been predicted from performance on the exercises designed to measure the skills which were being assessed by the teachers. These analyses were conducted first using the combined scores from the assessments and exercises administered in the first year (listening skills, concentration, following instructions, etc.) and then for the mathematics skills assessed during the second year.

The results of the analysis using the first year data are presented in the top half of Table 9.6. The top row of the Table shows that pupils from non-manual occupational backgrounds, and particularly pupils from professional and managerial backgrounds, received much more favourable assessments than pupils from manual occupational backgrounds. The second row shows how much more or less favourable these assessments were than would have been predicted on the basis of the pupils' scores in the tests of basic skills. These results, expressed as residual assessment scores, show that non-manual pupils were more favourably assessed than their basic skills performance would justify. This result is statistically significant not only when all four groups are being compared but also when the combined manual and combined non-manual groups are compared. The third row of the Table repeats this analysis using performance on the exercises specifically designed to measure the abilities being assessed, rather than scores on the basic skills, to predict the assessments. The results from this analysis show even more clearly that pupils from non-manual backgrounds, and in particular pupils from professional and managerial backgrounds, are given more favourable assessments than their actual performances justify, while pupils from manual occupational backgrounds are given poorer assessments than would have been expected on the basis of their performance.

However, this result is not repeated when the assessments of mathematics abilities are considered. As can be seen in the bottom half of Table 9.6, pupils from non-manual backgrounds receive more favourable assessments for their mathematical abilities than do pupils from manual backgrounds. But, after performance on the maths tests has been taken into account, when the residual assessments are compared, the differences no longer reach statistical significance; when performance on the mathematics exercises taken into account they disappear altogether. In the case of mathematics, the better assessments received by middle-class pupils can be entirely accounted for by their better performance in this area. This is in sharp contrast to the result from the combined first year assessments where middle-class pupils can be seen to be much more favourably assessed than their performance justifies.

Table 9.6   Social class and teacher assessments

	Profes- sional and managerial (n = 13)	Other non- manual (n = 25)	Skilled manual (n = 37)	Other manual (n = 32)		All non- manual (n = 38)	All manual (n = 69)	
Combined assessments								
Raw assessments	47.73	42.63	34.84	35.20	**	44.45	35.0	**
Residual using basic skills as covariate	6.69	3.09	−2.38	2.26	**	4.33	−2.3	**
Residual using exercises as covariate	8.45	3.53	−3.47	−2.19	**	5.30	−2.93	**
Mathematics assessment	(n = 16)	(n = 33)	(n = 41)	(n = 36)		(n = 49)	(n = 76)	
Raw assessment	14.5	13.9	12.3	11.5	*	14.1	11.9	*
Residual using maths test as covariate	1.35	0.85	−0.53	−0.78	NS	1.05	−0.65	NS
Residual using maths exercises as covariate	−0.21	0.05	0.29	−0.28	NS	−0.03	0.01	NS

* Statistically significant at 5 per cent level.
** Statistically significant at 1 per cent level.

The reason for this difference probably lies in the nature of the areas being assessed. The first year assessments were experimental in nature and represented an attempt at the systematic evaluation of areas not normally subjected to such evaluation but, nevertheless, regarded as important by teachers. In contrast, the mathematics assessments obtained in the second year were much closer to the subject matter of conventional assessment methods. Related to this is the amount of time spent on different areas of the curriculum as described in 'Inside the Primary Classroom'. Although teachers value the skills assessed by the experimental assessment procedures, they nevertheless spend the great majority of their time dealing with the basic skills. About a third of lesson time is spent on mathematics and it seems likely that this allows the teacher to become familiar with pupils' abilities in this area, while very little time is devoted to the skills assessed during the first year. It seems likely that teachers found it easier to relate their assessments directly to the performances of their pupils in mathematics than in less familiar areas where they were more likely to be influenced by other factors including those associated with social background.

SUMMARY AND CONCLUSIONS

The ORACLE findings support the conclusions of other studies which have shown that pupils from middle-class backgrounds have, on average, higher achievement levels than pupils from working-class backgrounds. The comparison of the different achievement quartiles shows that this is a relationship which is apparent within school classes as well as across very large samples. However, other differences between social groups which might have been expected from claims made in previous studies were not found. Pupils from different backgrounds had similar attitudes towards school, had similar levels of involvement in their school work and received similar levels and types of interaction with the teacher. It is this last point which is of most interest, particularly with regard to its relationship to the findings of other studies. A number of previous studies of classrooms, including those discussed above, have claimed that pupils from working-class backgrounds receive less teacher help and are less favourably treated than pupils from middle-class homes. The first point which needs to be made is that exact comparisons between the ORACLE study and these other studies are not possible. The most relevant of them were conducted either in America or with infant-aged pupils (Rist 1970; Sharp and Green 1975). It should also be emphasized however that the ORACLE study was on a much larger and more representative scale than these previous studies, and that it gathered systematic and quantifiable observational data, rather than relying on informal impressionistic methods.

It is this last point which may lead some people to question the validity of the ORACLE results. It may be argued that the limitations imposed by a pre-coded systematic observation system prevented the observers from noting the subtleties and nuances of interaction by which pupils from different backgrounds were actually differentiated. To some extent this is a valid criticism, although, of course, it refers equally to the results of any obser-

vational exercise, systematic or informal. It is always possible
that the research has missed key elements in the situation and no
conclusions from this sort of research can be regarded as final.
However, it must be emphasized that the amount of teacher interaction received by a pupil and the extent to which it is concerned
with his work is an important element of the treatment he receives
in class. It should also be said that most of the arguments about
differential treatment in studies such as those of Rist, and Sharp
and Green, go very little beyond assertions about dramatic differences in the amount of interaction received by pupils of different
backgrounds or abilities. It has recently been pointed out that
most examples of qualitative research in the classroom in fact depend heavily on quantitative assertions ('most of the time', 'rarely',
'unusual' etc.) albeit of an imprecise and unverifiable nature
(McIntyre and MacLeod 1978).

These assertions about differential attention given to pupils
from different social backgrounds cannot be supported by the data
from the present study. The ORACLE study found differences in
attainment between middle-class and working-class pupils, and
differences in rates of progress. But it did not find differences
in treatment which would account for these. Although the ORACLE
results give some support to the claim that middle-class pupils
are more favourably perceived by their teachers than their actual
achievements justify, this conclusion holds only in the areas where
teachers are likely to find it difficult and unfamiliar to make
assessments and were not repeated in a more central and familiar
area such as mathematics. These findings suggest that it is very
unlikely that, in general, the poorer performance of working-class
pupils compared with middle-class pupils attending the same
schools can be explained by reference to conscious or unconscious
unfairness on the part of teachers.

Despite the negative conclusions which arise from this analysis
of social class differences, the results underline the value of
direct observation of classrooms and of systematic observation
methods. Findings from the use of these methods, as reported in
'Inside the Primary Classroom', showed that popular notions about
primary schools as unruly and disorganized and as having abandoned the basic skills were unfounded. In a similar fashion, the
present analysis makes highly questionable some explanations for
social class differences in school performance that have recently
been gaining credence among educational researchers and sociologists.

NOTES

1 The analyses in Tables 9.1 to 9.6 were repeated for those
classes having between 50 and 80 per cent of pupils from
manual occupational backgrounds and gave very similar results. Full details are available from the author.
2 Sample difference scores (obtained by subtracting the pre-test

from the post-test score)   have low reliability and are nega-
tively correlated with the pre-test score. See Chapter 4 of
'Progress and Performance in the Primary Classroom' (Galton
and Simon 1980) for a discussion of the issues involved in
measuring change in test scores.

3   The measures of pupil attitudes and the results obtained from
them are discussed more fully in Chapter 8 of 'Progress and
Performance in the Primary Classroom'.

4   This result is similar to the analysis of teacher-pupil interactions and achievement level. A result not included in 'Inside
the Primary Classroom' was that the extra individual attention
received by low-achieving pupils came about as a result of the
teacher seeking them out, while high-achieving pupils were
rather more likely to initiate interactions themselves.

The percentages for pupil-initiated and teacher-initiated
interaction add up to a higher value than that for all individual interaction. Individual pupil-teacher interactions were
always coded as pupil- or teacher-initiated, but it was also
possible, though fairly unusual, for a group or class interaction to be so coded.

Part III
RESEARCH AND THE TEACHER

10 CURRICULUM CHANGE AND RESEARCH IN A MIDDLE SCHOOL

David Johnston

Boniface School was built to cater for 480 children between the ages of five and twelve in a northern, industrial city. The new building, opened in September 1975, was to provide education in an area where previously children had travelled to six other schools, none of which was in the immediate locality. The need for a new school had been felt many years earlier when parents' concern over the time lost in travelling each day led to public meetings with elected members and officers of the local authority. A decision was eventually taken to build a first and middle school complex under one Headmaster. Boniface is situated on a council development built in the early 1950s, although most of the catchment area consists of private property, mainly semi-detached houses.

In order to cope with the 365 children expected on the opening day, fourteen teachers had to be appointed: eight to work in the first school and six in the middle school. There was not enough time before opening to advertise for a Deputy Headteacher or for any posts of special responsibility. It was therefore necessary to interview staff in local schools who requested a transfer because their schools were losing children to Boniface. Nine teachers were recruited in this way following interviews with the Headteacher and the local education authority's staffing officer. Three probationary teachers were allocated to the school, and, following interviews, the two remaining vacancies were filled by experienced teachers who were moving into the authority's area. The position of Deputy Headteacher was to be advertised during the first term.

The school was described as 'open-plan' by the architect although, compared with some other schools built before Boniface, it would be more accurate to call it 'semi-open-plan'. The nature of the building required all teachers to work in very close physical proximity to one another. In the first school especially, the teachers would of necessity have to co-operate a great deal; and with such organization the respective strengths of each teacher could be used to the full. In fact, working in this way would be a necessary part of all the teaching in both parts of the school, although in the middle school bays it was possible for teachers to work alone on certain occasions. For some teachers this was an option which they preferred, but a great deal of co-operation did develop among all the staff.

Primary teachers are usually given a great deal of freedom in curriculum matters, and should therefore have considerable res-

ponsibility for decisions about their curriculum. The Headteacher
wanted to work out how to initiate and maintain a programme of
conscious curriculum planning and review. All too often primary
teachers have followed their own ideas to the exclusion of other
influences from within the school; consequently, when children
have changed teachers, the work has become fragmented and
there has been a lack of continuity. In a school where teachers
have to work in close proximity, with children at similar ages and
stages of development, it would seem sound for them to share
their thoughts and use their strengths for the benefit of all concerned. It was the Headteacher's view that the whole staff needed
to develop a clear awareness of the strengths and weaknesses
of the curriculum and to consider these against the background of
the needs of the children.

Looking back over the first four years of the school's existence
it seems that the programme of school-focused, in-service activity
fell into five stages. The account which follows describes the
middle school curriculum programme in some detail. The first
school staff were involved in similar activities.

STAGE 1: THE FIRST TERM OF THE FIRST YEAR

This stage was characterized by a definite lack of curriculum
development and by a concentration on establishing the school as
an operational unit. In the staff meetings before the beginning of
the term, a set of curriculum guidelines was handed out for the
key areas of language and mathematics. These were content-based
and had been drawn up by the staff of a school in a similar socio-
economic area where the present Head had previously been Headteacher. It was recognized that there were shortcomings in these
guidelines for the needs of Boniface children. Nevertheless, they
provided teachers with a framework which could be used as a
starting point. All decisions relating to the management of the
curriculum were at this stage taken by the Headteacher alone:
for example, a wide range of books was purchased to form the
basis of the reading and mathematics programmes. The teachers
agreed that the challenge of planning the curriculum could begin
once they felt that the initial organizational problems had been
ironed out.

The Headteacher wanted to pursue this challenge by drawing on
the curriculum development experience that the teachers had
had in other schools. The appointment of the Deputy Head was
crucial, and fortunately someone with wide experience and an
interest in this area was found to fill the post. Once the Deputy
had taken up his appointment, the Headteacher wanted to ensure
that the staff identified strongly with him as the key link in the
intended curriculum development programme: the Deputy was taking over a full-time teaching role and consequently would be
closer to the needs of the staff and children in what would be a
crucial time of curriculum innovation. It was also very important

that the Head and Deputy agreed on the approach to be used in producing a worth-while in-service course for the staff. The whole programme had to be carefully planned.

STAGE 2: THE SECOND TERM OF THE FIRST YEAR

Decisions had to be made as to how the teachers should be introduced to ideas of rational curriculum development. There seemed no point in attempting to discuss one specific curriculum area until firm foundations had been laid which would set the pattern for development in all subject areas. Meetings were held after school when hand-outs which had previously been distributed were discussed. Each meeting was chaired by the Deputy Head with the Head present on the majority of occasions. The intention was to create an awareness that there was an alternative to a content-based approach to the curriculum. The Headteacher was aware that teachers would probably feel insecure with an objectives-based approach, as his previous experience had been that teachers preferred to develop content-based ideas which they felt had more relevance to their needs. A clear suggestion was made to the teachers that structure should be introduced and that child-centred and structured approaches were not mutually incompatible.

These initial meetings, when all staff were able to question and discuss the proposals brought before them, led to some frustration for all concerned. The jargon of curriculum development confused many teachers and, as a result, many of the hand-outs were redrafted in terms with which staff were familiar. Some teachers did not at first appreciate the relevance of this type of approach and wanted to reject the use of aims and objectives. However, many talked informally to the Head and Deputy about the possibilities of the approach that was being adopted. Certainly, most of the staff were being challenged to question their basic thinking about the ways in which they planned their work with children. The limited time available for detailed discussion at the end of a busy school day added to the frustration. Nevertheless, the discussions continued over six weekly meetings, during which time the Headteacher was carefully monitoring the reactions of the staff to these new proposals.

STAGE 3: THE THIRD TERM OF THE FIRST YEAR

The beginning of this stage marked the time in the school year when a number of teachers were upgraded from Scale 1 to Scale 2 to undertake specific curriculum responsibilities. Those teachers who were upgraded were fully aware that they would have to co-ordinate activities in developing curriculum guidelines for their subject area: all the work that would be undertaken in any area would be done by all the staff working together. Although this might be very time consuming, it was thought that the discussions which would take place would enrich the experience of every teacher, provide a greater understanding of the different levels at which each subject can be studied and give an impetus for the staff to work as a team.

At this point the Deputy Head had been in post for only one term, and it was now very necessary for discussions to take place between him and the Head as to the strategies that would be employed to manage the curriculum meetings. Many hours were spent talking through the issues and, once the priorities had been considered, a pattern of organization was developed. All the staff were consulted about which curriculum area they wished to begin with, and language development was the unanimous choice. They were then divided into two groups, one led by the Deputy and the other by the curriculum specialist. Teachers from each year group in the school were divided between the curriculum groups; and an attempt was made to separate those teachers who might have tended to dominate discussions, any very quiet teachers and specialists in the particular discipline under discussion. Ranging in size from four to six, the groups were small enough to allow a substantial contribution from each member. Everyone had to feel that his or her efforts were of value, even though the experience of the group members differed a great deal. It was important to avoid a situation where some teachers might become frustrated because of the efforts of others.

All the meetings were held after school rather than in school time, on the same day of each week. They began at 4 p.m. and were planned to finish at 5 p.m., though they often overran by 10 or 15 minutes. A time limit was also set in terms of the number of weeks in which meetings would be held: it was anticipated that two terms would be given to each curriculum area.

The curriculum specialist was responsible for defining the curricular objectives which would be discussed at each meeting. During the meetings a great deal of time was devoted to talking about the teaching styles adopted when working with the children. All the teachers were keen to exchange experiences with the group leaders, and even the young probationers were drawn into the conversation. At the end of each meeting, the two groups met in plenary session, and each group leader gave a brief report of the group's discussions. A list of relevant skills was thus obtained, relating to each specific curricular objective. Obviously, similar ideas were often reported from each group. It was left to the group leaders, when they met separately from the main groups at a later stage in the overall development, to evaluate the ideas raised in the discussions. The teachers accepted the fact that the group leaders would have final responsibility for the presentation of the finished product. The Headteacher adopted a relatively passive role, spending time with both groups, though he held informal discussions with the group leaders at regular intervals to discuss progress.

After one term it was clear that there was some concern about the way the meetings were developing. Two main points arose.

First, they were taking far too long, especially as so many other areas were to be discussed. Second, a written summary was requested after each meeting in order that teachers could keep a careful check on previous discussion. In addition, during the meetings, the Headteacher became more and more conscious of the fact that the staff were working at many different levels.

It was at this point that a decision was made to become involved in a Schools Council project, 'Progress in Learning Science'. The fact that science was the subject for consideration was not of major importance. There were several reasons for adopting this project before the first series of curriculum meetings had been concluded. First, it offered a child-centred approach to the development of a curriculum area which was weak in the school. Second, the staff, with such wide but unrelated experiences of working with primary children, were at very different levels of expectation about styles of teaching and children's needs. Third, the Head felt that the basic philosophy of the project was sound. Fourth, its application spanned the full primary age range: it therefore provided an opportunity to involve all the staff of the first school in discussions with middle school staff. Fifth, the emphasis of the project materials required teachers to look closely at the children under their care. It was the last of these reasons that the Head felt was the most relevant to the development of the teachers' attitudes towards their work in the school.

Early in the term the Head had been approached by the local authority's Senior Research Adviser to ask whether the school would be willing to be involved in the ORACLE project. A brief outline of the nature of the research was given at this stage with a view to the directors of the project visiting the school at a later date, if in principle it was accepted that the school's participation in the project was viable. The Head agreed to see the researchers who visited the school and gave more details about the practical implications for those teachers who would be working alongside the project team. The Head was enthusiastic about a research project of this type at this stage in the school's development as it would probably contribute to an analysis of styles of teaching and classroom organization. This would link closely with the work in curriculum development and thus provide valuable information on which to base future plans for an effective teaching programme. However, there was no point in opting to be part of the research programme unless the staff concerned with the age group under review were themselves willing to be involved. Consequently, the teachers concerned were approached by the Head, who explained the nature of the research. The teachers also met the project directors before reaching a decision. There were some reservations expressed by the teachers but nevertheless they were prepared to accept the project and were pleased to give it full support.

STAGE 4: THE FIRST AND SECOND TERMS
OF THE SECOND YEAR

The staff who were to be involved in the ORACLE project for
the two years in which it would operate in the school were all
very experienced middle school teachers. They had taught in
other schools and included the Deputy Head and two Scale 3 post-
holders. The four teachers who made up the group were all part
of the third and fourth year middle school year team, with one of
the members a specified team leader responsible for co-ordinating
the curriculum and organizational developments. Consequently,
they met frequently to discuss a variety of issues relevant to the
needs of the children under their care and were able to share
their thoughts before and during the research programme. After
the acceptance of the project the teachers had more time to talk
among themselves, and it then became clear that some of their
reservations were actually fears of a number of situations which
they felt could arise. Comments were made to the Headteacher,
namely:
1   Unfamiliar features of the research methodology. For example,
    concern was expressed about whether the use of observers
    in classrooms would create a threatening situation for even
    the most confident teacher. This situation may be frustrat-
    ing when the teacher does not know who or what the observer
    is observing.
2   How the eventual findings would be interpreted. There was
    some concern as to whether teachers or schools might be com-
    pared for effectiveness.
3   A genuine feeling that teaching styles might alter, because
    of the presence of an observer in the classroom.
It was the Head's view that, given the situation, the teachers'
reactions were both normal and understandable. Any innovation,
research or otherwise, can expect a cool reception because by
implication it appears to be critical of teacher performance. Perhaps the fears expressed could have been reduced if there had
been a slower build-up to the introduction of the project when
the research team could have given the teachers more time to ask
questions about their reservations.
    Once the project had commenced, the key link with the research
team was through the observer who was working in the school.
She was quickly accepted by the staff because of her unobtrusive
personality and subtle approach which, combined with her understanding of the unforeseeable problems arising from daily school
life, such as timetable changes, made her an ideal choice. It was
suggested by the staff that this stemmed from the fact that she
herself was an experienced teacher. As the two years progressed,
the observer blended into the school, offering assistance to the
teachers in several areas and participating in various school
activities. The initial reservations were soon transformed into a
most successful and friendly working relationship.
    The interest and enthusiasm of the observer in turn fired the

interest of the teachers who would discuss the relevance of the
structured activities and test materials which from time to time
they had to administer as part of the research programme. The
written materials were favoured by the teachers who were generally impressed by the way in which fundamental skills and their
application were encompassed in each test. However, there was a
feeling that, because the tests were administered out of the context of normal work, the children had very little motivation to
succeed since they realized they would receive no feedback about
their performance on the tasks. They seemed to realize that all
their efforts were connected to the same project because of the
similarity of presentation.

The children involved in the project were used to having many
visitors in the school and so accepted the observer with the
minimum of disturbance. One member of staff had been concerned
about the possible effect of an observer's presence on the behaviour of some of the children in her class who tended to be
easily distracted. Although this initial worry was unfounded, it
did stimulate discussion about problems which might occur in a
more formal situation with less adaptable pupils; problems relating
to both the children's work and the flexibility of the monitoring.

While the ORACLE project was under way the Schools Council
project, 'Progress in Learning Science' had been undertaken with
all the staff of the school. This project aimed not so much to provide teachers with suggestions for learning activities as to help
them 'match' activities more closely to individual pupils' levels of
development. It set out to help teachers to base their classroom
decisions on more systematic information about pupils' attributes.
This information was to be collected by teachers through their
observations of individual pupils in the naturalistic setting of the
classroom.

As a guide to the observation and recording of pupil progress,
the project provided checklists with items on attitudes (e.g. curiosity, co-operation, open-mindedness), enquiry skills (e.g. observing, finding patterns in observations, communicating), and
concepts (e.g. time, length, life cycle).

The decision of the Boniface staff to engage in 'Progress in
Learning Science' (while continuing their other school-based
curriculum meetings) led to a series of twelve additional $1\frac{1}{2}$-hour
sessions at weekly intervals after school. The Head and Deputy
acted as group leaders, each working with two groups of six. In
addition to the staff of Boniface first and middle schools, the
groups included observers from six other schools within the local
education authority. The authority's Science Adviser also attended
almost all the meetings, taking a low-key role as a group member.

The Head and his Deputy, in leading the meetings, emphasized
that they were not sold on the project and did not want to sell it
to the staff. Rather, they presented it as raising a number of
issues which were of concern to the staff, and therefore worth
exploring, even if the conclusion drawn was that the project's
solutions were inadequate. Thus the aim was understanding of

issues rather than commitment to the project. The Headteacher
made it very clear to the project evaluators that his primary aim
in introducing his staff to the project was to encourage them to
think more deeply about the educational issues it raised concerning teaching styles, classroom organization, and assessment. He
saw these issues as congruent with the existing concerns of the
staff, who were discussing them as part of their attempt to
evolve policies for the new school.

As the ORACLE project continued the teachers began to discuss the underlying principles behind many of the materials. They
challenged not only each other but also the research techniques
and a wide range of activities relating to methods of assessing
various attitudes and abilities. There was strong staff disapproval
of the questionnaire concerned with attitudes to school – the
answers certainly seemed to reflect the children's light-hearted
approach rather than their true feelings. The whole issue of
teacher assessment of children arose when the teachers were
asked to grade children's skills on a three-point scale. It was
felt that although research by its very nature has to be objective,
an impressionistic comment can be far more valuable than a simple
numerical rating. On one occasion the objectivity of the research
was called into question when staff were asked to quantify and
compare a set of abstract qualities. However, as the project continued, the teachers were very willing to try to understand what
the project was doing even if there was some disagreement on
certain details.

A project like ORACLE needs to keep back information from
teachers about target pupils and about what is being looked for.
This can lead to frustration on the part of the teachers involved.
They want to know specific details about their pupils and the
relevance of their own teaching methods, and in the early stages
these cannot be made available. This is a problem which is not
easy to overcome as there is an incompatibility between the
wishes of the participants and the requirements of the research
design. The feedback from the project can add to the teachers'
frustration if there is a long time-lag between the tasks undertaken in the classroom and communication of the results. There is
a danger of a credibility gap existing between researchers and
practitioners, unless a clear pattern of communication is built up
that allows for relationships at a formal and informal level. As the
personal relationship with the project team developed, so the
staff felt at ease to express their opinions and therefore clarify
issues which may not have been initially too clearly understood.

The element of trust is an essential factor in a research programme of this type and can be genuinely developed only by
regular contact with all members of the project team. As the project proceeded the Head and Deputy had frequent contact with its
directors which led to a firm understanding of the nature of the
research and its findings. What was more important, however, was
that a set of personal relationships had formed between the
teachers and the team which probably led to a more honest, pro-

fessional and reliable evaluation of all that was being developed
in the school.

Towards the end of the second term of the second year the
teachers in the middle school had begun systematically to consider ways in which they could overcome a range of problems
including:
- the adoption of less formal approaches to teaching
- the use of more practical activities for pupils
- the elimination of patterns of classroom organization
  which obstruct observation of pupils
- the formulation of teachers' questions which encourage
  pupils to express themselves
- the problem of pupils who are normally unable to cope
  with tasks selected by their teachers
- the collection of information about individual pupils
  through observation.

The influence of the two projects, although difficult to assess
in specific terms, was certainly creating among the teachers a
genuine awareness of the need to consider carefully both the
curriculum and classroom organization.

STAGE 5: THE THIRD TERM OF THE SECOND, THIRD AND FOURTH YEARS

At this stage in the school's development the 'Progress in Learning Science' project had been concluded. There seemed a greater
awareness among the staff of the need for a rational approach to
the curriculum which gave rise to a wish by the middle school
staff (now nine teachers) to push ahead with other curriculum
areas using an objectives-based model. The first area for study,
language development, had taken nearly three terms, which was
longer than expected. It was agreed by the staff that the second
area, mathematics, ought to begin straight away, and this resulted
in further weekly meetings after school. In the meantime the
teacher responsible for the first area began to compile all the relevant material which had been produced in order to formulate a
policy for the middle school staff to consider. This document was
presented for discussion some weeks later, and after minor altera-
tions was agreed and implemented.

The second area of study, which was being led by the curriculum specialist in this field, had been running for one term when
the staff approached the Deputy Head to ask if a week-end conference could be organized on environmental studies. The reason
for this was to speed up the curriculum development programme.
The Headteacher was able to gain sponsorship from the local
authority for a residential week-end. The strategies employed
in this course were those which had been found effective in previous school-based in-service work, namely:
1 The leaders of the development (which should include either
   the Headteacher or Deputy Head and, where appropriate,

one other member of staff) must define their roles: they
must perceive themselves as learners, refrain from selling
ideas, and allow staff to elaborate those ideas they see as
relevant to the needs of the school;

2 Two team leaders are of great help in the planning stage to
ensure a breadth of experience to the development of the
programme and to provide opportunities to discuss the work
undertaken when each session is concluded;

3 Before the course begins there must be a slow build-up to
the first session, during which time staff are given the
opportunity to become acquainted with the philosophy involved;

4 The involvement of teachers from other schools within an
area can broaden the discussion and prevent staff from becoming too inward-looking;

5 A thorough preparation of the materials under discussion is
essential;

6 Group sizes for discussion should be kept to a minimum of
three and a maximum six: this results in greater teacher participation and thus study of the ideas in greater depth;

7 In order to ensure full involvement by each course member,
it is desirable to appoint individuals on a rota basis to act
as rapporteur to plenary discussions.

All the middle school staff attended and they were joined by
the majority of the first school staff. In two hard-working days
more was achieved than in the previous two terms. A programme
of environment studies for the whole school was set out. During
the week-end, staff had worked in small groups, had undertaken
some practical field-work, and had been visited by the local
authority's geography adviser, who gave a brief talk on the value
of an objectives approach to curriculum development.

The week-end away provided the impetus for continued activity.
Other subject areas still had to be studied, and even after four
years these were still not completed. In addition, when policy for
one curriculum area has been identified, work in that area has
not ceased. There has to be built into the system some element of
review of current work. The curriculum specialists now formally
undertook this task on a yearly basis although it is going on at
an informal level most of the time. There was also the problem of
assimilating new staff into the curriculum model that had been so
well accepted. Responsibility for this task was delegated to the
Deputy Headteacher. Another problem which arose was the need
felt by many staff for new skills in certain areas to help them
teach some subjects more effectively. To meet this need, teachers
continued to attend the local authority's in-service courses and
advisers ran evening courses in the school.

Towards the end of the third year the ORACLE research team
were still working in the school, although the project was now
drawing to a close as the children under review were soon to
transfer to the local comprehensive school. The research team had
throughout the exercise made efforts to report back to the teachers

involved in order that the results of the research could be discussed. On reflection it seems that the teachers at Boniface would have enjoyed the opportunity of even more feedback than the other local schools. This is probably due to the nature of the developments which had taken place in establishing an effective teaching programme in a new school. In the circumstances, at Boniface there was an eagerness to see any reflection of the change from mixed-ability class teaching to ability group work which took place after one year of the research. There was also considerable interest in how the children adapted to life in the comprehensive school where the environment seemed more impersonal and structured. Nevertheless, the experience gained from contact with the project enriched the awareness and outlook of a group of teachers who were eager to ensure that their teaching programme was meeting the needs of the children in the most efficient, professional manner. After the research project ended there was still a great deal of interest in the findings of the research, and the staff were keen to read the published reports.

It is difficult to specify the precise nature of the effects of any single project on the teachers involved. However, the overall programme of in-service work which took place in the school yielded tangible results:

1   The staff developed, and implemented with conviction, new approaches to basic areas of study; and this led to curriculum continuity throughout the school.

2   Those teachers with specialist curriculum responsibilities were able to share their expertise with every other teacher; they were thus more effective in carrying out their delegated responsibilities and in addition created an environment in which other teachers readily turn to them for guidance.

3   Relevant approaches to recording and assessing the work in each curriculum area were considered.

4   There was a willingness on the part of teachers to evaluate their own styles of teaching as well as different patterns of classroom organization.

5   There was an increased awareness that resources must be used to good purpose.

6   There was a recognition that curriculum development and staff development can be rewarding and enjoyable experiences.

11 TEACHERS' ASSESSMENTS IN CLASSROOM RESEARCH

Anne Jasman

The assessment and evaluation of self, others and the physical environment is an important part of any area of human behaviour. We all use our senses to monitor situations before making even such simple choices as what to eat or drink, as well as major decisions which may result in changes in life-style, and in the continuing process of personal growth and development. Assessment is particularly important in educational settings where it contributes to the decision-making which is calculated to assist children's learning.

Teachers are confronted by many sources of information. By observing and interacting with pupils in the classroom, a teacher acquires information about how they relate to her, to their peers and other adults, and about the quality of their work and the way in which they approach it. Other information is available from record cards, children's parents and other teachers. A teacher may want to organize all this available information systematically so that an accurate and coherent picture emerges of each child's characteristics, behaviour and performance.

There is a considerable literature on measurement and evaluation in psychology and education (Thorndike and Hagen 1969; Guilford 1973; Mehrens and Lehmann 1978; Cronbach 1970). The kind of assessment most familiar to teachers is the standardized test in which an individual pupil's score is compared to the performance of a large group (norm-referencing) or to some predetermined level of achievement (criterion-referencing). This form of test has been used to diagnose learning difficulties, and to measure achievement, aptitude or intelligence.

A variation is the 'teacher-made' test such as the CSE or the GCE 'O' and 'A' level examinations. Here the standardization of pupils' scores is not related to an external norm or criterion, but rather to the scores of other pupils taking the examination at the same time. Teachers often use such methods to test the content of pupils' learning and their application of knowledge in the classroom.

Questionnaires are less frequently used by teachers. This approach often requires a written response to a series of questions related to the area being studied. A similar format can be used in interviews where the information is given orally, and the technique is most commonly used to measure attitudes and personality variables.

In the classroom, the teacher also has access to all the pupils' work. This is a potentially valuable source of information, and a technique for assessing such products is described in 'Progress and Performance in the Primary Classroom', pp. 113-17.

An alternative approach is the use of structured activities where, instead of assessing a piece of work arising from normal class activities, the teacher decides what skills she wishes to assess and then devises an appropriate task. It is only when the criteria for assessment have been formulated that the task is developed to match those criteria, so that scoring the activities is straightforward.

The methods described have been concerned mainly with written responses. However, the teacher gains other information from talking with pupils and observing them whilst they engage in their classwork. There are various techniques for collecting and recording this knowledge systematically. Most schools devise a record-keeping system where such information is noted. More recently two Schools Council projects, 'Progress in Learning Science' (Harlen et al. 1977) and 'Communication Skills in Early Childhood' (Tough 1976), have developed a new approach for monitoring pupil progress. The materials consist of an in-service training programme and checklists which facilitate the development of teachers' observation and questioning skills and provide a framework for making their assessments. There is no scoring system, but teachers usually quantify their assessments by using a rating scale.

Unobtrusive measures such as those described by Webb (1975) provide a novel approach to solving some of the difficulties associated with data collection. The strength of such measures is that they do not require the active participation of the pupils. For example, physical evidence was used by Mosteller (1955) to investigate the usage of sections in an encyclopedia by noting differential wear and tear, dirty edges, finger markings and underlinings on the page. Information on grouping, movement and pupil behaviour can be obtained by such unobtrusive observation.

It is necessary to consider four major issues which influence the choice of an assessment technique, before describing the particular methods used in the ORACLE study. These issues involve purpose, validity, reliability and practicality; and they are interrelated in complex and dynamic ways which often require that compromises be made.

PURPOSE

Assessments are made with some purpose in mind, generally to provide information for decision-making. As pupils move through the school, assessments are used for selection, streaming and grouping, and to give information to other teachers and schools. Other reasons for measuring performance relate to groups of pupils rather than to individuals. Data on pupil achievement, attitudes, personality, etc., are used to monitor national trends and to compare, for example, the performance of groups subjected to different curricula, organizational policies, and styles of teaching. The methods described previously are not all appropriate for each of these purposes and this will affect the choice made. If a suitable procedure is not available for a particular purpose, an alternative may have to be devised.

VALIDITY

In either case, the validity of the technique has to be investigated. In questioning validity the teacher or researcher is essentially asking if the procedure measures what it is designed to measure and nothing else. Validity is a relative concept since measurements are made for a particular purpose. In engineering, for example, a micrometer is appropriate for measuring a thin sheet of steel but not the length of a girder.

Authors have used different terms to describe the types of evidence of validity. Thorndike and Hagen (1969) refer to content, criterion-related and construct validity, while Guilford (1973) describes predictive validity and factorial validity. The type of validity to be demonstrated and the method which is used depends on the assessment procedure being investigated.

Predictive or criterion-related validity is involved where the results are to be used to predict future performance. A measure is valid, in this sense, if the pupils who have achieved highly can be shown to go on to success in particular careers, higher education or the next stage of schooling.

Construct or factorial validity is the degree to which certain explanatory concepts or constructs account for performance on a test. An example of such a construct is sociability. By rational analysis of this construct, certain predictions can be made. For example, sociability would be expected to relate to the quantity and quality of interactions in a group setting. A test is said to have construct validity if the correlations between the test and other measures occur as predicted by the underlying theory.

Content validity is related to how adequately the items or content of a test sample the area under consideration. No numerical procedure is generally used to demonstrate content validity, since it is essentially a matter of judgment whether the items are sufficiently representative to allow generalizations to be made about pupil achievement on the basis of one particular test.

These three aspects of validity - predictive, construct and content validity - are independent only at a conceptual level. In practice, one or more may be relevant to a particular assessment procedure, and it is the purpose of the measure which determines the kind of evidence of validity that is required. Once the measure has been shown to be valid the next issue is one of reliability.

RELIABILITY

The reliability of an assessment procedure provides an estimate of how much confidence can be placed in its precision. Unlike measuring tools such as rulers or micrometers, tests are not absolute standards, but vary in themselves. Errors in measurement arise in a number of ways. The pupil may actually change from one occasion to another, the measuring instrument may be different on two occasions, and an inaccurate picture of pupil performance may result if a limited range of behaviour is sampled. A measure is said to be reliable if a pupil's performance remains the same or nearly the same in repeated measurements, so that the correlation coefficient between the two scores is high. Comparisons are generally made in one or more of three ways.

The first procedure, known as test-retest reliability, is concerned with variations in response to the test at a particular time, and also variations in individuals from time to time. There are, however, sources of unreliability which arise from the method rather than the test itself; for example, there may be memory or practice effects which can give rise to higher scores on the retest. The same method can be used to compare teacher ratings to establish their reliability. Here the same group of pupils are assessed on separate occasions by the same teacher.

This method does not identify any errors which arise from the particular set of tasks or items which have been chosen to represent the area of behaviour. This is an important aspect of reliability, since items must often be restricted in number but still be representative of a large body of knowledge to be tested. This aspect of reliability can be investigated by correlating two equivalent forms of test, or both halves of one test. The third method is termed inter-judge reliability. It is specifically related to subjective assessments and works in a rather similar way to the parallel test method. Two or more teachers assess the same pupils and their assessments are then compared.

PRACTICALITY

The last issue concerns the practicality of the assessment technique which has been chosen, taking into account its purpose, validity and reliability. Practical considerations will include the cost of materials used in the assessment, the time available for administration, the availability of teachers and others to administer the test or make the assessment, and the ease with which the test can be scored and the data organized into a usable form.

Each of these four issues has been treated separately. However, in practice they are all interrelated. The nature of such interrelationships can best be understood with reference to a particular example. The development of the teacher-based assessment techniques used in the ORACLE research programme will be discussed here in relation to these issues.

ORACLE began in 1975 as a five-year, process-product study of primary classrooms, and has been fully described in 'Inside the Primary Classroom' (Galton et al. 1980) and 'Progress and Performance in the Primary Classroom' (Galton and Simon 1980). The teacher-based assessment techniques discussed here were developed as part of this research. The intention was to develop methods for assessing aspects of pupils' development other than those which have been traditionally accepted as amenable to assessment, but which are considered important by teachers, so that when teaching styles were investigated in relation to differential pupil learning, achievement in the areas of these broader aims would be taken into account.

Before 1975 there had been no systematic survey of teachers' perceptions of the purposes of primary education. However, the Ashton survey - 'The Aims of Primary Education: a Study of Teachers' Opinions' (1975) - was the starting point for specifying in detail what was to be measured so that an appropriate method of assessment could be chosen.

In the Ashton research, teachers' groups were asked to formulate aims for primary education. By a process of discussion and constant refining, they finally produced a list of seventy-two aims relating not only to areas which have traditionally been accepted as a major part of the curriculum within the primary school, but also certain wider purposes, for example, the development of a pupil's ability to carry out independent work, make reasoned judgments and apply mathematical techniques to everyday situations. By means of a survey of teachers, the list of seventy-two aims was ranked in order of importance.

In the present study, since it was clearly impractical for the research team to attempt to monitor performance in each of these seventy-two areas, the investigation was restricted to the twenty-three aims which were related to intellectual development. Some of these were covered by basic achievement tests, and from the rest the choice of what to assess was given to a group of interested teachers. Those who wished to participate were asked to indicate three aims of their choice in order of preference. As a result of their choices, working groups of teachers were established to investigate ways of assessing the following five aims, one group dealing with each area.

1 The child should be able to listen with concentration and understanding.
2 The child should develop some inventiveness and creativity in some fields: for example, by painting, music, mechanical things, poetry, movement.
3 The child should know how to acquire information other than by reading; for example, by asking questions, by experimenting, from watching television.
4 The child should be able to:
   (a) compute the four arithmetic rules using his knowledge of number, multiplication tables and different units of measurement.

(b) use mathematical techniques in his everyday life i.e.
     estimating distances, classifying objects, using money.*
5 The child should know how to convey meaning clearly and
   accurately through speech for a variety of purposes; for
   example, description, explanation, narration.
At this stage, the purpose of the assessment had been defined
by the research team and what was to be assessed decided by the
teachers' groups. The next step was to consider which of the
assessment techniques already described would be most appropriate.
  Standardized tests were rejected for two reasons. There were
few, if any, existing tests which matched precisely the specifica-
tion of each aim. In some cases, it was difficult to see how a set
of items could actually be devised. Second, the fact that teachers
are critical of using only standardized tests to describe pupil performance contributed to the decision to pursue an alternative
approach.
  A questionnaire to collect information in these areas seemed
totally inappropriate, as this method could not provide information on pupil performance. However, as will be seen later, questioning pupils orally, as in an interview, can give the teacher a
clearer picture of a pupil's achievement. The assessment of pupils'
classwork was rejected, mainly for practical reasons. First, there
was no certainty that every teacher in the study would be engaged
in classwork related to each of the aims. Second, the ages of the
pupils in the study ranged from eight to eleven years, and differences of content and level of difficulty would have made the
task of ensuring comparability of assessments extremely difficult,
if not impossible. Third, the practical problem of handling such a
large number and variety of products was considered too great.
However, an alternative to classwork as the product to assess
was some form of structured activity specially devised to ensure
that the nature of the task would be the same for each pupil.
  Standardized tests, questionnaires, classwork and structured
activities all rely on some kind of product which is assessed.
However, the teacher also has knowledge of her pupils' performance based on observation and questioning. This information can
be recorded systematically using a record card or checklist, the
level of performance being indicated by rating on a three- or
five-point scale. The technique was particularly attractive in the
present study, as it could take into account a larger number of
criteria than could be covered by written responses. In the case
of 'conveying meaning accurately through speech' it was the only
viable approach. Unobtrusive measures in themselves could not
tap all the aspects which were to be assessed, but observing
pupils would obviously play an important part in teachers' assessments using a checklist.
  The techniques of assessment chosen for monitoring pupil per-

*Here two aims were amalgamated and tackled by one group of
teachers interested in mathematics assessment.

formance for the five aims listed were thus checklists of abilities
for each area. Teachers would assess the performance of their
pupils on the basis of the criteria given on the checklist; and
structured activities, developed to match these criteria, would be
given to the pupils. There were few examples of these techniques
available at that time. The decision to use the aims as formulated
in the Ashton survey as the starting point meant that appropriate
materials had to be developed within the research.

The first stage was to help teachers conceptualize what they
understood by each aim so that a framework could be devised for
their assessments. Each group of teachers observed the pupils in
their classes during a week, making notes on pupil performance
and listing examples of activities which might foster the abilities,
skills and attitudes associated with the aim. By a process of discussion, trial and feedback the final checklists of abilities were
produced for each of the five aims.

The second stage was to devise the structured activities to
match the criteria on the checklist. For example, as part of the
aim, 'the child should be able to acquire information other than by
reading', the teachers thought that a pupil should be able to make
independent observations. This was included on the checklist and
a spot-the-difference cartoon was subsequently devised as the
structured activity to match this criterion.

Before these materials could be used within the schools, it was
necessary to ensure their validity and reliability. The three aspects of validity - predictive, construct and content - may not
be equally relevant to a particular assessment procedure since
the validity of the measure is dependent on its purpose. The
most important aspect in this case is content validity as the purpose of checklists was to tap a broader range of product measures
for the ORACLE study. To some extent, the content validity of
the checklist had been ensured by the way in which it was developed. The aims used were taken from a large-scale survey of
teachers in England and Wales, and the decision relating to which
of the intellectual areas were to be investigated was also made
by teachers, as were the criteria on the checklist.

In addition, teachers whose classes were observed during the
ORACLE programme were asked to complete an open-ended
questionnaire giving their opinions of the appropriateness and
range of criteria for each aim. Most of these teachers, who had
not been involved in developing the checklists, found that the
abilities listed were helpful to them in making assessments and
appropriate to the five aims. This evidence suggests that the
checklists were representative of the area being studied and that
the content was valid.

In the case of the structured activities both construct and content validity are relevant. Two methods were used to demonstrate
construct validity. First, a factor analysis was carried out to
provide evidence that the constructs measured by these exercises
were those which they had been designed to measure. Second,
the relationship between the scores obtained on these exercises

and those on other similar measures was investigated.

A factor analysis was carried out on achievement test scores in basic skills and the three sets of structured activity scores obtained in the first year of the study; this yielded five factors. The principal factor was made up of all the achievement test scores. The remaining factors related to different elements of the structured activities: comprehension by looking and listening, formulation of questions, sequencing and creativity. This supports the construct validity of the structured activities, in that parts of the exercises designed to measure different abilities emerged as separate factors. It also supports the validity of the checklist itself, as these activities were measuring different qualities from the achievement tests.

The data collected in the second year of the study related to the everyday mathematics structured activities. The scores were factor analysed with the achievement test data and two factors emerged, the first consisting of items related to arithmetic competence, and the second consisting of those exercises dealing with the organization and presentation of data. This indicates that the activities did tap a different skill from that assessed by traditional tests and supports the construct validity of these exercises.

The second method of analysis involved comparisons with other similar measures. This presented problems as few appropriate measures were available. Materials from the Schools Council Oracy Project (Wilkinson et al. 1976) which tested listening comprehension were administered to seventy-four pupils who also completed the structured activities for 'listening with concentration and understanding'. Given that the skills assessed by the Schools Council tests did not exactly overlap those measured here, the correlation coefficient of 0.4 which was obtained (and which was statistically significant at the 1 per cent level) provides further evidence of construct validity.

The content validity of the structured activities in relation to abilities on the checklist was more problematic. For practical reasons, the structured activities were designed so that the evidence of pupil performance was available in written form. This meant that certain abilities on the checklist were not tapped by a structured activity. As the content validity of the checklist depended on the inclusion of all the abilities thought to represent the aim, the structured activities had limited content validity. Teachers in the classroom were, however, able to observe and question pupils in order to make assessments of the abilities which are not measured by the structured activities. The main difficulty, then, is to ensure that the assessments can be made reliably, since teacher ratings have generally been found to be inconsistent over time and between individuals.

The reliability of the teacher assessments was investigated in two ways in this study. First, different teachers assessed the same pupils using the 'listening with concentration and understanding' checklists, while other teachers assessed taped examples of pupils talking for the 'conveying meaning clearly and accurately through speech' checklist. Interclass correlation coefficients for the three abilities on the 'listening' checklist were 0.81, 0.87 and 0.83 respectively. For the four criteria on the 'conveying meaning' checklists, the interclass, correlation coefficients were 0.93, 0.96, 0.95 and 0.89. Second, teachers made independent assessments of their pupils using the 'acquiring information' checklist on two occasions separated by a four week interval. The correlation coefficients obtained on the ten criteria assessed by the teachers ranged from 0.58 to 0.96 with most of the values lying between 0.70 and 0.88. These correlation coefficients are relatively high and indicate that teachers were able to use the checklists reliably.

In general, the validity of ratings is accepted since it is difficult to test their validity statistically. As Thorndike and Hagen (1969) point out, 'The very fact that we have fallen back on ratings usually means that no better measure of the quality in question is available.'

Such is the case with some of the abilities on the checklists and all aspects of the aim: 'conveying meaning clearly and accurately through speech'. Although Thorndike and Hagen (1969) go on to say that 'there is usually nothing else against which we can test the ratings', in the teacher-based assessment programme some teacher assessments could be directly compared with appropriate structured activities, and the overall teacher rating could be correlated with achievement in the basic skills. This analysis enabled both the validity and the reliability of the teachers' ratings to be investigated.

The correlation coefficients given in Table 11.1 are statistically significant in all cases except the two elements of the creativity exercise. It will be seen that the teacher assessments correlate more highly with achievement on the basic skills than with the specific, structured activity, except in the case of arithmetic competence. Thus, either the structured activities did not measure the abilities or the teachers were not assessing according to the criteria. However, it has already been shown that the structured activities were reasonably valid measures of the abilities they were designed to assess so that the inference must be made that the teachers were not making valid assessments. Nevertheless, in small-scale studies carried out to investigate the reliability of teachers' assessments, they were able to reach agreement with each other and be consistent in their assessments. It is suggested, therefore, that other pupil characteristics besides achievement may contribute to the teachers' assessments of pupil performance.

Since performance on both basic skills and structured activities correlates significantly with teachers' assessments, it is necessary to take achievement into account before the significance of these other characteristics can be determined. Under experimental conditions, pupils receiving different treatments would have been matched on initial achievement so that the differences between groups could be investigated directly. The statistical technique of covariance analysis is used to control for those factors which cannot be kept constant except in experimental research. In this way, comparisons are possible between the assessments made by teachers outside an experimental setting when pupils are grouped by their age, sex, social class and type, even though initial performance on basic skills or structured activities may be different for each group of pupils.

Table 11.1 Correlation coefficients for teacher assessments with total achievement test score and structured activity score

Teacher assessments	Achievement test score	Structured activity score
Creativity		
originality	0.30*	−0.07
appropriateness	0.30*	0.14
Sequencing	0.40*	0.26*
Following instructions	0.40*	0.21*
Formulating questions	0.32*	0.17*
Comprehension	0.46*	0.17*
Arithmetical competence	0.44*	0.50*
Organization and presentation of data	0.41*	0.36*

* Statistically significant at or beyond the 1 per cent level.

An analysis of covariance was carried out on the assessments made for the two aims which correlated significantly with the structured activities. Although each ability on the checklist was assessed separately, the ratings have been aggregated in this analysis since the high intercorrelations suggest that the teachers did not discriminate between them.

Mean teacher assessment scores for pupils of different age, sex, social class and type were adjusted to take into account the different levels of achievement on basic skills and structured activities within each group. The resulting differences are expressed as residual assessments in Table 11.2. By referring to the first column of this table it is seen that the raw teacher assessment scores differ significantly for pupil age, social class and type, but not for pupil sex. It should not be assumed that these assessments reflect real differences in the performance of the groups, since even when pupil achievement in basic skills and structured activities is taken into account there is still a significantly different residual assessment. The teachers were therefore over- and under-estimating pupils relative to their actual performance.

Table 11.2   Analysis of covariance of teacher assessments by sex, age, social class and type of pupil with basic skills scores and structured activity scores as covariate

Pupil characteristics		Raw teacher assessment	Residual assessments		n
			Basic skills as covariate	Structured activities as covariate	
Sex	Boys	39.07	0.39	. 0.71	155
	Girls	38.35	−0.37	−0.68	165
Age*	9+	40.33	7.29	2.33	140
	10+	39.78	−1.22	0.73	87
	11+	35.40	−9.66	−4.20	93
Social class*					
	Non-manual	44.45	4.33	5.30	42
	Manual	35.00	−2.33	−2.9	79
Pupil type*					
Attention-seekers		37.58	1.36	−0.39	63
Intermittent workers		36.03	−2.92	−2.49	123
Solitary workers		40.75	0.65	1.53	89
Quiet collaborators		45.00	4.76	4.31	45

* Significant at or beyond the 1 per cent level

Younger pupils are over-rated whilst older pupils are under-rated relative to their actual performance. It should be remembered that each teacher assessed a particular group of pupils, generally of the same age, while the achievement tests and the structured activities were completed by the whole age range. The abilities of the younger pupils tended to be over-estimated by the teachers, since they compared an individual's performance with that of his peers rather than the whole age range. Similarly, older pupils were under-estimated since the teachers rated performance without reference to the poorer performance of younger pupils elsewhere.

Teachers over-estimated the performance of pupils whose parents were in non-manual occupations, and under-estimated pupils whose parents were in manual jobs. Previous work has suggested that middle-class pupils tend to do better than expected from their IQ scores, while working-class pupils tend to do worse than expected. This matter is discussed at length by Paul Croll in Chapter 9 of this book, but it is interesting to note here that the teachers reflect this trend in their assessments. It is suggested that middle-class pupils more closely match the stereotype of a 'good' pupil, and that teachers may often equate their social competence with success on tests and, therefore, over-estimate their cognitive abilities, while under-estimating those of pupils from working-class backgrounds for the same kind of reason. It should be noted, however, that the ORACLE teachers' interactions with pupils from different social classes did not differ in any way which was tapped by the observation instruments.

The influence of pupil behaviour on teacher assessments was investigated by considering the differences between the various ORACLE pupil types described by Galton et al. (1980 pp. 142 ff.). Quiet collaborators received the highest ratings, followed by solitary workers, attention-seekers and intermittent workers in that order. When achievement in basic skills was taken into account, attention-seekers came second to quiet collaborators; and the abilities of these two pupil types were over-estimated as were those of solitary workers, while the abilities of intermittent workers were under-estimated. It might be expected that teachers made their assessments in relation to the basic skills in the light of their interactions with individuals or groups of pupils. Quiet collaborators who had the highest contact time with the teachers were over-estimated to the greatest degree. Attention-seekers were second in terms of contact time and again their abilities were over-estimated. Solitary workers did not have as much contact with the teacher and were only slightly over-rated. Intermittent workers tended to avoid contact with the teacher and were under-estimated in relation to their performance on basic skills. It appears that contact with the teacher is equated with pupil success and results in an over-estimation of pupil ability.

When performance on structured activities was taken into account, residual assessments of the various pupil types differed from those obtained when basic skills were used as the covariate. In this new analysis, attention-seekers and intermittent workers were under-estimated. The structured activities had been devised to relate to aspects of independent study, and the teachers seem to have assumed that these pupils were ill equipped to pursue their work independently. Both quiet collaborators and solitary workers were over-estimated; their behaviour, quietly concentrating on the task in hand, was perceived as closely related to success in independent study.

Although teachers' assessments were related to various pupil characteristics, it seemed possible that certain features of particular teaching styles might also affect the bias of the teachers' assessments. An appropriate analysis to control for the relationship between teaching style and pupil type is a two-factor analysis of covariance. As before, the covariates were basic skills and structured activity scores, and the joint effects of pupil types and teaching styles on teachers' assessments were considered. The question of interaction between the variables was examined, but no significant interactions were found. Thus, in this analysis any differences between the assessments of different pupil types or of those by different teaching styles could be treated with confidence. The results are summarized in Table 11.3.

Table 11.3   Two-way analysis of covariance of teacher assessments by pupil type and teaching style

Pupil type (adjusted for teaching style)	Residual assessment (basic skills score as covariate)	Residual assessment (structured activity score as covariate)
Attention-seekers	3.03	0.34
Intermittent workers	−1.45	−1.82
Solitary workers	−0.79	0.61
Quiet collaborators	1.41	3.27
Significance	*	NS
Teaching style (adjusted for pupil type)		
Individual monitors	−7.66	−1.71
Class enquirers	7.60	4.28
Group instructors	7.64	2.64
Infrequent changers	3.74	2.18
Rotating changers	−0.51	−2.18
Habitual changers	−4.20	−2.68
Significance	**	**

* Significant at the 5 per cent level.
** Significant at and beyond the 1 per cent level.
NS Not significant.

This table shows that with basic skills scores as covariate, the significance of the pupil type effect was reduced and the degree of over- or under-estimation was altered when teaching style was taken into account. With structured activity scores as covariate the differences between assessments of the pupil types were no longer significant. Teaching style thus reduced the significance of the previous results in Table 11.2. When basic skills were used as covariate, attention-seekers and quiet collaborators were over-estimated, but solitary workers and intermittent workers were under-estimated in relation to their performance. The difference between teachers' assessments of these pupil types was previously explained in terms of the quantity of teacher interaction with individuals and in groups. Removing the influence of teaching style effectively accounted for the teacher-pupil interaction in groups so that the range and order of teacher assessments of

the pupil types in Table 11.3 matched the quantity of teacher
interactions with individual pupils. Attention-seekers and quiet
collaborators, who interacted with the teachers as individuals on
more occasions than the solitary workers and intermittent workers,
were over-estimated in relation to their performance on the basic
skills tests. In some way, their teachers were equating successful
pupil performance with the amount of interaction they had with
pupils as individuals.

In the second part of the analysis teachers were grouped by
style and pupil type controlled for, instead of grouping by pupil
type and controlling for teaching style.

From this analysis, two groups of teaching styles emerged,
those which over-estimated performance: class enquirers, group
instructors and infrequent changers, and those which under-
estimated performance: rotating changers, habitual changers and
individual monitors. The teachers in the first group have been
shown elsewhere to place greater emphasis on basic skills, and
this may have led to a devaluation of the skills associated with independent study and an expectation that pupils would acquire
them without specific teaching. The second group of teachers
placed more emphasis on individualization and independent study,
but under-estimated pupil performance in these areas. It should
be remembered that this group had difficulty in effectively organizing their classes and were not the most successful style in terms
of their pupils' performance on structured activities or basic
skills. Nevertheless, they used more independent work and were
more aware of the problems involved, so that their assessments
of their pupils were generally rather harsh.

In the second year of the study, the aim assessed by teachers
was concerned with 'everyday mathematics'. The group of teachers
was different from the previous year's group, and results cannot
be directly compared. Since pupils had completed a set of structured activities as well as a Richmond mathematics test, it was
possible to carry out a similar analysis of covariance to investigate
the differences between teachers' assessments of pupils of different age, sex, social class and type. Since no significant differences were obtained it can be concluded that teachers, besides
being more accurate in their assessments, were not taking into
account the pupil variables mentioned. They were able to assess
'everyday mathematics' more accurately because, in this area,
achievement can be readily quantified in terms of the number of
'right' answers. However, the correlations between teachers'
assessments and children's scores on Richmond Tests and structured activities (0.44 and 0.40 respectively) did suggest a source
of error. An analysis of covariance was again used to investigate
whether there were significant differences between assessments
when teachers were grouped by style. It was considered appropriate to use structured activity scores as the covariate as they
incorporated two factors: 'arithmetic competence' which was highly
correlated with the Richmond maths test and 'manipulation and
presentation of data' which was unique to the structured exercises.

The variation in pupil types within each teaching style was again taken into account, and the results are summarized in Table 11.4.

Table 11.4   Teachers' assessments by teaching style adjusted for pupil type in everyday mathematics

Teaching style	Residual assessment, significant at or beyond the 1 per cent level (structured activity score as covariate)
Individual monitors	1.90
Class enquirers	−0.13
Group instructors	−0.89
Infrequent changers	0.51
Other changers	0.36

Again two groups of teaching styles emerged. The teachers who over-estimated pupil performance in relation to the structured activities included the individual monitors, infrequent and other changers, and those who under-estimated pupil performance included class enquirers and group instructors. This supported the view that those teachers who had placed greater emphasis on particular skills, whether in mathematics or in independent work, tended to under-estimate their pupils' performance. For example, the class enquirers and group instructors under-estimated pupil performance in mathematics whilst placing greater emphasis on this area in class.

The results of the investigations into the validity of teachers' assessments are summarized as follows. The teachers' assessments on the checklists were highly intercorrelated and tended to relate to pupil performance on achievement tests rather than to the matched structured activities. Other factors such as the age, sex, social class and behaviour of pupils were related to teachers' assessments particularly with respect to pupils' independent work. However, some characteristics of teachers themselves also related to their assessments so that those who emphasized either basic skills or independent study tended to under-estimate the performance of pupils in areas which they valued more highly.

These results raise problems for both the researcher and the practising teacher. Both forms of assessment are to some extent unsatisfactory; the structured activities are valid measures but limited in their scope; and the teachers' ratings are not made on the basis of the specified criteria, since other pupil qualities affect them. Both procedures developed in this programme provided useful information on pupil performance, despite their limitations. They can, however, be improved. Further structured activities can be developed to tap abilities such as oral communication and practical mathematics, and programmes can be devised to help teachers make more valid assessments.

As a result of the work with teacher groups in this study, an in-service programme was devised to provide teachers with practical experience in developing their own checklists and alternative assessment strategies. For example, a number of teachers considered the assessment of topic work, approaching the question by considering their intentions that the child should have an immediate purpose in mind and be able to scan a reference book. A series of questions was devised, field-tested and rephrased until it was appropriate for on-the-spot assessment in the classroom.

The disadvantage of this method is obvious. It requires committed teachers who are prepared to give up their own time. However, it is necessary to reach the wider audience of teachers who are not able to spend time devising their own techniques but who wish to assess skills and abilities which are not tapped by traditional achievement tests. The use of structured activities can help in this situation. If they can be incorporated into the materials used in the classroom, teaching and assessment will come together and this will help teachers to provide activities appropriate to an individual or group of pupils.

The exercises on 'applying mathematical techniques to everyday situations' furnish an example of a useful procedure. The children were encouraged to do as much as they could, but to approach the teacher for help if necessary. Each problem had previously been broken down into its component stages. The teacher simply had to mark on a key what help had been given. Credit was given not just for arriving at the right answer but also for carrying out stages of the problem. This type of approach can be incorporated by teachers into their own materials and is amenable to wider application in curriculum development.

In this chapter an attempt has been made to describe a range of valid and reliable assessment techniques. The reliability of teachers' assessments has been considered as well as some possible factors influencing the valid application of checklists of ability. Strategies have been briefly described for improving the validity of teacher assessments, and the application of structured activities in the classroom.

Throughout the ORACLE research, teachers have referred to their limited expertise in the area of assessment. They have received little training in the range and application of formal and informal assessment techniques. It is, perhaps, only to be expected that the rapid expansion in the 1960s left teachers a little bewildered and confused. Particularly, they are uncertain of the ways to monitor and assess the performance of the pupils in their class.

Even in a time of economic restriction, those engaged in education - teachers, trainers and researchers - can take up this challenge using a variety of approaches. Some teachers are willing and able to develop their own techniques with help and consultation from those who have expertise in the field. Others, lacking resources of time and money, may require ready-made assessment

techniques related to classroom practice. Teachers are expected
to make judgements for a variety of purposes and help is needed
on a broad front. This can operate through initial and in-service
training and within curriculum development projects using such
procedures as have been briefly described here.

The consequence of inaction is likely to be the placing of the
responsibility for monitoring pupil performance with external
agencies. Meanwhile, teachers have knowledge, based on their
constant interactions with pupils, which can be used to provide
children with the opportunity to make the most of their potential.
This knowledge may be ignored if teachers do not acquire the
means to collect it systematically and share it with their colleagues.

12 EMPIRICAL RESEARCH AND EDUCATIONAL THEORY

Ruth Jonathan

During the past two decades there has been growing debate and criticism about the assumptions and methodology of educational research, and about the part its findings have to play in the generation and implementation of practical policies in education. The aim of this chapter is to examine and clarify some of these issues, though justice cannot be done to their complexity in the space available.

Education, considered not as a subject for academic study, but as a process which affects our lives, is a practical activity, like medicine or engineering. This is not to say that it does not need a theoretical basis - for only from such a basis can we give reasons for our actions - but its theory base will be very different from that of pure science. A scientific theory simply tells us what occurs under certain given conditions, and enables us to throw up and test hypotheses as to why it occurs. During its early stages, a science describes; when interrelated theories in a field are more fully articulated, they explain; they can never prescribe. It is thus axiomatic that no amount of improvement or advance in the fields of psychology, sociology, classroom studies or statistical analysis could, of itself, provide us with solutions to educational problems. There are inescapably three strands to theorizing about practical activities: an understanding of what states of affairs exist, the articulation of what causal factors bring them about, and our logically quite separate evaluation of these states of affairs. The descriptive and explanatory strands in our theorizing are the province of the factual; the prescriptive strand is strictly evaluative. Thus, practical activities demand a particularly complex kind of theorizing in which empirical enquiry and speculative thought both play an essential part.

This point, though simple, has to be made at the outset, since educational philosophers and other 'armchair theorists' have long protested that they alone cannot justify educational decisions. All too frequently this has mistakenly been taken to imply that somebody else can. It would seem prima facie unnecessary to demonstrate that a decision for action cannot issue solely from a value judgment, since educational philosophers assure us repeatedly that 'it is not possible to deduce statements about the aims of education or its curriculum from any philosophical statements' (O'Connor 1957). Since, however, such disclaimers have been taken to imply that there is some other single logical sphere from which decisions can be deduced, it is necessary to show that the disclaimer reflects not merely on the nature of philosophy, but

more importantly on the nature of decisions for action. Thus, in
order to claim that a value judgment alone could generate a decision for action, one would have to argue that the value judgment
was based on a moral principle considered to be ultimately good,
and that this moral principle ought therefore always to be applied.
However, knowledge of empirical data would still be a prerequisite
for the application of such a moral principle. It would be vacuous
to suggest that 'principle x should be applied regardless of circum-
stance' because the very notion of applying a principle implies a
consideration of its relationship to states of affairs in the
world.

Empirical theorists have typically been rather less modest in
issuing disclaimers about the substantive implications of their
findings, and assertions that 'every decision can be rationally
justified in the light of the evidence' (Christopherson 1964)
abound in the literature. Such an assertion is problematic to say
the least. Suppose that on the basis of evidence which shows that
children from the lower socio-economic groups underachieve in
education relative to those from higher socio-economic groups, a
decision is made to improve the educational chances of the former
group. Of course, this decision has been made 'in the light of the
evidence', in the sense that no empirical data may have been considered except those related to the correlation between socio-
economic grouping and educational achievement. None the less
a value judgment is also involved, since the assumption has been
made that it is not desirable that educational achievement be a
function of socio-economic status. Since in effect, most of us
share that assumption, this may seem like a quibble. But suppose
that further empirical research revealed that the most efficient
way to equalize achievement was to remove all children in handi-
capped groups from their natural parents; would we consider a
decision to act in this way to be rationally justified in the light of
the evidence or would we not seek further justification of a moral
kind by re-examining our objectives? Decisions cannot be fully
justified by factual evidence, since full justification implies strict
deduction, and no deductive conclusion can contain any element
that was not present in the premises of that deduction. Decisions
about what we ought to do can therefore never be justified solely
by considerations of how things are, or why they are, just as
they could never be rationally based solely on our desires about
how we would like the world to be.

All the above is intended to put into perspective the controversy which has raged for the past twenty years about whether
educational theory is worthy of the name. It is all too often assumed that unless theorizing in education can be shown to approximate to theorizing in pure science, it must be considered a rather
disreputable enterprise. It is a long time since Aristotle cautioned
that one of the hallmarks of an educated man is that he seeks, in
any area of enquiry, only so much precision as the nature of that
enquiry permits. None the less, the spectacular rise of science in
modern times has led to the popular acceptance that scientific

reasoning should be the paradigm of rational thought, and that
empirical enquiry itself holds the key to progress in the social
field. Thus E.L. Thorndike (1962) boldly claimed that
   the profession of teaching will improve (i) in proportion as its
   members direct their daily work by the scientific spirit and
   methods and (ii) in proportion as the leaders in education direct
   their choices of methods by the results of scientific investigation rather than by general opinion.
The assumption here seems to be that just as 'health' is better
served by scientific medicine than by the trial and error traditional remedies of the village wise woman, so 'education' will be
better served by the application of the results of scientific investigation than by the dictates of general opinion. Though both
medicine and education are practical activities in so far as empirical studies inform us as to the means by which desired ends can
best be achieved in all these fields, the analogy is poor. First,
whilst we might reasonably secure consensus on what constitutes
'good health', most educational debate is precisely over the question of what constitutes 'good education'. In a democratic society,
decisions about the latter - with information provided, to be sure,
by experts in both the empirical and normative spheres of reasoning - are indeed the province of 'general opinion'. Second it is
by no means clear that in a complex normative field of activity
like education, 'methods' (means) can be neatly separated from
'aims' (ends). The example above of the means by which we might
eliminate underachievement as a function of socio-economic status
serves to illustrate the complexity of this relation.
   Patently extravagant claims like Thorndike's have led some
educationalists to dismiss empirical studies in education rather
hastily. The truth of the matter is more complex than either side
in the debate allows; of course empirical studies cannot alone
provide the answers to our problems, but, equally obviously, no
such answers can be reached without descriptive and explanatory
data. The establishment of this point, though it clears the ground
a little, simply points the way to a further controversy. We have
established that in the field of education we should not expect
empirical enquiry to fulfil functions for which it was never intended: it is a further question whether, in this particular field,
it can fulfil the functions for which empirical studies are generally
intended.
   We began with the premiss that education is a practical activity,
like medicine or engineering, and it is frequently assumed that
we can apply the findings of empirical research to the activity of
education in a similar way to that in which advances in biochemistry or metallurgy are applied to medical or engineering problems.
The application of science to practical activities appears straightforward, provided only that one understands the nature of practical activities and the nature of science and boundaries of its
scope. Practical activities result from the making of decisions and
their subsequent implementation. Science describes and explains:
it tells us which of our decisions are feasible, and advises us on

the factual consequences of implementing them in a variety of
ways. Potential parents would consult a genetics expert to discover what the consequences, in genetic terms, of their bearing
a child might be. A community would consult a civil engineer to
discover what exactly would be involved, from the engineering
viewpoint, in constructing a bridge over a river, or building a
tunnel beneath it. Whether or not the couple wished to have a
child, or the community a particular type of river-crossing,
would depend upon many factors, on only a limited range of
which the empirical theorists are qualified to pronounce. The
empirical experts provide certain factual data, and those who
consult them go away and make decisions in the light of this data
and other relevant considerations. It is often suggested that the
problematic status of educational theory will be obviated if educational decisions are taken in exactly this way. Let philosophers
of education, politicians, practising teachers or the general public decide on their aims, then go to psychologists, sociologists or
educational researchers for the facts, in the light of which they
can come to informed decisions.

It is at this point that the analogy between education and medicine or engineering breaks down, and the second difficulty
appears. The 'facts' of psychology, sociology or other educational
research findings are simply not like the 'facts' of biochemistry
or metallurgy. The objects up for empirical investigation are not
cell structures, whether animate or inanimate, but individual
people and interacting groups and individuals. The research
enterprise, therefore, is not simply much more complex, but is
quite different in kind: there is no procedure by which a qualitative difference can be assimilated to a series of quantitative differences, and to suppose otherwise is to fall into reductionism.
Critics of empirical research in education have thus been quick to
point out that research into human behaviour in any sphere,
whether for purposes of explanation, or for the more limited function of simple description, will necessarily be fraught with implicit assumptions, uncontrollable variables and problems of replicability not associated with the aseptic procedures of pure
science. Their conclusion is that such a methodologically suspect
procedure should be abandoned as fundamentally flawed. Many
empirical workers in the field typically share the assumption of
their critics that approximation to the procedures of the natural
sciences is a standard measure of rational respectability. Thus
the case for the defence generally takes the form of protestations
of objectivity, assurances that sophisticated statistical analyses
will eliminate uncontrolled variables, and suggestions that large
samples will mitigate the problems of replicability.

Both parties to the debate need again to be reminded of Aristotle's warning that 'the man of education will seek exactness so
far in each subject as the nature of the thing admits' ('Nichomachean Ethics', I (iii) 4). Just as it is foolish to maintain that
educational theory is worthless unless it is strictly analogous to
scientific theory, so it is mistaken to suppose that empirical re-

search in the behavioural sciences must either conform to natural
science research, or be abandoned. That scientific certainty
would be desirable in all fields of enquiry is debatable: that it is
not to be had cannot be disputed, nor is this fact a function of
the state of development of the fields of study in question. Some
of the problems that beset the behavioural sciences *are* methodological. Researchers are restrained by limitations on experimen-
tation and problems of duplicating investigations to test the predictive power of explanations. It is quite conceivable that, as
these studies develop, sophisticated techniques of one kind or
another will overcome such problems. However, it can only lead
to confusion if it is assumed that progress in techniques of observation or analysis can overcome all the difficulties that differen-
tiate the behavioural from the natural sciences. It is not that we
don't yet have frameworks for description and explanation in the
behavioural field which reach the heights of precision we expect
of the natural sciences; it is rather that these could never possibly be had. The crucial differences between the two areas of
enquiry are not methodological, they are logical.

Looking at what happens in classrooms is not analogous to looking at what happens in test tubes, and to suggest that we should
proceed as if it were, since science is the norm of all our thinking,
is radically to misunderstand science. Science is the study of
matter, and matter is all that test tubes contain. Classrooms also
contain minds. When molecules collide, they do not do so either
unintentionally or deliberately; they simply collide. When people
interact, they do not simply interact; there is meaning in their
interaction. If we ask why molecules collide, we are asking for
reasons, all of which will be causal. If we ask why a particular
human interaction took place, some but not all of the reasons asked
for will be causal. There are reasons, which we can search for
and find, why molecules collide; but the molecules themselves do
not collide for a reason. There are reasons, similarly, why people
interact in given ways, but they themselves have reasons for
their actions which are not co-extensive with causal explanations.
If we observe a child's arm rise in a classroom, a scientific explanation for this can be offered in terms of electrical impulses in
the brain, neural messages to the muscles in the arm and bio-
chemical changes in these contracting muscles. This is an explanation of how and why his arm rises. To understand why he
raises his arm we can only speculate about shared social conven-
tions and their application to this particular incident. The answer
to 'why did his arm rise' can be fully given in physiological terms.
The answer to 'why did he raise his arm' is quite other: he is
requesting permission to visit the lavatory - but he might just be
fooling. Any description or explanation of an action which fails
to take account of its purposiveness is an incomplete description:
to suppose otherwise is to overlook the fundamental difference
between actions and happenings, between people and things.

Any idea that empirical research in education will gradually
evolve towards the heights of precision reached by pure scientific

research, provided its methodology is improved, is therefore a gross oversimplification. Science is the province of causal explanations: statements of the reasons for actions will only sometimes be identical with statements of the causes of actions. That the reasons we need to elucidate in an educational situation will be more logically complex than in the study of nature should not lead us, however, to abandon the search for reasons altogether. When crossing the Channel in a biplane it would be foolish to bale out on discovering that we are not travelling by jet. Though decisions cannot be based solely on evidence, we do not decry evidence, since, without it, no decision can be taken. Though the evidence thrown up by empirical research in the behavioural sciences will never have the explanatory or predictive powers of evidence in the natural sciences, it is the only evidence relevant to our enquiry. The most we can ask of evidence is that it be as sound as possible in the circumstances. The best sort of evidence on which to base educational decisions will therefore simply be the soundest that the nature of empirical research in education allows. The best possible empirical research in education would not be work which rested on no prior assumptions, controlled every variable and had a fully articulated explanatory and predictive framework. In the nature of the enterprise, this is not an ideal, but an impossibility – a contradiction in terms. Any work which claimed to exhibit these characteristics would be radically misconceived. The most exemplary empirical research in the field of education would simply be work in which prior assumptions were made explicit, uncontrolled variables were allowed for in alternative explanations, and the predictive limitations of the findings were clearly indicated.

In order to counter the charge that educational theory in general, and empirical research in the field in particular, should be abandoned as inevitably disreputable, since they are not 'truly scientific', I have made the following points. (1) That to expect empirical theorizing to generate, of itself, the rationale for policies is radically to misunderstand the nature of practical activities. (2) That the findings of empirical enquiry provide a necessary, though not a sufficient, condition for decision-making. (3) That the explanatory power of the empirical contribution to decision-making in education cannot mirror that of the natural sciences. (4) That this is not a methodological problem but follows from the nature of the study: education is an activity followed purposively by human beings. (5) That an acceptance of these points leads to the conclusion that research in education is incurably complex. (6) That the search for 'scientific' validity is misdirected if it is seen as an 'all or nothing' goal. Of course confusion is avoided if questions of fact and questions of value are separated wherever possible. But where assumption and inference inevitably colour the 'facts' at every turn, these turns should not be glossed over or avoided, for they cannot be; they must simply be clearly signposted. For we cannot refrain from action, and actions imply decisions. Rational decisions imply good reasons for our actions, and

empirical research in education is simply the search for reasons.
The best reasons we can get in any situation are simply the best
that are to be had. If these do not have the hard status of
science, that is simply a further fact which we must take into consideration.

With all the above in mind, I should like to look at some aspects
of the ORACLE research project undertaken at the Leicester University School of Education, 1975-80, under the direction of
Brian Simon and Maurice Galton. I wish to make references to the
research design and findings of this project, not to assess the
validity of that particular piece of research, but to highlight some
of the logical and methodological problems I take to be inherent in
work of that nature. I chose this particular piece of work for
three reasons: (1) I was involved in it myself at the 'fact-gathering'
level as a classroom observer from 1976 to 1978. (2) This paper is
published in conjunction with work related to the project. (3)
More importantly, the ORACLE project was a sophisticated and
sustained attempt to overcome the primary problem of empirical
research in education, namely subjectivity in initial judgments
and subsequent inferences. No doubt some of its minor shortcomings will be its own, and hence avoidable, but most of the
crucial problems can be shown to be inevitable accompaniments
of this genre of research.

The aim of the project 'Observational Research and Classroom
Learning Evaluation' was to carry out a process-product study of
children in approximately 100 primary school classrooms to ascertain what connections there might be between particular learning
situations and particular learning outcomes. The first step towards this aim was seen to be to find out what is actually going
on in classrooms. One way to do this might simply be to ask
teachers to report on their teaching aims and methods and their
pupils' response to them, checking the former against the opinion
of an outside observer – LEA adviser or educational researcher,
and the latter against standardized tests. This approach was followed by the Lancaster Study (Bennett 1976) and is open to the
objection that teachers' perceptions of their own performances
are highly subjective, that people may not always be doing what
they claim to be doing, or even what they believe they are doing,
and that outside assessment of the flavour of a classroom by an
adviser or researcher is equally idiosyncratic and lacking in a
basis for comparison with other subjective reports. Systematic
observational procedures involving time-sampling, such as those
employed by ORACLE, are an attempt to overcome this subjectivity
in initial judgments and to let the facts speak for themselves.

Since it is not possible to keep track of everything that is going
on in a classroom, some data must be selected for observation.
Under normal circumstances an observer in any situation picks
out those actions or events which he finds particularly striking,
interesting or relevant. Perceptions are thus inevitably coloured
by expectation, presuppositions, prejudices and past personal
experience. This is overcome in low-inference observation using

time sampling techniques by directing what the observer should focus his attention on at any given time, to the exclusion of all else. The ORACLE observers thus monitored in each classroom the activities of eight randomly preselected pupils and of the teacher, focusing on the teacher for approximately 20 minutes and each pupil for approximately 5 minutes per hour, by coding on a specially prepared individual record sheet precisely what the pupil or teacher under observation was doing at the exact time of a prerecorded time signal which was fed into the observer's ear every 25 seconds from a portable cassette tape-recorder. The length of time the observer should focus on an individual was thus determined in advance, which individual should be the focus at any given time was a function of a predetermined arbitrary order, and what should be recorded at each time signal was a function, therefore, not of the observer's personal idiosyncracies, but of the mutually discrete categories on the prepared coding sheet. Does such a procedure overcome the problem of observer-subjectivity, and if so at what cost?

In one sense, the 'facts' or data that the observer collects in this way are free of subjective bias, but it is a further question whether they are therefore uncoloured by assumptions and presuppositions. To the extent to which a time-sampling observer is properly trained in the use of the coding instrument, and following the rules for its use in good faith, his personal idiosyncracies will not be reflected in the raw data of the research. Provided that the instructions for coding happenings and observable behaviour on the coding instrument are understood and followed, observer agreement on situations which are similar in relevant respects is axiomatic. The definition of what these relevant respects are to be, however, is co-extensive with the discrete categories which represent the only code in which the observer can report what he sees. Since these categories are dependent upon the priorities, assumptions and interests of the research designers, the facts collected by systematic observation are as much personal constructs as any other 'facts' that people 'observe'. Though this method of observation overcomes many of the problems associated with subjective accounts, it does not provide us with data uncoloured by assumptions. Since what we observe is a function of what we look for and at, in such a situation observations are not coloured by the differing observers' personalities, for the observers are not really observing at all. They are simply acting as the eyes and ears of the research designers, and therefore the assumptions implicit in the data collected will be those of the research designers, as reflected in the construction of the coding instruments, and instructions for their use.

The first and major advantage of data collected in this way is that an event recorded at place A and time X by observer M is strictly comparable with an event recorded at place B and time Y by observer N, since all such events will be judged according to criteria laid down by research designer R at a time and place unrelated to any specific event. We therefore have comparability in data reportage uninfluenced by differing personalities or by the changes in criteria and mood which would inevitably colour the reportage of a single individual over a period of time. Thus random time-sampling techniques ensure standard criteria in observation, the lack of which standard criteria is the primary methodological weakness of subjective accounts. But the more fundamental problem of subjectivity, namely that we can only see in any given situation a combination of the possibilities of which we are aware, is as much a central feature of this type of procedure as it is of more obviously idiosyncratic reportage.

Describing a situation, whether in words or in the code of a series of ticks in category boxes, is a matter of deciding what are relevant respects for judging that situation. Just as a description in words will depend on the possibilities of which the writer is aware, so a coded description in ticks will be a function of what categories exist, and of what the rules are for picking out certain ones to the exclusion of others. Thus some coding instruments will have more explanatory power than others, just as some languages are more capable than others of reflecting fine conceptual discriminations. In time-sampling the observer's task is not to make his own discriminations, but to reflect faithfully on the coding schedule the discrimination previously made by the research designers. But, by definition, a pre-arranged coding schedule can pick up in the classroom only those activities which it is expecting to find, and can record them as exhibiting only those characteristics which are built in to their definition. No refinement in the recording instrument can overcome this fundamental problem, since all one could say about an event not catered for in the definition of categories is that it is anomalous - its characteristics, though not its occurrence, go unrecorded.

It might be countered that if a significant number of events fell into this 'unrecorded anomaly' category, researchers would know that something was going wrong, and amend the research design. Aside from the methodological problem that if the design were changed in the course of research, comparability with previously collected data would be lost, there is a more fundamental reason why this state of affairs cannot in fact occur. An observer would only ascribe large numbers of events to the 'unrecorded' category if he ceased to abide by the rules of the game, since a set of discrete categories which aims to cover all significant eventualities must define those categories in terms of each other. Thus if the coding schedule allows fourteen possible ways, A - N, of describing the pupils' activity, category B will be partially defined as not (C - N)ing, category L as not (A - K)ing, and so on.

Thus the establishment of standard criteria for judging and reporting events, which characterizes low-inference, observational procedures involving time-sampling, ensures strict comparability over a large sample of observations and overcomes one of the primary problems of subjectivity in reportage. Though researchers in the field are aware that comparability is thus achieved only through shared subjective agreements between research designers and classroom observers, the layman must be reminded that data collected in this way can be evaluated only in terms of these articulated agreements. It must not be assumed that when individual subjective impressions are not allowed to colour the data, 'the facts speak for themselves' somehow, for what is to count as a relevant fact, is predetermined. One cannot express in a language any concepts for whose utterance that language does not allow: a pre-arranged coding schedule is a very precise language, whose precision is bought at the expense of its vocabulary. A minute vocabulary, precisely defined, allows maximum mutual understanding, but only within the close limits of articulated shared agreements.

In a technical sense, of course, these are problems inherent in any taxonomic exercise; that we call dolphins mammals and not fish is a function of a taxonomy which uses methods of reproduction, not habitat, as its defining characteristic. 'Looking at the facts' does not reveal that dolphins have a similarity to cats which obviously overrides their differing similarities to tunny fish. We simply agree in this case on the convention by which we choose to group living creatures. Debate over the taxonomy would be debate only over its descriptive convenience, since it is established only for purposes of description. The same is not true of a taxonomy developed for the purposes of educational research. In setting up categories to identify the activities of children in classrooms we are concerned with observable behaviours, some of which are assumed to be representative also of mental activity, and this apparently descriptive exercise has strong normative implications. For purposes of simple description we could define 'working', 'wasting time', 'disrupting', etc., in a particular way, and simply refer enquirers to the original definition to ensure that they did not draw false inferences from the data. But educational research is not produced to enlighten educational researchers in the way that biological taxonomies are established for the convenience of biologists. It is undertaken to provide evidential backing for the formation and implementation of practical policies by teachers, administrators and politicians. Unless the shared subjectivity of researchers, which defines and ascribes behaviour to the category 'working', exactly mirrors the general consensus of what counts in a pupil as 'working', only misunderstanding can result from reportage culled from the agreed taxonomy about how much pupils 'work' in particular types of situation.

Since completely shared agreement on what counts as 'working' is not to be had in everyday terms, this problem can be overcome as far as is humanly possible by extreme caution and precision in the presentation of research findings. Comments on 'how much' children 'work' must be accompanied by reminders of what activities are being referred to as work in that particular context. Exactitude can be bought at the price of a certain amount of pedantry; there is a point beyond which accessibility of findings leads to distortion and misunderstanding. This is no criticism of the research in question: if we want scientific precision in educational research, we cannot expect it to be presented without those qualifying clauses which characterize accurate reportage.

Presentation of findings is a methodological problem, and as such is capable of solution, but it points the way to a further logical problem which cannot be resolved by refinements within the methodology. What counts as 'working' or 'wasting time' is a qualitative judgment about an activity which takes place purposively over a period of time: time-sampling is a quantitative procedure which categorizes what is actually happening at an instant in time. Any strictly monitored version of my activity as I write this paper would necessarily distort events if only my observable actions were taken into account. At any given moment I may be making coffee, lighting a cigarette or gazing out of the window – none the less I have been working all day, for there is more to writing this paper than wielding a pen. In the same way, a child who is doodling while the teacher is talking may well be attending to her words more closely than another child who is gazing in her direction, hands folded. There is no way, by observation, that the child's degree of attention can be assessed or recorded, since an observer who allowed inferences about the child's supposed mental activity to override prior definitions of its observable features, would be departing from the agreed criteria, and negating the methodological advantages of the code.

This is a serious problem at the fundamental stage of data collection; further logical problems become apparent when we manipulate the data to generate research findings. Activities take place over time; time-sampling records what is taking place at a given instant. At a theoretical level this procedure assumes that the whole is merely the sum of its parts, irrespective of how these parts are arranged to make up the whole. In practice the assumption is that inherently qualitative behaviour can be accurately reflected by the aggregation of a series of discrete quantitative measurements. Given the difficulty already alluded to that 'behaviour' is necessarily characterized by intention in so far as it is an action not a happening, it must be inferred to have many components, some of which are not observable, and therefore not even candidates for quantification. Thus a characterization of the whole of behaviour in terms of its observable parts is incomplete in principle. Incompleteness in descriptions of observed behaviour is an inescapable feature of any method of observation, and limits the validity of inferences drawn from such descriptions. However, observation by random time-sampling also distorts this already incomplete description, in two specific ways.

One of the findings of the ORACLE project which may surprise teachers until they are familiarized with the research design is the very small proportion of time which children spend 'partially working and partially distracted'. This finding is a function of the time-sampling procedure. Though the coding schedule allows for such behaviour, having a category defined precisely thus, observers must judge at the instant of any given time-signal whether a child is working, distracted from work or 'partially

working and partially distracted'. Unless the child is doing two
observable thing simultaneously at that instant, say working out
a sum on paper and talking about a football result, he will not be
classified as partially engaged on his work. If, at the instant of
the time-signal, he is writing a figure and not speaking, he is
seen to be working; if he is saying 'Arsenal two . . .' and not
writing, he is seen to be distracted. It will be argued that when
the whole interaction is coded over a period of 5 minutes, this
problem resolves itself, since the child who is altnerately working
and alternately distracted from work can be interpreted as working desultorily over the whole period. In the aggregated conclusion, however, there is no way in which 5 minutes of desultory
engagement can be contradistinguished from 2.5 minutes of conversation, and 2.5 minutes of unrelated talk.

Fragmentation and subsequent aggregation of observable behaviour simply does not offer the overall description of actions
which appears to emerge, and a thorough understanding of the
implications of time sampling is essential to interpret correctly
the finding that for three-fifths of all observation time the 'typical' pupil is task-oriented, just as an understanding of averag-
ing procedure is essential to interpet the statement that in the
year X the average life expectancy was forty years. With no
understanding of how aggregation distorts events located over a
period of time, the layman might assume that pupils typically
worked for three-fifths of their time in the classroom, and were
otherwise engaged for two-fifths. The facts in both cases are
much more complex than the conclusions indicate. If a pupil is
observed every 25 seconds, and is alternately looking at his work
without speaking, or fighting over a ruler with his neighbour, he
will appear on aggregate to be working for half the time, though
he is probably not 'getting on with his work', in terms that a layman understands, at all. Moreover, the amount of time perceived
to be task-oriented will rise in inverse proportion to the complexity of the task. A child discussing the football results whilst putting a colour wash on a wall poster, if he continues to wield the
brush, is task-oriented; a child discussing the football results
while working out a sum is distracted from his task. Thus a statement about how much of a child's time is task-oriented may reflect
either on the child's own activity or on the nature of the task itself. In the raw data, where the nature of the task is recorded,
this is allowed for: in generalizations to children's activity as a
whole, the distinction is lost.

The problems of fragmentation become acute when conversation
is the focus of enquiry, since conversation involves more than
active speech and obvious listening. The findings of this project
show children to spend one-fifth of their classroom time talking,
and the surprising smallness of this finding depends partially
upon the statistical use made of the raw data. Monitored over a
5 minute period, a child in a group of four children may be actually speaking, or listening with all other activity suspended, for
only two out of the possible ten time-signals. But a desultory

conversation between the four children, during which work is repeatedly glanced back to, may well be taking place throughout
the period. The other time-signals will probably be coded as routine or task-oriented since categories, as previously stated, are
necessarily defined in terms of each other.

When a series of many such interactions are aggregated to give
a picture of the typical child, the opportunities for misunderstanding are multiplied. An everyday example may serve to illuminate
this. Suppose that after time-sampling the conversational habits
of my family, it is suggested that the typical family member is
engaged in conversation for two-fifths of his time. This tells me
very little about the conversational habits of the family unless
many other variables are at my disposal. I need first to know how
many of us there 'typically' are. If there are two of us, it is relatively simple: each of us spends all of his time actively or pas-
sively in the conversation. If there are five of us, the situation
is more complex: do we all converse two-fifths of the time, or
does the 'typical' member engage one or several of us simultaneously for this period, or two of us separately for one-fifth of
each of our time, or even four of us individually for one-tenth?
Aside from this variable, which can be specified and accounted
for in the initial data, but which is lost in generalization, how
is the conversation distributed, not between individuals, but
through time? Is there a qualitative difference between a 5-hour
period characterized by pauses when no one is obviously speaking
or listening to speech, and the same period made up of 3 hours
of silence and 2 hours of heated debate? Distinctions of this type,
though not of this magnitude, are blurred in generalizations
from the original data, but this blurring is also an inherent
feature in the principle of time-sampling, even at the initial stage
of data collection. The findings of time-sampling generalize from
a series of individual events: the procedures of time-sampling
also entail that the 'events' themselves are generalizations - statistical constructs produced by aggregation from a series of dis-
continuous observations.

These points, about the reflection in research findings of the
aseptic procedure of systematic observation by random time-
sampling, should serve to throw some light on the debate sur-
rounding the validity of such research. To evaluate the first criticism of educational research - that it cannot have the objectivity
of science - demands a brief clarification of what scientific objectivity consists in. If a particular gas is oxygen, that is a fact,
not because 'the facts speak for themselves' in science but because all interested parties have agreed upon the defining characteristics that are relevant to picking out one gas from others and
labelling it. The label 'oxygen' is simply a convenient shorthand
for that particular set of defining characteristics. In the same
way, a description of the observable behaviour of children in
classrooms can be expressed in terms of a given set of specified
criteria which allocate actions to categories and thus label them,
provided that all interested parties have agreed upon the defining

characteristics that are relevant to each category. In both science and educational research, objectivity is little more than the outcome of shared subjective agreement and to this degree the procedures of both may be objective. Beyond the confines of the research itself, the analogy breaks down.

The findings of science are destined for scientists – parties to the shared agreements of the activity in question by definition. The findings of educational research are destined for teachers, politicians and administrators who do not necessarily share the taxonomic agreements of researchers. However valid or otherwise inferences from research data may be, they will be quite irrelevant or actively misleading when the findings are reviewed by the layman whose conception of 'working', 'wasting time' or 'talking' differs significantly from the agreed definitions of researchers. Thus research methodology cannot be merely a means to research findings, but must appear as an integral part of those findings. No doubt educationalists would like to read the findings of research in everyday language, free from tedious references to methodology. Such a method of presentation must misrepresent and distort their import. Scientific findings cease to be valid when they cease to be science; the findings of educational research cease to be valid when they are removed from the context of the research design which gives them meaning. Science escapes confusion in description or explanation by using its own vocabulary, understood by fellow initiates. When educational research describes or explains it employs concepts like 'working', 'talking' or 'wasting time' which have their own meanings in ordinary language. In so far as these are used in a special and restricted sense in the research, its findings are clear. Confusion follows from extrapolating from the special to the everyday meaning of such concepts. Everyday meanings are more complex, fluid and varied than the researcher's taxonomy of measurable behaviour implies, since in everyday terms 'working' in the cognitive sense is characterized by many non-observable processes, and this mismatch in conceptualization will encourage invalid inference unless its dangers are stressed in the findings. Pointing out the mismatch is the most researchers can do, since they logically cannot remove it. One can measure only what is measurable, and in no field of enquiry is this co-extensive with what the lay person perceives as relevant.

Similarly, a researcher observing behaviour, if he refrains from guessing about its intention, can observe only its outward characteristics. If the activity in question, say 'getting on with one's work', has qualitative implications which are not outwardly manifested, these will simply be overlooked. If enquirers interpret statements about 'how much time a pupil spends engaged upon his task' as if they were equivalent to statements about 'how much the pupil is working', quite false inferences might be drawn from the data. If readers of findings obtained from quantitative measurements are reminded of how they have been obtained, their validity within their own terms of reference will be protected. It will also be clear which items of information in the findings most accurately reflect everyday reality. Since some types of activity are more open to measurement than others, quantitative information will more nearly tell the whole story about such activities. Thus we can measure how much time children spend waiting for the teacher, since we can see when they are waiting, and we can add up each incidence of waiting to get a meaningful proportion of their total time. It is therefore possible to paint a picture of how different styles of classroom management affect the proportion of the average child's total time spent waiting for the teacher.

It is much harder to paint a reasonably accurate picture about 'working-time', since 'working' is a qualitative concept, not all of whose characteristics are observable, and an aggregate of separate incidences of working leaves unanswered just those questions about the pattern and quality of work activity which are of probably greatest interest to educators. To avoid mistaken extrapolation from research findings, it must be stressed that if the original data are quantitative, they can only be looked to for answers to quantitative questions. There may be educational situations in which it is most pertinent to know how much of the typical pupil's total time is spent not visibly engaged on anything other than his allotted task. If proportions of time thus spent can be shown to correlate with measurable learning outcomes, inferences of a causal nature could be drawn between these two factors, if all other variables - personality, innate ability, environmental factors, etc. - could be kept either constant or measurable. We do not of course cease to search for reasons where measurement breaks down - we may have good reasons to suppose that something is the case. But it is the hallmark of good reasoning to point out where inferences are based on measurable correlations or causes, and where they are based, as they must sometimes be in an imperfect state of knowledge, on good grounds for supposition.

To ask that empirical research in education should answer all the questions, even those of a strictly factual nature, posed by educational problems is to seek the impossible. Hunches, intuition and reports of personal experience give us only clues to how differing children acquire particular abilities and dispositions in a variety of circumstances. The alternative approach is to dissect and measure the learning situation. Such a procedure gives us real information about what is measurable, and further clues about the measurable accompaniments of abilities and dispositions which we can judge only qualitatively in a quite different way. To reject this information on the grounds that it is only part of the story would be as misguided as to assume conversely that it constituted the whole story.

13 ORACLE: its implications for teacher training

Maurice Galton and
Brian Simon

INTRODUCTION

The significance of the ORACLE research for teacher training
lies in its focus on the classroom, and specifically on teachers'
strategies and tactics and on the interaction processes which go
on in the classroom. Thus the focus of interest is strictly on what
may be called pedagogical issues – issues which, surprisingly,
have often been neglected in teacher training over the last few
decades.

This ties in with the increased concern in colleges and universities with the professional aspects of training. Over the last few
years there has been a distinct move away from what is called the
'concurrent' model (whereby professional training for class teaching is integrated diffusely with the students' general education)
to the 'consecutive' model, whereby the students' professional
education takes place at a separate time, and is distinct from the
students' more general education. This move has taken root as a
result of the introduction, and now full adoption, of the BEd, together with the phasing out of the Certificate. As a result of this
shift, which is widespread, colleges (and polytechnics) are beginning to focus on the professional aspects of training for a full
year, so that their approach begins to approximate to what has
long been the system on postgraduate teacher education courses
at universities.

This shift means that a full year is given in teacher education
both to school practice and to related professional studies.
Recently there has been a further shift within the organization
of the colleges,which is bringing the English colleges closer to
the pattern which has long obtained in the Scottish colleges of
education. This is the organization of a new department, parallel
with the education studies department, specifically concerned
with professional training, the induction of the student into the
actual practice of teaching. It is our contention that the ORACLE
findings are of particular concern to such departments in the
colleges.

Previously the induction of the student to the practice of teaching was regarded as largely the responsibility of education departments, assisted by the subject departments. This departmen-
talized structure of colleges was a product of the enormously rapid
expansion of the colleges in the 1960s. In the situation that developed, responsibility for the induction of students into teaching
was normally shared between the subject departments (all students

studied one or more usually two main subjects as part of their
personal education) and the education department. The former,
often largely staffed by ex-grammar school teachers, were at a
disadvantage in assisting their students to prepare for primary
school teaching. The latter, the education departments, under
the influence of the move towards more rigorous studies in education related to the establishment of the BEd degree, now began
(in the late 1960s) to focus major attention on the theoretical
study of education, in particular on the history, sociology, psychology and philosophy of education. In this sense the focus
tended to move away from concern with the actual practice of
classroom teaching.

Supervision of the student when on teaching practice, though
normally the responsibility of the education department, was
shared with members of staff of the main subject departments.
This, of course, had evident advantages in that advice from lecturers with varied experience was available. Nevertheless the net
result, as brought out in the Area Training Organization enquiries of the early 1970s, was that actual responsibility for the student teacher's classroom practice tended to fall between two
stools, neither the education department on the one hand nor the
subject departments on the other being directly concerned with
classroom practice. These conditions may, perhaps, to some extent account for the widespread criticism of the products of the
colleges which developed in the early 1970s.

It is true that, alongside specialists in the basic disciplines
related to education (for instance, history and psychology), education departments included staff members with special expertise
in such matters as the teaching of reading and mathematics, both
of which subjects figure largely in the primary school in that
every teacher spends a considerable amount of her time in the
areas of numeracy and literacy. Special attention has undoubtedly been given to these areas in the colleges in the past and still
is, but each of these has tended to be treated as a specialist
activity, so that no one has had specific responsibility for inducting students into overall procedures relevant to classroom teaching and management. This has been the weak link in the teacher
training process in the colleges as they have developed over the
last two decades.

The difficulties are compounded, to some extent, by the dual
responsibility of colleges to produce both primary and secondary
school teachers. While the bulk of the students, probably about
80 per cent, have been prepared for primary teaching, a minority
have also been prepared for secondary teaching, and there has
been a natural tendency to devote special attention to the latter,
if only for status and prestige purposes.

The proportion of primary and secondary students, of course,
has varied between colleges. Also the colleges have been well
aware of the problem here, and have tended to develop specific
programmes within education departments for students concentrating on either primary or secondary teaching (and middle school

teaching more recently). However, the fact remains that teaching
in the primary sector, where class teaching is the rule (in the
sense that the individual teacher is still normally responsible for
all subject areas), differs qualitatively from the job of the secondary teacher who is normally a specialist in one, or at the most,
two subjects. For this reason the training of primary school
teachers presents different problems from those of secondary
teachers - in particular in relation to classroom procedures and
management.

In our view, the recent shift towards the development of professional studies departments (whatever they may be called) is
important and positive, in that it provides the conditions whereby
the focus on teaching becomes a primary centre of concern in the
professional year. There is, of course, a problem in the separa-
tion of theoretical studies in 'education departments', from practical studies in 'professional studies departments', and ideally
there must be a close relationship between the work of the two
departments. But the formation of professional studies departments at least gives the conditions where greater emphasis can be
put on this side of the work.

It has been strongly urged, for instance by the Universities
Council for the Education of Teachers Working Party's Report on
teacher education for secondary schools, that teacher trainers
need to know in as specific detail as possible what is actually de-
manded of the beginning teacher in terms of his activities and responsibilities. It is our contention that the ORACLE findings can
be of considerable assistance here. Also that these findings, in
that they present and analyse differing teaching 'styles' as actually used by primary teachers, provide a basis for the serious
discussion and analysis of the very complex problems involved in
teaching primary classes of the sizes now existing.

ISSUES ARISING FROM THE 'ORACLE' FINDINGS

In the first place, the ORACLE findings indicate that forms of
classroom organization and consequent teacher-pupil and pupil-
pupil interaction patterns are important in terms of educational
outcomes. Thus certain of the teaching styles identified have been
shown to be more effective than others on the criteria used in the
study. Previous studies have sought to show that one method is
superior to all others. The assumption behind the ORACLE study
is that all teaching methods have something to be said for them
but that circumstances are often such that they prevent the
teacher from fulfilling the potential of the particular approach
used. It is on these matters, it is suggested, that the students'
attention should be directed.

The ORACLE evidence underlines the extreme complexity of the
primary school classroom, a dynamic organization requiring both
intensive thought and the development of a variety of skills on
the part of the teacher. Of particular significance here are the

findings concerning widespread reliance on individualization of
the teaching/learning process. This issue is discussed in some detail in 'Inside the Primary Classroom', where it was shown that
individualization was the most popular method used by teachers
across all styles, and in the case of one style, 'individual monitors',
almost the only method used. Given the existing average size of
primary classes - thirty pupils - it is not surprising that the
dominant mode of teacher-pupil interactions is didactic. The promotion of discovery or enquiry, the stimulation of pupils to thought
and creativity, seem to be minimized in this situation. This must
surely be a matter of concern.

A second main finding concerns what was found to be a minimal
use of collaborative group work on the part of pupil groups by
teachers. While it was found that pupils are normally seated in
groups around tables or desks, the work on which the pupils
were engaged remained overwhelmingly individualized. In spite,
then, of all the rhetoric in the literature, for instance, in the
Plowden Report, about the importance of collaborative group work,
in the ORACLE sample of over 100 teachers, few actually operated
this system. Those teachers who were clustered together under
the style entitled 'group instructors' were also primarily didactic
in their interactions with their groups. Few 'higher order' questions or statements were made to the groups as a whole, and, although in the second year of the study the proportion of group
instructors increased substantially, while the proportion of higher
order questions also marginally increased, the picture overall
revealed a situation where collaborative group work of the kind
emphasized by Plowden was minimally represented. This also
seems to raise important questions which will again be referred
to later.

Third, the paradoxical finding was made that probing and stimulating questions and statements of the 'higher order' kind were
maximized by teachers of whatever style in the class-teaching
situation. The Plowden Committee, perhaps rightly, argued for a
reduction in the amount of class teaching going on in primary
school classrooms. Yet it seems that it is only in this situation,
at present, that teachers generally promote enquiry-type thinking,
and seek to stimulate their pupils by probing questioning and
similar techniques.

The analysis of successful teaching in 'Progress and Performance
in the Primary Classroom' indicates that the use of challenging
questioning techniques is an important ingredient of such an
effective teacher's style. When such questioning is carried out
during class teaching, however, there is always a danger that
some pupils will be left out of the discussion. A crucial issue,
therefore, is how to promote the use of such questioning techniques within settings other than class teaching, involving fewer
pupils.

Although many other issues arise from the ORACLE findings,
these three points, (i) the nature of individualization, (ii) the
scope and character of group work, and (iii) the place and role

of class teaching, seem to be of primary importance. The behaviour of both teachers and pupils in the classroom will necessarily be determined (to some extent at least) by the teacher's decisions both concerning her overall strategy, and concerning her tactics - that is, the minute by minute interactional process that takes place in the classroom. Six different styles were identified in the ORACLE research, each derived from analysis of interactional data obtained through systematic observation. These set out a wide variety of alternative strategies and tactics available to the teacher, but each of these has been shown to have certain definite implications having an educational significance. It is our contention that serious consideration needs to be given by teacher trainers and their students to the implications of these differing styles, so that a more penetrating awareness can be developed of the significance of the teacher's decisions in these respects.

'In Progress and Performance in the Primary Classroom', (Chapter 11), we have already made the suggestion that, if the stimulating character of teacher-pupil interactions is to be enhanced, there must be a move away from individualization as the main approach towards a combination of collaborative group work and class teaching, using individualization mainly as a technique for monitoring individual pupils' progress. It is our view that total individualization is impractical both from a theoretical and practical point of view; theoretically, because, if Piaget's views are taken seriously, the teacher should monitor individual pupils' development in detail across a variety of subject areas and there simply is neither the time nor the resources to carry this through effectively; and in practice, because with an average of thirty pupils in the classroom, individualization means that the amount of time the teacher can devote to each individual pupil is severely circumscribed (an average of 2 minutes in every hour must be the absolute maximum).

If, on the other hand, the technique of collaborative group work can be extended, this would allow the teacher more time to focus her attention on each of the four to six groups in the classroom, and thus to engage in extended educational interactions more effectively with members of the class as a whole. If this is combined with some class teaching, which also allows this possibility, the general level of stimulation, of enquiry and discovery in the classroom could be raised.

It is important in this respect to analyse why teachers in fact do not appear to use collaborative group work in primary classrooms today, and conversely to develop deliberately the necessary skills both in the teachers (and students preparing as teachers), and among the pupils. This matter is discussed to some extent in Sarah Tann's chapter in this volume, but clearly teachers need a great deal more help in the development of this work than they have been given in the past - they also need the resources which must be carefully structured and developed. Further, the necessary skills both cognitive and social, need consciously to be developed in the pupils. In our analysis of pupil-pupil interaction within the seated groups in the ORACLE sample certain striking features have emerged, particularly relating to the relative lack of interactional contacts between members of the opposite sex. The whole question of the principles underlying the composition of groups in primary classrooms is clearly an important one, to which, we suggest, attention also needs to be devoted. Certainly, further research needs to be carried out in this field.

PUPIL TYPES AND TEACHING STYLES

The ORACLE research collected data derived from the observation of a sample of eight pupils in each classroom. These were selected in such a way as to provide a representative sample both in terms of achievement and sex. From the analysis of this data it was possible to identify four distinct types of pupil and it is clear that the proportions of different types in each class is largely dependent on the teacher's style. Attention-seekers, for example, tend to flourish in classes of the infrequent changers who spend almost 90 per cent of the time in normal lesson sessions interacting with their pupils. Intermittent workers, on the other hand, who tend to avoid the teacher's attention and chatter to each other when her back is turned, are more usually found in classes where individualization of the learning process is the main organizational strategy. Solitary workers, who are model pupils (if the aim of the teacher is to have a well-ordered, quiet classroom), are found mostly in classes where the teacher stands in the front and interacts with all the pupils, as is more often found at secondary level. The last pupil type, the quiet collaborators, are very similar to the solitary workers in that, left to themselves, they are reluctant to engage in conversation with other pupils preferring to concentrate on their work. They differ from the former type, however, in that whereas solitary workers receive most of their share of teacher attention as part of a class audience the quiet collaborators receive theirs as part of a group. Quiet collaborators are therefore found mainly in the classes of the group instructors and their identification within the pupil typology provides striking confirmation of the earlier assertion that the Plowden prescription of collaborative learning in groups is not a widely implemented strategy within the primary classroom of today. These pupils, although they share materials, rarely converse about their work with other pupils either when the teacher is present or when she is engaged elsewhere in the class.
 Given these varied patterns of pupil behaviour and the fact that it is heavily influenced by teaching style, it is of interest to enquire what takes place when particular types of pupils transfer to teachers using a different style, as many of the ORACLE sample did in the second year of the study. The results show that attention-seekers and intermittent workers are more likely to change type than are solitary workers and quiet collaborators. When, for example, attention-seekers move to a teaching style

which does not single out as many pupils as possible for attention, only 14.3 per cent of children remain in the same type. In a similar manner when intermittent workers are taught by teachers using a style different from the individual monitors, only 26 per cent continue to sustain the high level of distraction characteristics of this type. Solitary workers and quiet collaborators on the other hand appear much more stable in their behaviour from year to year. Nearly 60 per cent of pupils who belong to these types in the first year continue to do so even when they are no longer in classes taught by a teacher using the class enquirer or group instructor style.

The presence of a large proportion of solitary workers and quiet collaborators would appear to be an essential requirement for the successful management of the relatively large-sized classes which exist in primary schools today. Without the presence of these pupils, who need the minimum of help and attention, it would be impossible for the teacher to cope with the children with special needs. Yet it must be a source of concern that so many children in primary classrooms spend the greater part of their days without the stimulus of conversation either with the teacher or with fellow pupils.

Given the fact that teachers are rarely seen teaching by others, judgments about the effectiveness of a new recruit to the staff room can be made only superficially by the head, for example, observing that when he passes by in the corridor the children are working conscientiously with the minimum of noise and movement. If in addition to this outward show of control there are regular wall displays and at the end of the year most of the children are above-average for their age on the reading test, the young teacher may feel that she has done all that is required of her. In this situation the new teacher therefore comes under considerable pressure to increase the number of solitary workers in her class.

But the ORACLE findings demonstrate that such results are often achieved at the expense of providing a stimulating and challenging learning environment for the pupils. The study shows that children spent a considerable proportion of time writing and completing mathematical worksheets - perhaps because this was the easiest way for the teacher to keep the pupils fully occupied and so present the outsider with the image of a business-like atmosphere; but there is abundant evidence from the study that such practices fail to capitalize on the children's full potential. Intermittent workers, faced with a repetitive diet of exercises and worksheets, find ways to pass the time by talking behind the teacher's back. It is not that they are less-able pupils who find difficulty in concentrating for longer periods; in fact they make exactly the same progress as do the solitary workers who spend nearly one day a week more on these exercises. Our analysis of the most successful teachers in the study indicates that all of them try in various ways to increase the amount of interaction which they have with the pupils, in particular engaging in conversations of a challenging and stimulating kind. In year two of the study, when the number of teachers engaging in these types of 'higher order interactions' increased, the number of intermittent workers decreased - presumably because they find the environment more stimulating.

RECENT DEVELOPMENTS IN TEACHER TRAINING

These and the other matters raised earlier, warrant serious consideration by teachers and teacher trainers. In the induction of the student into teaching, an analytical approach based, perhaps, to some extent, on the ORACLE findings, could provide a useful basis for the 'school experience' that many colleges provide, not only in the professional year, but to a lesser extent throughout the three or four years of professional training. Such school experience, if properly organized, and using video tape - as many colleges do - could usefully take account of the ORACLE findings concerning, for instance, the different teaching styles found actually to occur in primary classrooms, and of related matters. The findings could be used to heighten the student's awareness of the options open to the beginning teacher and to the different combinations of forms of classroom organization and teaching styles which are available. The general aim here might be to promote reflection about the significance of different approaches, preparatory to the students undertaking actual teaching practice in the schools themselves. Relevant here is the use of micro-teaching, as developed particularly at the University of Stirling, the New University of Ulster, at Coleraine and at some colleges. The objective of this technique includes the deliberate development of certain specific teaching skills. Micro-teaching may prove to be an effective approach also in inducting students into the skills required for effective collaborative group work by pupils.

This approach differs somewhat from that adopted by, for instance, Richard Mills who, in a recent study (1980), provides a number of 'blow by blow' accounts of classroom life of six children. Between these descriptions the author gives his own opinion about, for example, the value of competition and the use of activities such as collecting data for drawing up graphs. These comments appear to lack the objectivity which results from the systematic method of data collection used during the ORACLE study and many of the author's observations seem relatively unimportant when put beside the ORACLE findings relating to the distribution of teacher time, the imbalance in the curriculum in favour of written work and the problems of intermittent and solitary working discussed earlier. Mills's discussion of written work, for example, is concerned only with issues such as whether material with no technical errors should alone be displayed or whether written work should whenever possible arise from the task in hand and not be determined by the teacher. While these

issues are no doubt important it would seem more urgent, in the
light of the ORACLE study, to begin any discussion of written
work with an analysis as to why the majority of children observed
in our study spent so much time on activities such as copying,
sentence completion and comprehension exercises. Student
teachers often criticize generalized discussion about the value of
certain teaching approaches when such discussions are unrelated
to the practical realities of classroom life. We would argue that
the kinds of discussions that Mills's book seeks to promote would
become more profitable if the problems which a teacher faces
when attempting to structure the learning of thirty children or
more are continually kept in mind. The ORACLE study highlights
the value which teachers place on 'busyness' and in such an environment an excessive concentration on writing seems necessary
to keep the majority of children occupied while the teacher attends
to those with special needs. Findings such as these provide a
useful way of bridging the gap between theory and practice. Not
only do they encourage college tutors to be more realistic in the
tasks that they set students but they can also help the students
to realize that the problems experienced during their first en-
counters with children are shared by the majority of the profession.

TEACHERS' RHETORIC

So far the issues discussed have dealt with student training. We
now turn to the implications of the research findings for more
experienced teachers. Just as the ORACLE findings have cast a
good deal of doubt on the value (or accuracy) of much of the
rhetoric about primary school teaching - for instance, that propagated by the Black Papers on the one hand, and by the Plowden
Committee on the other - so they bring into focus the value (or
otherwise) of what may be called teacher rhetoric about teaching.
This is the supposition that penetrating analysis of interactional
processes in classrooms has nothing to offer to teachers who, as
one put it recently, 'believe that they know when they are teaching effectively'. Teachers, it is claimed, 'have their own checks.
General class response, individual pupil interest, the work pupils
produce, the progress they make all indicate whether things are
going well.' It is argued that 'by and large teachers acquire their
skills pragmatically. They learn to vary their approach to meet
different types of problem' (Spooner 1980). By the same token
the focus on analysis of actual classroom process is regarded as
unnecessary, and even ludicrous. 'The ambition is to achieve out
of classroom observation "the development of professional studies
as an academically rigorous, practically useful and scientifically
productive activity".' The idea that from an analysis of good practice a science of 'teacher craft' can be constructed is regarded as
ridiculous. The author concludes that fortunately 'there are rich
elements in our heritage which should protect us from the worst
excesses of educational research.'

Our experience stands in direct opposition to this standpoint. Practising teachers, in a series of meetings in the short period that has elapsed since the publication of 'Inside the Primary Classroom', have shown enormous interest in the findings of the research. This is understandable in view of the fact that the research seeks only to reflect, or hold a mirror up to, existing teacher and classroom practice. The individual teacher, segregated in her own classroom (or area of an open-plan school) has little opportunity either of knowing or of finding out what other approaches are used by teachers in other schools (or even in her own school). It has also been our experience that, so demanding is the job of the primary school teacher, so highly active the teachers themselves (interacting with pupils for 80 per cent of the time), that it is difficult, even impossible for them to know what individual or even groups of pupils elsewhere in the classroom are doing when their attention is focused on a specific individual or group. While the teacher certainly develops a close awareness of the total activity within her classroom (this is an essential skill developed by teachers), and while she responds to certain signals with great rapidity, her main concern is and must be to ensure that everybody is working as productively as possible in the circumstances, that disruption is held to a minimum and that things proceed normally. Of course the teacher develops very specific professional skills. But the claim that everything is proceeding with maximum effectiveness in all the classrooms of whatever type of school throughout the country due to the teachers' professional expertise developed individually in separate classrooms cannot stand up as credible.

In 'Progress and Performance in the Primary Classroom' we have argued that such attitudes have arisen in part because of the continuous sniping at primary teachers by certain sections of the media. This has been reinforced by the feeling that much of the debate about teaching methods seems to have little to do with the problems encountered day by day in the classroom. The danger, which can arise if teacher rhetoric of the kind used by Spooner becomes widespread, is that it places increasing pressure on the young relatively inexperienced teacher. The argument that the teacher alone, often in isolation, is capable of solving all her own problems inevitably means that where an individual knows in herself that she is failing with some of the pupils she will be even more reluctant to appeal to colleagues for help in case this is interpreted as a sign of lack of professionalism. The data provided in the ORACLE studies is useful here in that it indicates that the problems such teachers encounter are not unique but are common to the profession as a whole.

IS THIS APPROACH TOO BEHAVIOURIST?

The use of interaction-analysis techniques allied to micro-teaching has been criticized both in the United States and in this country.

It is argued that the approach is behaviourist and that, in seeking to break down the art of teaching into a number of discrete
skills, one loses sight of the fact that the effective teacher offers
his pupils more than simply a sequence of well-executed program-
mable actions. Teaching teachers, these critics argue, is not the
same thing as training rats to pass successfully through a series
of hoops in a maze.

Some of these concerns seem justified when set against the
practices of some American educationists. In some parts of the
United States so-called 'teaching laboratories' have been set up
where the student interacts with a small group of children while
his supervisor watches from behind a glass screen or a two-way
mirror. The student teacher is in continuous contact with the
supervisor by means of a small hearing aid which is wired to a
microphone. Using some interaction system, such as that developed by Flanders, the supervisor records on a key the precise
category of interaction taking place every 3 seconds. The impulse
from the key is fed directly into a computer and the aggregate
totals displayed on a video screen. The supervisor gives immediate
feedback to the student while he is actually teaching, telling him
which categories to use and which to avoid.

This seems an abuse of the technique and we doubt whether
such prescriptive methods are practised anywhere in Britain.
Examples of the best kind of practice include the work of Brown
(1975) at the New University of Ulster and McIntyre and MacLeod
(1978) at the University of Stirling, both of whom used interaction
analysis and micro-teaching techniques in their schemes of teacher
training. In both cases the role of the supervisor is crucial. He
is not there to make certain that the student sticks to the prescription but to offer feedback to the trainee in a way which allows
him to identify his own weaknesses and consider how these can be
overcome. The supervisor then enters into a dialogue with the
student and in the light of his own greater experience helps him
to select and evaluate the particular procedures most suited to
the task in hand.

In adopting such approaches those who use the techniques of
interaction analysis and micro-teaching are not so naive as to
claim that teaching consists merely of a composite collection of
disparate skills. The reason for selecting certain skills for practice, for instance questioning or specific techniques for introducing a topic, lies rather in the belief that focusing on such skills
plays a crucial role in encouraging students to re-think their
total approach to teaching.

For instance, open-ended questioning requires pupils to draw
conclusions about evidence, suggest ways of testing out specific
hypotheses or engage in related types of enquiry activity. To
increase the use of such questioning may have a considerable
influence on children's intellectual development. In the ORACLE
study questions of this type are referred to as 'higher order'
interactions and it is a feature of the junior school classrooms
studied that, although the greater the use teachers made of this

type of questioning the more successful the pupils were in terms
of progress in basic skills and in other measured outcomes, little
use was made of these teaching tactics by most of the teachers in
the sample. Similar findings are found in research carried out in
American classrooms. One American researcher recorded and
analysed the time that children were given to answer a teacher's
question (Budd-Rowe 1974). She was interested in two kinds of
wait-time. The first concerned the time which was allowed to
elapse between the teacher asking the question and the pupil
beginning an answer. The second consisted of the period between
the pupil completing his answer and the teacher making a further
comment by way of feedback. Budd-Rowe found that both wait-
times were characteristically less than 1 second's duration in the
average classroom. The normal sequence was for the teacher to
repeat or rephrase the question if the pupil hadn't answered
within 1-second interval or·in some cases (as discussed in
Chapter 8), simply to pass on to another pupil. With the second
type of wait-time the teacher usually followed up the pupil's
answer immediately either by repeating it, by ignoring it if she
felt it inappropriate, or by changing it by commenting 'in other
words what you really meant was . .'. Not surprisingly most of
the transcript of pupils' answers consisted of one-line reporting
of information or simple descriptions of observations.

Budd-Rowe then trained a group of teachers to alter one single
aspect of behaviour; namely to extend the time in which they
allowed pupils to answer and also the time before the teacher
responded from 1 second to 3. The effect was particularly dramatic in respect of the second wait-time period, that between the
pupil finishing his answer and the teaching making a further
comment. When this period was extended, a whole range of
answers began to emerge, irrespective of the question asked.
Budd-Rowe used interaction analysis to document these responses
for the teachers. They were amazed to find pupils who previously
had given very stereotyped answers begin to hypothesize, speculate and offer a variety of opinions and insights into problems.
Yet, apart from following the suggestion of giving pupils more
time, the teachers had done little in the way of changing their
teaching method. In response to these new initiatives by the
pupils, however, they were impelled to make radical changes in
their approach. For example, they found themselves ceasing
simply to repeat the student's answer and were, indeed, led to
ask further probing and stimulating questions.

In retrospect it is easy to imagine why things happened in this
way. When the teacher first began to give pupils more time, students no doubt continued to give the same type of answers as
before. When the teacher did not immediately respond, the pupils
began to think that the answer given was not that required; so
they tried again, hesitatingly at first, but with renewed confidence when their replies elicited surprised pleasure from the
teacher and resulted in further interesting discussion. Budd-Rowe
claims to have used these simple techniques very successfully in

training primary teachers to use enquiry approaches in science.
There seems to be no reason why similar training strategies
should not be equally successful in this country provided that
teachers can be persuaded to open themselves to these experiences.

THE MODIFICATION OF PRACTICE

This perhaps raises a central issue; the problem of bringing
about change among the less enthusiastic members of the profession. For instance, Budd-Rowe reported that she was unsuccessful in persuading a minority of her sample of teachers to give
pupils more time even when they were faced with the evidence
from a series of small-scale, micro-teaching studies clearly showing how successful the practice was. Our experience with the
teacher-based assessment work reported on by Jasman in this
volume suggests that it is not simply a result of mistrust between
researcher and teacher which lies at the heart of this dilemma.
Jasman was very successful in running in-service training programmes which resulted in a number of teachers returning to
their schools with a firm commitment to persuading colleagues to
adopt some of the strategies which had been developed as part of
this aspect of the ORACLE research. They were signally unsuccessful in their attempts and, when later they were visited by
another member of the team, many of the teachers who had originally taken part in the in-service training were no longer making
use of the checklists in their own assessment procedures. All
thought that the techniques were valuable, most looked back on
the in-service experience as worth while, but had abandoned any
further work in these areas either because of the lack of sympathetic support within the school or because they had been persuaded to put all their spare energy into developing some other
aspect of the school curriculum. In general we found that there
was warm appreciation of our efforts as researchers, but that
teachers regretted that the daily pressure of teaching prevented
them from giving time to this kind of activity. The same is true
of the project assessment techniques discussed by Leith in
Chapter 5.
   This suggests that wide-scale changes will come about only if
small groups of committed teachers in collaboration with researchers
can produce materials incorporating desired improvements, but at
the same time covering content areas which are familiar parts of
the general curriculum. Two examples can be found in the structured activities which were developed alongside the teacher-based
assessment checklists. For 'acquiring information other than by
reading' an activity was designed which required teachers to give
pupils opportunities for asking probing questions. In the exercise
using the four rules of number to solve everyday practical problems such as measuring, shopping, reading timetables and so on,
questions were not marked right or wrong but according to the
kind of help which a pupil needed in order to obtain a correct

answer. Every time the teacher was called upon by a pupil she simply marked the appropriate letter of a simple code in the margin according to the type of help which was needed. This required no more effort on the part of the teacher than if she had marked the sum right or wrong with a tick or cross. When the pupil finally brought the exercise for marking the teacher could see at a glance the kinds of remedial help that the particular pupil had required in the course of his work.

More elaborate extensions of these techniques are to be found at secondary level in the work of Sutton and Wragg in the Teacher Education Project (Wragg 1977), which is modelled on an earlier curriculum development by Haysom and Sutton (1974), the Science Teaching Education Project. In his recent work, Sutton has addressed himself to the problem of implementing a language across the curriculum policy and of training students to extend the responses of pupils in their writing and their spoken language. In each case, whether it be an exercise in creative writing or simply a way of marking a descriptive essay or judging the relevance of a particular text, Sutton provides specimen exercises which students can try out in the course of their teaching practice. In helping students to evaluate the success of such exercises, both Wragg and Sutton incorporate schemes of interaction analysis.

There are as yet no similar developments in the field of primary education. Given the evidence from the ORACLE series of studies of the need for modification of existing patterns of teaching there is a strong case for developing similar types of curriculum material at the primary level.

Several other issues arising from the ORACLE studies have a clear relevance to teacher education; for instance the need to develop skills of teacher-based assessment, as discussed in Jasman's chapter in this volume. Enough has, however, been said to bring out the close relevance of the ORACLE analysis to this important field of activity. In their recent primary school survey (1978), HMIs called for a closer monitoring by teachers of their pupils' overall development in order to achieve a match between this development and the tasks set. They do not, however, indicate how this may be done. If teacher educators are to take up this challenge they may find it helpful to take into account the ORACLE findings concerning classroom organization, teaching styles, pupil types and related matters.

BIBLIOGRAPHY

Abercrombie, J.M.W. (1960), 'The Anatomy of Judgement', Hutchinson, London.
Aristotle (1947), 'The Nichomachean Ethics' with English translation by H. Rackham, Heinemann, London.
Ashton, P., Kneen, P., Davies, F. and Holley, B.J. (1975), 'The Aims of Primary Education: a Study of Teachers' Opinions', Schools Council Research Studies, Macmillan Education, London.
Barker Lunn, J.C. (1970), 'Streaming in the Primary School', NFER, Slough.
Barnes, D. and Todd, F. (1977), 'Communication and Learning in Small Groups', Routledge & Kegan Paul, London.
Bassey, M. (1978), 'Nine Hundred Primary School Teachers', NFER, Slough.
Bealing, D. (1972), The Organization of Junior School Classrooms, 'Educational Research', 14, pp. 231-5.
Bennett, N. (1976), 'Teaching Styles and Pupil Progress', Open Books, London.
Bernstein, B. (1974), 'Class, Codes and Control', 2nd ed., Routledge & Kegan Paul, London.
Biggs, E. (1965), 'Mathematics in Primary Schools', Schools Council Curriculum Bulletin no. 1, HMSO, London.
Blackie, J. (1967), 'Inside the Primary School', HMSO, London.
Blackie, J. (1974), 'Changing the Primary School: an Integrated Approach', Macmillan, London.
Boydell, D. (1975), Pupil Behaviour in Junior Classrooms, 'British Journal of Educational Psychology', 45, pp. 122-9.
Boydell, D. (1978), 'The Primary Teacher in Action', Open Books, London.
Boydell, D. (1980), The Organization of Junior School Classrooms: a Follow-up Survey, 'Educational Research', 23.
Brophy, J. and Good, T. (1970), Teachers' Communication of Differential Expectations for Children's Classroom Performance: Some Behavioural Data, 'Journal of Educational Psychology', 61, pp. 365-74.
Brophy, J. and Good, T. (1974), 'Teacher-Student Relationships: Causes and Consequences', Holt, Rinehart & Winston, New York.
Brown, G. (1975), 'Microteaching: A Programme of Teaching Skills', Methuen, London.
Brown, M. and Precious, N. (1968). 'The Integrated Day in the Primary School', Ward Lock Educational, London.
Budd-Rowe, see Rowe, M.B.
Bullock Report (1975), 'A Language for Life', HMSO, London.
Byrne, D. and Williamson, W. (1972), Some Intra-Regional Variations in Educational Provision and their Bearing upon Educational Attainment in the Case of the North East, 'Sociology', 6, no. 1, pp. 71-87.
Byrne, D., Williamson, W. and Fletcher, B. (1973), Models of Educational Attainment: a Theoretical and Methodological Critique, 'Urban Education', 8.
Chanan, G. and Delamont, S. (eds), (1975), 'Frontiers of Classroom Research', NFER, Slough.
Christopherson, D.G. (1964), The Education of Britain's Scientists who are Teachers, 'Education for Teaching', 65, November, pp. 6-9.
Clegg, Sir Alec (1971), 'Revolution in the British Primary School', National Association of Elementary School Principals, Washington, United States.
Cowen, E.L., Zax, M., Klein, R., Izzo, L.D. and Trost, M.A. (1965), The Relation of Anxiety in School Children to School Record, Achievement and Behavioural Measures, 'Child Development', 36, pp. 128-32.
Croll, P. and Willcocks, J. (1980), Pupil Behaviour and Progress, in Galton, M. and Simon, B. (eds), 'Progress and Performance in the Primary Classroom', Routledge & Kegan Paul, London.

Cronbach, L.J. (1970), 'Essentials of Psychological Testing', 3rd Edition, Harper & Row, New York.
Daniel, M.V. (1947), 'Activity in the Primary School', Blackwell, London.
DES (1977), 'Education in Schools; a Consultative Document', Cmnd 6869, HMSO.
Donnison, D. (1972), 'A Pattern of Disadvantage', NFER, Slough.
Douglas, J.W.B. (1964), 'The Home and the School', MacGibbon & Kee, London.
Dusek, J.B. (1975), Do Teachers Bias Children's Learning?, 'Review of Educational Research', 45, no. 4, pp. 661-84.
Featherstone, J. (1971a), 'Schools Where Children Learn', Liveright, New York.
Featherstone, J. (1971b), 'An Introduction' in the series British Primary Schools Today, Macmillan Education, London.
Fielder, W., Cohen, R. and Feeney, S. (1971), An Attempt to Replicate the Teacher Expectancy Effect, 'Psychological Reports', 29, pp. 1123-8.
Fischer, W.F. (1970), 'Theories of Anxiety', Harper & Row, New York.
Flanders, N.A. (1960), 'Teacher Influence on Pupil Attitudes and Achievement', Final Report, Co-operative Research Programme Project no. 397, University of Minnesota, Minneapolis.
Floud, J. and Halsey, A.H. (1957), Intelligence Tests, Social Class and Selection for Secondary Schools, 'British Journal of Sociology', 8, no. 1.
Galton, M. and Simon, B. (eds), (1980), 'Progress and Performance in the Primary Classroom', Routledge & Kegan Paul, London.
Galton, M., Simon, B. and Croll, P. (1980), 'Inside the Primary Classroom', Routledge & Kegan Paul, London.
Garner, J. and Bing, M. (1973), Inequalities of Teacher-Pupil Contacts, 'British Journal of Educational Psychology', 43, no. 5, pp. 234-43.
Gaudry, E., and Spielberger, C.D. (1971), 'Anxiety and Educational Achievement', Wiley, Sydney.
Goldsmith, J. and Fry, E. (1970), The Test of a High Expectancy Prediction on Reading Achievements and IQ of Students in Grade 10 (or Pygmalion in puberty), Research Report summarized in Elashoff, J. and Snow, R. (1971), 'Pygmalion Reconsidered', C.A. Jones, Worthington, Ohio.
Goldstein, K. (1939), 'The Organism', American Book Company, New York.
Good, T. (1970), Which Pupils do Teachers Call On?, 'Elementary School Journal', 70.
Goodacre, E.J. (1968), 'Teachers and Their Pupils' Home Backgrounds', NFER, Slough.
Gosden, P.H.J.H. and Sharp, P.R. (1978), 'The Development of an Education Service: the West Riding 1889-1974', Martin Robertson, Oxford.
Grieger, R.M. (1971), Pygmalion Revisited: a Loud Call for Caution, 'Interchange', 2, no. 4, pp. 78-89.
Griffin-Beale, C. (ed.), (1979), 'Christian Schiller in his Own Words', privately printed.
Guilford, J.P. (1973), 'Fundamental Statistics in Psychology and Education', 5th ed., McGraw-Hill, New York.
Haggitt, E.M. (1975), 'Projects in the Primary School', Longman, London.
Halsey, A.H. and Gardner, L. (1953), Selection for Secondary Education and Achievement in Four Grammar Schools, 'British Journal of Sociology', 4, pp. 60-77.
Halsey, A.H., Heath, A.F. and Ridge, J.M. (1980), 'Origins and Destinations', Clarendon Press, Oxford.
Harlen, W., Darwin, A. and Murphy, M. (1977a), 'Match and Mismatch: Raising Questions, Leader's Guide', Oliver & Boyd, Edinburgh.
Harlen, W., Darwin, A., and Murphy, M. (1977b), 'Match and Mismatch: Raising Questions, Oliver & Boyd, Edinburgh.
Harlen, W., Darwin, A. and Murphy, M. (1977b), 'Match and Mismatch: Raising Questions', Oliver & Boyd, Edinburgh.
Haysom, J.T. and Sutton, C. (1974), 'Theory into Practice: Activities in School for Student Teachers', McGraw-Hill London.
Hillman, S.B. and Davenport, G.G. (1978), Teacher-Student Interactions in Desegregated Schools, 'Journal of Educational Psychology', 70, no. 4, pp. 545-53.
HMI Survey (1978), Department of Education and Science, 'Primary Education

in England: a Survey by HM Inspectors of Schools', HMSO, London.
Jackson, P. and Lahaderne, H. (1967), Inequalities of Teacher-Pupil Contacts, 'Psychology in the Schools', 4, pp. 204-11.
James, J. (1951), A Preliminary Study of the Size Determinant in Small Group Interaction, 'American Sociological Review', 16, pp. 474-7.
Just, M.R. (1974) An Environmental Approach to Mental Health, in Just, M.R., Bell, C.S., Fisher, W. and Schensul, S.L., 'Coping in a Troubled Society', D.C. Heath, Lexington.
Keddie, N. (1971), Classroom Knowledge, in Young, M.F.D. (ed.), 'Knowledge and Control', Collier Macmillan, London.
Keen, E. (1970), 'Three Faces of Being: Towards an Existential Clinical Psychology', Appleton-Century-Crofts, New York.
Kelly, G.A. (1955), 'Psychology of Personal Constructs', Norton, New York.
Kent, G. (1968), 'Projects in the Primary School', B.T. Batsford, London.
King, R. (1974), Social Class, Educational Attainment and Provision: an LEA Case Study, 'Policy and Politics', 3, no. 1.
Kogan, M. (1978), 'The Politics of Educational Change', Manchester University Press.
McGroskey, J.C. (1977), Classroom Consequences of Communication Apprehension, 'Communication Education', 26, pp. 27-33.
McIntyre, D. and MacLeod, G. (1978), The Characteristics and Uses of Systematic Classroom Observation, in McAleese, R. and Hamilton, D. (eds), 'Understanding Classroom Life', NFER, Slough.
Mason, S.C. (1960), 'The Leicestershire Experiment and Plan', Councils & Education Press, London.
Mehrens, W.A. and Lehmann, I.J. (1978), 'Measurement and Evaluation in Psychology', Holt, Rinehart & Winston, New York.
Mills, R.W. (1980), 'Classroom Observation of Primary School Children', Unwin Education Books, London.
Moran, P.R. (1971), The Integrated Day, 'Educational Research', 14, Part 1, November 1971, pp. 65-9.
Mosteller, F. (1955), Use as Evidence by an Examination of Wear and Tear on Selected Sets of ESS, in Davis, K. et al. A Study of the Need for a New Encyclopaedia Treatment of the Social Sciences, unpublished manuscript, pp. 167-74.
Murrow, C. and Murrow, L. (1971), 'Children Come First: The Inspired Work of English Primary Schools', American Heritage Press, New York.
Nash, R. (1973), 'Classrooms Observed', Routledge & Kegan Paul, London.
Nash, R. (1976), 'Teacher Expectations and Pupil Learning', Routledge & Kegan Paul, London.
O'Connor, D.J. (1957), 'An Introduction to the Philosophy of Education', Routledge & Kegan Paul, London.
Open University, prepared by Buckley, R., Massey, A. and Marshall, A. (1975), (PET 271), Technology for Teachers, Block 5, Unit 16, Curriculum Change and Organization III, 'Syllabus Building Assessment', Open University Press, Milton Keynes.
Peters, R.S. (ed.), (1969), 'Perspectives on Plowden', Routledge & Kegan Paul, London.
Plowden Report (1967), 'Children and their Primary Schools' (2 vols), Report of the Central Advisory Council for Education in England, HMSO, London.
Pyle, D. (1975a), Intra-Regional Variations in Educational Provision, 'Sociology', 9, no. 3, pp. 491-5.
Pyle, D. (1975b), Models of Educational Attainment, 'Urban Education', 10, no. 2.
Rance, P. (1968), 'Teaching by Topics', Ward Lock Educational, London.
Ridgway, L. and Lawton, I. (1968), 'Family Grouping in the Primary School', 2nd ed., Ward Lock Educational, London.
Rist, R.C. (1970), Student Social Class and Teacher Expectations: the Self-Fulfilling Prophecy in Ghetto Education, 'Harvard Educational Review', 40, no. 3, pp. 411-51.
Rogers, V. (1970), 'Teaching in the British Primary School', Collier Macmillan, London.

Rosenthal, R. and Jacobson, L. (1968), 'Pygmalion in the Classroom: Teacher Expectation and Pupils' Intellectual Development', Holt, Rinehart & Winston, New York.

Ross, A.M. (1960), 'The Education of Childhood', Harrap, London.

Rowe, M.B. (1974), Wait-Time and Rewards as Instructional Variables, their Influence on Language, Logic and Fate Control, 'Journal of Research in Science Teaching', 11, pp. 81-94.

Rudduck, J. (1978), 'Learning through Small Group Discussion', Society for Research into Higher Education, University of Surrey.

Sargant, W. (1969), Opening Presidential Address: Physical Treatments of Anxiety, in Lader, M.H. (ed.), 'Studies of Anxiety: Papers Read at the World Psychiatric Association Symposium, "Aspects of Anxiety", London, November 1967', Headley Brothers, Ashford.

Schachtel, E.G. (1963), 'Metamorphosis: On the Development of Affect, Perception, Attention and Memory', Routledge & Kegan Paul, London.

Schools Council Examination Bulletin 31 (1975), 'Continuous Assessment in the C.S.E.', Evans/Methuen Educational, London.

Schools Council Examination Bulletin 32 (1975), 'Assessment and Testing in the Secondary School', Evans/Methuen Educational, London.

Schrank, W. (1970), A Further Study of the Labelling Effects of Ability Grouping, 'Journal of Educational Research', 63, pp. 358-60.

Selleck, R.J.W. (1972), 'English Primary Education and the Progressives 1914-1939', Routledge & Kegan Paul, London.

Sharp, R. and Green, A. (1975), 'Education and Social Control: A Study in Progressive Primary Education', Routledge & Kegan Paul, London.

Silberman, M.L. (1969), Behavioral Expression of Teachers' Attitudes Towards Elementary School Students, 'Journal of Educational Psychology', 60, pp. 402-7.

Silberman, C.E. (1970), 'Crisis in the Classroom: the Remaking of American Education', Random House, New York.

Silberman, C.E. (ed.), (1973), 'The Open Classroom Reader', Vintage Books, New York.

Simon, B. (1953), Intelligence Testing and the Comprehensive School, reprinted in Simon, B. (1971), 'Intelligence, Psychology and Education', Lawrence & Wishart, London.

Spooner, R.T. (1980), Teacher Craft, a review of 'Focus on Teaching', Bennett, N. and McNamara, D. (eds), in 'Education', 27 June.

Taylor, E.S. (1974), 'Project Project', The Book Society of Canada, Agincourt, Canada.

'The Hornsey Affair' (1969), Penguin Education Special, London.

Thier, H.D. (1970), 'Teaching Elementary School Science: a Laboratory Approach', D.C. Heath, Lexington.

Thorndike, E.L. (1962), 'Psychology and the Science of Education: Selected Writings', ed. Jonich, G.M., Teachers College Press, New York.

Thorndike, R.L. and Hagen, E. (1969), 'Measurement and Evaluation in Psychology and Education', 3rd ed., Wiley, New York.

Tough, J. (1976), 'Listening to Children Talking: a Guide to the Appraisal of Children's Use of Language', Schools Council Communication Skills in Early Childhold project, Ward Lock Education in association with Drake Educational Association, London.

Tough, J. (1977), 'Development of Meaning', Allen & Unwin, London.

Tubiana, P. (1978), Psychoanalyse de l'Anti-science, 'Paris-Match', 1506, p. 114.

United States Office of Education (1970), 'Education of the Disadvantaged', US Government Printing Office, Washington DC.

Universities Council for the Education of Teachers (1979), 'The PGCE Course and the Training of Specialist Teachers for Secondary Schools: a Consultative Report'.

Webb, E.J. (1975), Unobtrusive Measures, in Payne, D.A. and McMorris, R.F. (eds.), 'Educational and Psychological Measurements: Contributions to Theory and Practice', 2nd ed., General Learning Press, Morristown, NJ.

Weber, L. (1971), 'The English Infant School and Informal Education', Prentice-Hall, Englewood Cliffs, NJ.

Wilkinson, A. Stratta, L. and Dudley, P. (1976), 'Learning Through Listening', Schools Council Oracy Project, Listening Comprehension Tests, Macmillan Education, London.

Wragg, E.C. (ed.), (1977), 'Talking to Learn: a Study Unit on the Role of Pupil Talk in School Learning', Teacher Education Project, Nottingham University and Leicester University Schools of Education.

INDEX